CORE SKILLS

S0-BFD-106

Math Review
Computation · Algebra · Geometry

ISBN 0-7398-8540-5

Printed in the United States of America.

3 4 5 6 7 8 9   054   09 08 07 06

Steck Vaughn™

A Harcourt Achieve Imprint

www.Steck-Vaughn.com
1-800-531-5015

Table of Contents

Preview 5–9

Unit 1 Whole Numbers

The Addition Facts **10**
Column Addition **11**
Reading and Writing Numbers **12**
Comparing and Ordering **13**
Rounding **14**
Adding Larger Numbers **15**
Addition with Regrouping **16**
More Addition with Regrouping **17**
Estimation of Sums **18**
Addition Practice With and Without
    Regrouping **19**
The Subtraction Facts **20**
Subtracting Numbers **21**
Subtracting Larger Numbers **22**
Subtracting with Regrouping **23**
Subtracting with Regrouping Hundreds **24**
Subtracting with Regrouping Twice **25**
Estimation of Differences **26**
Addition and Subtraction With and
    Without Regrouping **27**
Problem-Solving Strategy: Guess
    and Check **28–29**
Problem-Solving Applications **30**
Unit 1 Review **31**

Unit 2 Whole Numbers

The Multiplication Facts **32**
Multiplying Larger Numbers **33**
Multiplying with Regrouping **34**
More Multiplying with Regrouping **35**
Multiplication Practice **36**
The Division Facts **37**
Division with 1-digit Divisors **38–39**
Division Practice **40**
Division with 2-digit Divisors **41**
Division Practice **42**
Dividing Larger Numbers **43**
Dividing by Hundreds **44**
Multiplication and Division Practice **45**
Estimation of Products **46**
Estimation of Quotients **47**

Problem-Solving Strategy: Choose an
    Operation **48–49**
Problem-Solving Applications **50**
Unit 2 Review **51**

Unit 3 The Meaning and Use of Fractions

Proper Fractions **52**
Improper Fractions and Mixed Numbers **53**
Equivalent Fractions **54**
Simplifying Fractions **55**
Addition and Subtraction of Fractions
    with Like Denominators **56**
Addition of Fractions with Different
    Denominators **57**
Addition of Fractions Using the Least
    Common Denominator **58**
Adding Mixed Numbers, Whole
    Numbers, and Fractions **59**
Problem-Solving Strategy: Complete a
    Pattern **60–61**
Practice with Improper Fractions **62**
Problem-Solving Applications **63**
Subtraction of Fractions with Different
    Denominators **64–65**
Subtraction of Fractions and Mixed
    Numbers from Whole Numbers **66–67**
Subtraction of Mixed Numbers with
    Regrouping **68–69**
Problem-Solving Strategy: Make a
    Drawing **70–71**
Problem-Solving Applications **72**
Unit 3 Review **73**

Unit 4 Multiplication and Division of Fractions

Multiplication of Fractions **74**
Multiplication of Fractions Using
    Cancellation **75**
Multiplication of Whole Numbers by
    Fractions **76–77**
Multiplication of Mixed Numbers by
    Whole Numbers **78**
Multiplication of Mixed Numbers by
    Fractions **79**

Multiplication of Mixed Numbers by
    Mixed Numbers .80
Problem-Solving Applications 81
Problem-Solving Strategy: Write a
    Number Sentence 82–83
Division of Fractions by Fractions 84–85
Division of Fractions by Whole
    Numbers 86–87
Division of Whole Numbers by Fractions 88
Division of Mixed Numbers by Whole
    Numbers 89
Division of Mixed Numbers by Fractions 90
Division of Mixed Numbers by Mixed
    Numbers 91
Problem-Solving Strategy: Identify
    Extra Information 92–93
Problem-Solving Applications 94
Unit 4 Review 95

Unit 5 Working with Decimals

Reading and Writing Decimals 96
Compare and Order Decimals 97
Fraction and Decimal Equivalents 98
More Fraction and Decimal Equivalents 99
Addition of Decimals 100–101
Subtraction of Decimals 102–103
Problem-Solving Strategy: Work
    Backwards 104–105
Problem-Solving Applications 106
Estimation of Decimal Sums and
    Differences 107
Practice Adding and Subtracting
    Decimals 108
More Practice Adding and Subtracting
    Decimals 109
Multiplying Decimals by Whole
    Numbers .110–111
Multiplying Decimals by Decimals 112–113
Dividing Decimals by Whole Numbers 114
Dividing Decimals by Decimals 115
Dividing Whole Numbers by Decimals 116
Decimal Quotients 117
Multiplying and Dividing by Powers of 10 . .118
Estimating Decimal Products and
    Quotients 119
Practice Multiplying and Dividing
    Decimals 120

More Practice Multiplying and Dividing
    Decimals 121
Problem-Solving Strategy: Use
    Estimation 122–123
Problem-Solving Applications 124
Unit 5 Review 125

Unit 6 Percents

Meaning of Percent 126
Changing Decimals and Fractions to
    Percents 127
Interchanging Fractions, Decimals,
    and Percents .128
Percents Greater Than 100% 129
Percents Less Than 1% 130
Problem-Solving Applications 131
Problem-Solving Strategy: Use a Bar
    Graph 132–133
Using Decimals to Find a Percent
    of a Number .134
Using Fractions to Find a Percent of a
    Number 135
Finding What Percent One Number Is
    of Another 136
Finding a Number When a Percent of
    It Is Known 137
Simple Interest 138–139
Percent of Increase 140
Percent of Decrease 141
Problem-Solving Strategy: Use a
    Circle Graph 142–143
Problem-Solving Applications 144
Unit 6 Review 145

Unit 7 Algebra: Expressions and Equations

What is Algebra? 146
Sets of Numbers 147
Understanding Numbers and Absolute
    Value 148
Comparing and Ordering Integers 149
Adding and Subtracting Integers 150
Multiplying and Dividing Integers 151
Order of Operations 152
Evaluating Expressions 153

Writing Expressions with Variables **154**
Evaluating Expressions with Variables **155**
Finding Missing Addends and Missing
    Factors **156–157**
Problem-Solving Strategy: Use Logic . . **158–159**
Squares and Exponents **160**
Cubes and Exponents **161**
Scientific Notation **162**
Square Roots **163**
Solving Multi-Step Equations **164–165**
Collecting Like Terms in Equations . . . **166–167**
Solving Equations with an Unknown
    on Both Sides **168–169**
Using Equations to Solve Problems . . . **170–171**
Exponents in Expressions **172–173**
Problem-Solving Strategy: Use a
    Logic Chart **174–175**
Problem-Solving Applications **176**
Unit 7 Review **177**

Unit 8 Algebra: Functions, Graphs, and Inequalities

Functions and Relations **178**
Graphing Ordered Pairs **179**
Linear Functions **180**
Equations with Two Variables **181**
Graphing Solutions **182**
Graphing Linear Equations **183**
Slope **184**
The Slope Formula **185**
Inequalities **186**
Solving Inequalities with Addition and
    Subtraction **187**
Solving Inequalities with Multiplication
    and Division **188**
Solving Problems with Inequalities **189**
Problem-Solving Strategy: Use a Line
    Graph **190–191**
Problem-Solving Applications **192**
Unit 8 Review **193**

Unit 9 Geometry

Points and Lines **194**
Types of Angles **195**
Types of Triangles **196**

Polygons **197**
Perimeter of a Triangle **198**
Perimeter of a Rectangle **199**
Problem-Solving Strategy: Make
    a Table **200–201**
Formula for Area of a Triangle **202**
Formula for Area of a Rectangle **203**
Surface Area of a Rectangular Prism . . **204–205**
Area of Parallelograms and
    Trapezoids **206–207**
Formula for Volume of a Rectangular
    Prism **208**
Formula for Circumference of a Circle **209**
Formula for Area of a Circle **210**
Formula for Volume of a Cylinder **211**
Problem-Solving Strategy: Use a
    Formula **212–213**
Problem-Solving Applications **214**
Unit 9 Review **215**

Unit 10 Measurement, Ratios, and Proportions

Customary Measurement **216**
Metric Length **217**
Metric Mass **218**
Metric Capacity **219**
Ratios **220**
Ratios in Measurement **221**
Proportions **222**
Solving Proportions with an Unknown **223**
Using Proportions to Solve Problems **224**
Direct Variation **225**
Similar Triangles **226**
Using Similar Triangles **227**
Using Proportion in Similar Figures **228**
The Pythagorean Theorem **229**
Problem-Solving Strategy: Select a
    Strategy **230–231**
Unit 10 Review **232**

Final Review **233–236**

Glossary **237–240**

Answer Key

Answer Key **241–256**

Find the simple interest using Interest = principal × rate × time.

a	*b*
19. $175 at $3\frac{3}{4}\%$ for 2 years	$400 at 9.2% for 1 year

Find the absolute value of each number.

a	*b*	*c*	*d*
20. $\lvert {}^-3 \rvert$	$\lvert 2 \rvert$	$\lvert {}^-4 \rvert$	$\lvert {}^-601 \rvert$

Simplify.

a	*b*	*c*	*d*
21. ${}^-8 + 6 =$	${}^-20 - ({}^-9) =$	$13({}^-6) =$	${}^-76 \div ({}^-4) =$
22. $10 \div 2 + 6 =$	$12 - 21 \div 3 =$	$(7 - 2) \times 10 =$	$14 + 3 \times 12 =$

Write an algebraic expression for each verbal expression.

a	*b*
23. a number times 50 _____	17 less than z _____

Evaluate each expression if $m = 5$, $n = {}^-2$, and $p = 3$.

a	*b*	*c*	*d*
24. $n - 3p =$	$17 + mp =$	$n(2 + 2m) =$	$\dfrac{2mp + 5}{m} =$

Solve.

a	*b*	*c*	*d*
25. $x + 11 = 40$	$x - 7 = 17$	$9x = 45$	$3x + 5 = 32$
26. $3x + 4x = 84$	$15x - 3x = 72$	$42 + x = 81 - 2x$	$8x + 6 = 9x + 1$

Simplify.

a	*b*	*c*	*d*
27. $(6^2) =$	$({}^-2)^3 =$	$\sqrt{49} =$	$(9^7) \div (9^5) =$

Change each number from scientific notation to standard form.

a	*b*	*c*	*d*
28. 3×10^3	1.2×10^4	6.07×10^5	8.9×10^2

Circle which of the given points lie on the graph of the given function.

29. $3x - 3y = {}^-3$ $(2, 3)$ $(0, {}^-1)$ $({}^-4, {}^-3)$

Solve each equation using the given value of *x*.
Write the ordered pair which makes the equation true.

a	*b*	*c*
30. $2x + 2y = ^-4$ when $x = 2$	$x - 3y = 9$ when $x = ^-1$	$2x + y = 10$ when $x = 3$
Ordered pair _____	Ordered pair _____	Ordered pair _____

For each equation, find and graph three solutions.
Draw a straight line through those points.

a

31. $2x + y = 1$

b

$x - 2y = ^-2$

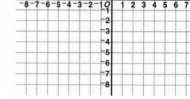

Find the slope of each line that passes through the given points.

a	*b*	*c*
32. $(1, 4), (2, 3)$	$(1, 0), (3, 7)$	$(^-2, 1), (5, 10)$

Solve.

a	*b*	*c*	*d*
33. $2x - 10 > ^-44$	$49 \geq x + 17$	$^-4x \leq 60$	$3x - 13 > 19 + 7x$

Classify each triangle. Write *right, obtuse, equilateral,* or *scalene*.

a	*b*	*c*	*d*
34.		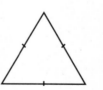	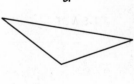
_____	_____	_____	_____

Classify each polygon. Write *regular* or *irregular*.

a	*b*	*c*	*d*
35.		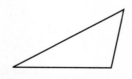	
_____	_____	_____	_____

Change each measurement to the unit given.

	a	b	c
36.	15 qt = _____ gal _____ qt	40 m = _____ km	32 oz = _____ lb
37.	40 in. = _____ ft _____ in.	56 kg = _____ g	334 mL = _____ L

Write a fraction for each ratio. Simplify.

38.

a — the ratio of pints in a quart to pints in a gallon

Ratio _____

b — the ratio of days in a week to months in a year

Ratio _____

Solve the proportion.

	a	b	c
39.	$\frac{7}{8} = \frac{x}{40}$	$\frac{x}{9} = \frac{10}{3}$	$\frac{x}{3} = \frac{12}{18}$

Solve.

40. Triangle ABC is similar to triangle XYZ. What is the length of XY?

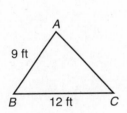 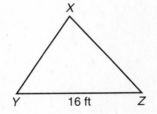

Answer _____

41. Triangle MNO is similar to triangle TUV. What is the length of MO?

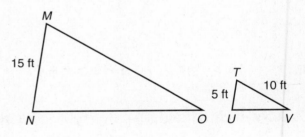

Answer _____

Find the length of the missing side in each right triangle.

	a	b	c
42.	$a = 3, b = ?, c = 5$	$a = 8, b = 6, c = ?$	$a = ?, b = 12, c = 13$

Solve.

43. What is the perimeter of a chalkboard that measures 7 feet by 3.5 feet? (Hint: $P = 2l + 2w$)

Answer _____

44. What is the area of a picture that measures 9 inches by 12 inches?

Answer _____

The Addition Facts

Shown below are some addition facts that you need to know
very well. Practice adding until you have the facts memorized.

PRACTICE

Add.

	a	b	c	d	e	f	g	h	i	j
1.	1 +1	2 +1	0 +1	4 +1	5 +1	7 +1	6 +1	3 +1	9 +1	8 +1
2.	5 +2	1 +2	2 +2	9 +2	7 +2	8 +2	0 +2	6 +2	4 +2	3 +2
3.	3 +3	0 +3	4 +3	1 +3	5 +3	2 +3	9 +3	6 +3	8 +3	7 +3
4.	5 +4	9 +4	7 +4	1 +4	2 +4	6 +4	4 +4	0 +4	3 +4	8 +4
5.	3 +5	5 +5	1 +5	9 +5	4 +5	2 +5	7 +5	6 +5	0 +5	8 +5
6.	6 +6	4 +6	0 +6	5 +6	9 +6	2 +6	8 +6	1 +6	7 +6	3 +6
7.	3 +7	1 +7	5 +7	8 +7	4 +7	7 +7	0 +7	9 +7	2 +7	6 +7
8.	0 +8	3 +8	9 +8	2 +8	7 +8	1 +8	6 +8	4 +8	8 +8	5 +8
9.	1 +9	6 +9	4 +9	2 +9	8 +9	0 +9	5 +9	9 +9	3 +9	7 +9

More Addition with Regrouping

Sometimes you must regroup more than once.

Find: 648 + 573

Add the ones.	Add the tens.	Add the hundreds.
8 + 3 = 11	1 + 4 + 7 = 12	1 + 6 + 5 = 12
Regroup.	Regroup.	Regroup.

Th	H	T	O
			1
	6	4	**8**
+	5	7	**3**
			1

Th	H	T	O
		1	1
	6	4	8
+	5	7	3
		2	1

Th	H	T	O
	1	1	1
	6	4	8
+	**5**	7	3
1,	2	2	1

✗PRACTICE

Add.

	a	b	c	d	e
1.	1 1 2 4 7 +6 8 3 *9 3 0*	5 7 8 +2 4 3	4 9 0 +2 4 7	8 4 6 +3 7 4	7 6 4 +2 8 5
2.	2 3 4 +3 6 8	6 0 7 +4 0 9	5 8 3 + 7 5	3 5 +1 6 7	8 7 2 +5 0 0
3.	3,2 3 4 + 4 3 9	6,4 6 4 +1,3 5 8	2 8 9 +7,5 1 5	3,0 0 5 +2,8 9 7	1 5,2 2 5 + 7,9 5 1
4.	2 3 4 2 1 0 +3 5 2	1 5 7 6 0 +1 6 4	2,3 9 5 2,7 0 8 + 4 3 1	6,3 9 4 2,1 8 2 +2,0 1 4	1 2,1 0 5 9,3 8 7 + 1,5 3 2

Line up the digits. Then find the sums.

a	b	c
5. 731 + 294 = _____	3,755 + 2,881 = _____	7,357 + 2,983 = _____

731
+294

6. 5,312 + 748 = _____	3,009 + 7,896 = _____	876 + 5,499 = _____

Estimation of Sums

To **estimate** a sum, first round each number to the same place.
Then add the rounded numbers.

Estimate: 856 + 431

Round each number to the same place. Add.

$$
\begin{array}{rcr}
8\ 5\ 6 & \to & 900 \\
+4\ 3\ 1 & \to & +\ 400 \\
\hline
 & & 1{,}300
\end{array}
$$

Estimate: 1,583 + 632

Round each number to the same place. Add.

$$
\begin{array}{rcr}
1{,}5\ 8\ 3 & \to & 1{,}600 \\
+\ \ 6\ 3\ 2 & \to & +\ 600 \\
\hline
 & & 2{,}200
\end{array}
$$

PRACTICE

Estimate the sums.

	a	b	c	d
1.	$327 \to 300$ $+492 \to +500$ $\overline{\hspace{2em}800}$	$253 \to$ $+485 \to$	$384 \to$ $+234 \to$	$265 \to$ $+341 \to$
2.	$728 \to$ $+371 \to$	$452 \to$ $+285 \to$	$167 \to$ $+462 \to$	$272 \to$ $+594 \to$
3.	$543 \to$ $+488 \to$	$754 \to$ $+376 \to$	$486 \to$ $+540 \to$	$535 \to$ $+480 \to$
4.	$924 \to$ $+668 \to$	$822 \to$ $+555 \to$	$733 \to$ $+248 \to$	$612 \to$ $+145 \to$
5.	$1{,}287 \to$ $+\ \ 739 \to$	$2{,}105 \to$ $+\ \ 618 \to$	$1{,}692 \to$ $+1{,}487 \to$	$3{,}492 \to$ $+\ \ 877 \to$

Addition Practice With and Without Regrouping

PRACTICE

Add.

	a	b	c	d	e
	$^1\ ^1$				
1.	6 5 7 +2 6 7 ――――― 9 2 4	7 6 8 + 9 4	9 8 7 +3 4 6	7 7 9 + 8 3	6 9 3 +8 3 5
2.	4 1 8 +7 9 3	8 4 6 +4 5 7	5 7 5 +7 7 7	7 0 4 +5 9 9	2 3 6 +4 2 1
3.	6 8 4 +2 0 3	7 9 6 +7 0 9	9 8 5 + 5 7	3 9 4 +5 0 5	7 5 6 +9 8 6
4.	6,7 7 9 +1,8 3 4	6,9 4 5 +2,2 4 3	4,9 6 7 +6,0 2 1	3,5 1 2 +3,8 9 4	3,8 5 2 +1,9 4 8
5.	4,3 9 7 +8,0 5 6	3,9 4 7 + 8 7 4	5,6 9 3 +1,8 7 6	3,2 0 7 +2,9 8 4	8,0 0 6 +3,9 9 5
6.	3,8 0 5 +4,7 7 8	6,7 8 4 +8,5 2 2	2,4 1 1 +6,2 2 8	3,5 2 8 +2,4 9 7	2,8 9 6 +1,1 0 5

Line up the digits. Then find the sums.

	a	b	c
7.	651 + 398 = _____ 651 +398	436 + 253 = _____	6,138 + 446 = _____
8.	2,968 + 1,885 = _____	4,008 + 2,995 = _____	4,321 + 2,859 = _____
9.	7,562 + 2,314 = _____	6,384 + 2,645 = _____	1,234 + 8,967 = _____

The Subtraction Facts

Shown below are some subtraction facts that you need to know very well. Practice subtracting until you have the facts memorized.

PRACTICE

Subtract.

	a	b	c	d	e	f	g	h	i	j
1.	6 −1	10 − 6	4 −0	6 −5	10 − 1	11 − 7	7 −4	2 −0	11 − 6	3 −0
2.	12 − 3	12 − 8	12 − 5	3 −1	14 − 5	8 −1	4 −4	10 − 5	9 −7	9 −8
3.	14 − 7	7 −5	13 − 6	11 − 8	8 −6	10 − 4	9 −6	11 − 9	7 −3	12 − 4
4.	4 −1	7 −7	11 − 2	11 − 3	15 − 8	7 −6	13 − 9	8 −7	8 −4	9 −3
5.	9 −2	17 − 9	13 − 4	10 − 3	14 − 6	17 − 8	11 − 5	16 − 8	16 − 7	11 − 4
6.	8 −2	9 −5	15 − 7	13 − 7	18 − 9	7 −2	5 −3	12 − 9	6 −4	4 −3
7.	15 − 6	16 − 9	15 − 9	10 − 7	5 −1	10 − 9	12 − 6	6 −2	8 −5	13 − 5
8.	14 − 8	3 −3	8 −3	9 −9	8 −8	6 −3	2 −2	12 − 3	14 − 9	12 − 7
9.	13 − 8	10 − 8	5 −5	2 −1	5 −2	9 −4	5 −4	9 −1	4 −2	10 − 2

Subtracting Numbers

Subtracting numbers with two or three digits is like subtracting basic facts two or three times. You start with the ones column.

Find: 168 − 23

Subtract the ones.	Subtract the tens.	Subtract the hundreds.

H T O
  1 6 **8**
−   2 **3**
       5
	H T O
	  1 **6** 8
	− **2** 3
	    4 5
		H T O
		  1 6 8
		− 2 3
		 1 4 5

PRACTICE

Subtract.

	a	b	c	d	e
1.	6 5 −5 2 **1 3**	8 9 −4 6	5 6 −4 6	9 8 −3 7	6 2 −4 0
2.	8 3 −2 1	7 6 −1 2	8 4 − 3	9 8 −1 5	5 6 − 5
3.	5 7 −3 3	9 8 −5 0	7 8 −1 3	9 7 −4 2	8 2 −2 1
4.	8 9 −6 2	6 8 −5 1	5 2 −4 2	5 7 − 7	6 7 −1 6
5.	1 2 3 − 1 1	5 9 6 − 6 2	2 4 7 − 1 4	4 9 8 − 8 7	1 6 6 − 4 0
6.	2 3 9 − 1 7	1 5 3 − 2 1	4 1 9 − 1 6	3 6 7 − 3 2	3 8 4 − 8 0

Subtracting Larger Numbers

Subtracting numbers with two or more digits is like subtracting basic facts again and again. Always start with the ones column.

Find: 5,864 − 2,143

Subtract the ones.	Subtract the tens.	Subtract the hundreds.	Subtract the thousands.
Th H T O 5, 8 6 **4** − 2, 1 4 **3** **1**	Th H T O 5, 8 **6** 4 − 2, 1 **4** 3 **2 1**	Th H T O 5, **8** 6 4 − 2, **1** 4 3 **7 2 1**	Th H T O **5,** 8 6 4 − **2,** 1 4 3 **3, 7 2 1**

PRACTICE

Subtract.

	a	b	c	d	e
1.	9 8 9 −7 5 6 *2 3 3*	3 4 6 −2 3 6	6 3 7 −1 2 4	8 7 5 −4 2 5	7 9 8 −3 5 0
2.	4 9 5 −1 3 0	7 5 2 −7 4 2	7 6 9 −4 5 2	8 3 6 −3 0 5	5 2 8 −4 1 2
3.	5, 3 9 8 − 1 7 5	6, 8 3 9 − 4 0 7	1, 7 6 5 − 2 4 5	3, 5 6 7 − 4 1 6	1, 9 9 8 − 3 6 2
4.	2, 2 8 6 − 2 1 5	1, 4 7 5 − 3 2 2	3, 8 5 4 − 7 0 1	1, 4 4 5 − 2 1 5	2, 6 9 0 − 5 8 0
5.	1, 5 8 4 −1, 4 2 3	3, 9 7 5 −1, 7 7 2	5, 3 9 1 −4, 1 3 1	2, 8 7 9 −1, 6 7 9	4, 1 5 5 −3, 0 1 5
6.	3, 8 7 5 −1, 5 6 2	2, 2 1 5 −1, 1 0 0	6, 4 8 9 −4, 0 5 0	5, 7 6 8 −1, 2 3 3	1, 9 9 5 −1, 9 8 5

Subtracting with Regrouping

Sometimes when you try to subtract in the ones column, you do not have enough to subtract. You must regroup a ten to get enough ones.

Find: 32 − 15

Can you subtract the ones? No.	Regroup.	Subtract the ones. 12 − 5 = 7	Subtract the tens. 2 − 1 = 1
Tens | Ones 3 | 2 −1 | 5	Tens | Ones 2 | 12 3̶ | 2̶ −1 | 5	Tens | Ones 2 | 12 3̶ | 2̶ −1 | 5 | 7	Tens | Ones 2 | 12 3̶ | 2̶ −1 | 5 1 | 7

PRACTICE

Subtract.

	a	b	c	d	e
1.	4 10 5̶ Ø̶ −1 2 3 8	8 1 −3 7	6 6 −3 9	8 1 − 7	5 0 −1 8
2.	8 1 −2 9	3 4 − 8	2 6 − 9	6 3 −1 7	5 7 − 9
3.	8 6 −3 9	7 6 −3 8	7 5 −2 8	9 6 −3 7	4 5 − 6
4.	4 2 −1 3	3 8 −1 9	8 6 −3 8	6 5 −3 9	8 2 − 5

If there are enough ones to subtract, then do so. If not, regroup first.

	a	b	c	d	e
5.	5 7 −1 5	6 0 −2 3	5 6 −2 4	9 2 −2 1	6 4 −2 9
6.	9 1 −4 3	6 7 −2 5	9 1 −4 2	5 7 −2 5	8 6 − 5

Subtracting with Regrouping Hundreds

Sometimes you can subtract in the ones column, but you do not have enough tens to subtract. Then you must regroup hundreds as 1 less hundred and 10 more tens.

Find: 329 − 146

Subtract the ones. $9 - 6 = 3$	Regroup the tens.	Subtract the tens. $12 - 4 = 8$	Subtract the hundreds. $2 - 1 = 1$
H T O 　3 2 **9** −1 4 **6** 　　　3	H T O 2 12 　ᴤ **2** 9 −1 4 6 　　　3	H T O 2 12 　ᴤ **2** 9 −1 4 6 　**8** 3	H T O 2 12 　ᴤ ᴢ 9 −1 4 6 **1 8 3**

PRACTICE

Subtract.

	a	b	c	d	e
1.	$\begin{array}{r} ^{5\ 16} \\ \cancel{6}\,\cancel{6}\,8 \\ -3\ 9\ 1 \\ \hline 2\ 7\ 7 \end{array}$	$\begin{array}{r} 4\ 4\ 9 \\ -\ \ \ 8\ 6 \\ \hline \end{array}$	$\begin{array}{r} 8\ 3\ 3 \\ -1\ 7\ 2 \\ \hline \end{array}$	$\begin{array}{r} 5\ 5\ 1 \\ -4\ 7\ 0 \\ \hline \end{array}$	$\begin{array}{r} 3\ 0\ 6 \\ -1\ 5\ 2 \\ \hline \end{array}$
2.	$\begin{array}{r} 9\ 8\ 9 \\ -1\ 9\ 7 \\ \hline \end{array}$	$\begin{array}{r} 9\ 1\ 9 \\ -7\ 2\ 2 \\ \hline \end{array}$	$\begin{array}{r} 3\ 6\ 0 \\ -2\ 8\ 0 \\ \hline \end{array}$	$\begin{array}{r} 5\ 5\ 6 \\ -\ \ 6\ 1 \\ \hline \end{array}$	$\begin{array}{r} 6\ 4\ 8 \\ -1\ 6\ 2 \\ \hline \end{array}$
3.	$\begin{array}{r} 8\ 4\ 8 \\ -2\ 9\ 0 \\ \hline \end{array}$	$\begin{array}{r} 8\ 7\ 8 \\ -6\ 9\ 7 \\ \hline \end{array}$	$\begin{array}{r} 4\ 3\ 1 \\ -1\ 5\ 1 \\ \hline \end{array}$	$\begin{array}{r} 8\ 7\ 9 \\ -1\ 8\ 0 \\ \hline \end{array}$	$\begin{array}{r} 2\ 2\ 2 \\ -\ \ 9\ 0 \\ \hline \end{array}$
4.	$\begin{array}{r} 3\ 2\ 9 \\ -\ \ 6\ 3 \\ \hline \end{array}$	$\begin{array}{r} 6\ 0\ 8 \\ -5\ 8\ 5 \\ \hline \end{array}$	$\begin{array}{r} 4\ 3\ 8 \\ -2\ 8\ 8 \\ \hline \end{array}$	$\begin{array}{r} 8\ 1\ 9 \\ -3\ 3\ 8 \\ \hline \end{array}$	$\begin{array}{r} 5\ 5\ 8 \\ -2\ 8\ 6 \\ \hline \end{array}$

If there are enough to subtract, then do so. If not, regroup first.

	a	b	c	d	e
5.	$\begin{array}{r} 9\ 2\ 2 \\ -7\ 3\ 2 \\ \hline \end{array}$	$\begin{array}{r} 7\ 3\ 9 \\ -5\ 2\ 4 \\ \hline \end{array}$	$\begin{array}{r} 9\ 0\ 2 \\ -1\ 2\ 1 \\ \hline \end{array}$	$\begin{array}{r} 4\ 2\ 3 \\ -2\ 1\ 8 \\ \hline \end{array}$	$\begin{array}{r} 8\ 6\ 8 \\ -5\ 2\ 3 \\ \hline \end{array}$
6.	$\begin{array}{r} 6\ 0\ 8 \\ -\ \ 5\ 3 \\ \hline \end{array}$	$\begin{array}{r} 4\ 7\ 2 \\ -3\ 8\ 1 \\ \hline \end{array}$	$\begin{array}{r} 9\ 7\ 6 \\ -2\ 1\ 5 \\ \hline \end{array}$	$\begin{array}{r} 8\ 5\ 9 \\ -3\ 8\ 4 \\ \hline \end{array}$	$\begin{array}{r} 5\ 1\ 1 \\ -3\ 7\ 0 \\ \hline \end{array}$

Unit 1 Whole Numbers

Subtracting with Regrouping Twice

When you subtract, sometimes you do not need to regroup at all. Sometimes you must regroup once. Sometimes you must regroup more than once.

Find: 320 − 158

Regroup 1 ten as 10 ones. Subtract. $10 - 8 = 2$	Regroup 1 hundred as 10 tens. Subtract. $11 - 5 = 6$	Subtract the hundreds. $2 - 1 = 1$

H | T | O
    1 | 10
3 | 2 | 0̸
−1 | 5 | 8
       | | 2
	H | T | O
	    | 11 |
	2 | 1̸ | 10
	3̸ | 2 | 0̸
	−1 | 5 | 8
	    | 6 | 2
		H | T | O
		    | 11 |
		2 | 1̸ | 10
		3̸ | 2 | 0̸
		−1 | 5 | 8
		1 | 6 | 2

PRACTICE

Subtract.

	a	b	c	d	e
1.	$\begin{array}{r} 9 \\ 5\,\cancel{10}\,10 \\ \cancel{6}\,\cancel{0}\,\cancel{0} \\ -2\,4\,1 \\ \hline 3\,5\,9 \end{array}$	$\begin{array}{r} 3\,5\,7 \\ -1\,6\,9 \\ \hline \end{array}$	$\begin{array}{r} 5\,1\,8 \\ -3\,2\,9 \\ \hline \end{array}$	$\begin{array}{r} 7\,3\,4 \\ -4\,6\,8 \\ \hline \end{array}$	$\begin{array}{r} 9\,5\,2 \\ -6\,8\,7 \\ \hline \end{array}$
2.	$\begin{array}{r} 9\,4\,6 \\ -8\,4\,7 \\ \hline \end{array}$	$\begin{array}{r} 5\,4\,2 \\ -2\,7\,5 \\ \hline \end{array}$	$\begin{array}{r} 5\,1\,6 \\ -1\,8\,9 \\ \hline \end{array}$	$\begin{array}{r} 7\,3\,4 \\ -\ \ 8\,7 \\ \hline \end{array}$	$\begin{array}{r} 3\,4\,2 \\ -2\,5\,6 \\ \hline \end{array}$
3.	$\begin{array}{r} 5\,6\,1 \\ -4\,7\,8 \\ \hline \end{array}$	$\begin{array}{r} 7\,8\,7 \\ -3\,8\,9 \\ \hline \end{array}$	$\begin{array}{r} 6\,3\,5 \\ -\ \ 5\,7 \\ \hline \end{array}$	$\begin{array}{r} 5\,3\,2 \\ -3\,4\,6 \\ \hline \end{array}$	$\begin{array}{r} 4\,3\,8 \\ -3\,5\,9 \\ \hline \end{array}$
4.	$\begin{array}{r} 6\,3\,2 \\ -1\,5\,9 \\ \hline \end{array}$	$\begin{array}{r} 4\,3\,4 \\ -1\,8\,9 \\ \hline \end{array}$	$\begin{array}{r} 5\,1\,1 \\ -1\,2\,8 \\ \hline \end{array}$	$\begin{array}{r} 4\,6\,2 \\ -1\,8\,9 \\ \hline \end{array}$	$\begin{array}{r} 4\,3\,5 \\ -1\,9\,8 \\ \hline \end{array}$

Line up the digits. Then find the differences.

a   b   c

5. 900 − 301 = _____   318 − 119 = _____   650 − 178 = _____

$\begin{array}{r} 900 \\ -301 \\ \hline \end{array}$

Estimation of Differences

To estimate a difference, first round each number to the same place. Then subtract the rounded numbers.

Estimate: 654 − 210

Round each number to the same place. Subtract.

$$
\begin{array}{rcr}
6\ 5\ 4 & \rightarrow & 700 \\
-2\ 1\ 0 & \rightarrow & -200 \\
\hline
 & & 500
\end{array}
$$

Estimate: 3,794 − 832

Round each number to the same place. Subtract.

$$
\begin{array}{rcr}
3,7\ 9\ 4 & \rightarrow & 3,800 \\
-\ \ 8\ 3\ 2 & \rightarrow & -\ 800 \\
\hline
 & & 3,000
\end{array}
$$

PRACTICE

Estimate the differences.

a	b	c	d
1. $\begin{array}{r} 482 \rightarrow\ \ 500 \\ -246 \rightarrow -200 \\ \hline 300 \end{array}$	$\begin{array}{r} 357 \rightarrow \\ -129 \rightarrow \\ \hline \end{array}$	$\begin{array}{r} 568 \rightarrow \\ -374 \rightarrow \\ \hline \end{array}$	$\begin{array}{r} 845 \rightarrow \\ -659 \rightarrow \\ \hline \end{array}$
2. $\begin{array}{r} 682 \rightarrow \\ -249 \rightarrow \\ \hline \end{array}$	$\begin{array}{r} 453 \rightarrow \\ -326 \rightarrow \\ \hline \end{array}$	$\begin{array}{r} 376 \rightarrow \\ -150 \rightarrow \\ \hline \end{array}$	$\begin{array}{r} 928 \rightarrow \\ -572 \rightarrow \\ \hline \end{array}$
3. $\begin{array}{r} 546 \rightarrow \\ -366 \rightarrow \\ \hline \end{array}$	$\begin{array}{r} 765 \rightarrow \\ -249 \rightarrow \\ \hline \end{array}$	$\begin{array}{r} 430 \rightarrow \\ -357 \rightarrow \\ \hline \end{array}$	$\begin{array}{r} 828 \rightarrow \\ -680 \rightarrow \\ \hline \end{array}$
4. $\begin{array}{r} 1,050 \rightarrow \\ -\ 726 \rightarrow \\ \hline \end{array}$	$\begin{array}{r} 1,473 \rightarrow \\ -\ 815 \rightarrow \\ \hline \end{array}$	$\begin{array}{r} 2,591 \rightarrow \\ -\ 866 \rightarrow \\ \hline \end{array}$	$\begin{array}{r} 2,283 \rightarrow \\ -\ 599 \rightarrow \\ \hline \end{array}$
5. $\begin{array}{r} 3,388 \rightarrow \\ -1,357 \rightarrow \\ \hline \end{array}$	$\begin{array}{r} 4,042 \rightarrow \\ -2,279 \rightarrow \\ \hline \end{array}$	$\begin{array}{r} 5,910 \rightarrow \\ -1,873 \rightarrow \\ \hline \end{array}$	$\begin{array}{r} 6,491 \rightarrow \\ -4,185 \rightarrow \\ \hline \end{array}$

Addition and Subtraction With and Without Regrouping

PRACTICE

Add or subtract. Watch the signs that tell you which operation to use.

	a	b	c	d	e
1.	9 6 +2 1	4 8 +3 7	5 1 4 +2 6 3	8 1 7 +1 4 6	7 5 3 +2 8 9
2.	5 7 −1 2	8 2 −2 7	6 5 8 −3 2 4	5 9 2 −2 5 7	8 0 0 −5 3 6
3.	6,1 4 2 +3,7 5 6	9,6 2 5 +4,2 1 3	2,3 5 8 +4,1 3 5	6,8 3 4 +8,8 7 9	5,7 0 5 + 9 8 6
4.	8,6 5 4 −2,4 3 1	9,6 4 2 −6,4 2 5	7,1 9 4 −3,4 5 7	9,4 8 6 −3,2 5 4	9,0 0 0 −5,4 2 7
5.	5 8 2 1 4 3 +2 1 4	8 6 1 4 9 5 +8 2 7	7 7 9 8 2 7 +5 7 9	9 2 6 7 9 +6 5 8	4,2 1 4 3,0 4 2 +2,7 4 3
6.	3 8,7 6 2 −2 6,5 2 1	4 5,9 6 2 −1 2,5 3 5	3 7,4 2 4 −1 5,2 5 8	7 6,2 0 0 −4 1,3 5 0	9 0,0 0 0 −1 2,5 4 2
7.	2 7,4 5 4 +4 1,3 4 5	7 6,6 3 3 +8 3,6 9 8	9 4 6 +3 0,3 0 6	3 5,2 7 8 +6 3,6 2 1	9 2,0 2 7 +2 1,9 7 3

Line up the digits. Then add or subtract.

a

8. 9,787 + 1,578 + 463 + 9,242 = _____

b

750,000 − 7,500 = _____

Problem-Solving Strategy: Guess & Check

The Celtics and the Lakers have won more NBA championships than any other basketball teams. Together, they have won 28 championships. The Celtics have won 4 more times than the Lakers. How many times have the Lakers won an NBA championship?

Understand the problem.

- **What do you want to know?**
  how many times the Lakers have won an NBA championship

- **What information is given?**
  Clue 1: Lakers wins + 4 = Celtics wins
  Clue 2: Lakers wins + Celtics wins = 28

Plan how to solve it.

- **What strategy can you use?**
  You can guess an answer that satisfies the first clue.
  Then check to see if your answer satisfies the second clue.

Solve it.

- **How can you use this strategy to solve the problem?**
  Try to guess in an organized way so that each of your guesses gets closer to the exact answer. Use a table.

Guess Lakers Wins	Check Clue 1	Clue 2	Evaluate the Guess
10	10 + 4 = 14	10 + 14 = 24	too low
15	15 + 4 = 19	15 + 19 = 34	too high
14	14 + 4 = 18	14 + 18 = 32	too high
13	13 + 4 = 17	13 + 17 = 30	too high
12	12 + 4 = 16	12 + 16 = 28	satisfies both clues

- **What is the answer?**
  The Lakers have won an NBA championship 12 times.

Look back and check your answer.

- **Is your answer reasonable?**
  You can check addition with subtraction.

  16 − 4 = 12   Celtics wins − 4 = Lakers wins
  28 − 16 = 12   28 − Celtics wins = Lakers wins

  The addition checks, and the number of wins satisfies both clues. The answer is reasonable.

Use guess and check to solve each problem.

1. Earl is 8 years younger than Denise. The sum of their ages is 42. How old is each?

   Answer _____

2. What two numbers have a sum of 123 and a difference of 7?

   Answer _____

3. In all, Jupiter and Saturn have 34 moons. Saturn has 2 more moons than Jupiter. How many moons does each planet have?

   Answer _____

4. In the basketball game, Anita scored 37 points on 2-point and 3-point goals. She scored 6 more 2-pointers than 3-pointers. How many of each did she score?

   Answer _____

5. Sea otters and seals can stay underwater for a long time. Together, they can last 27 minutes without taking a breath. Seals can stay under 17 minutes longer than otters. How long can otters stay underwater?

   Answer _____

6. Sound is measured in decibels (dB). The sound of loud rock music is 30 dB less than the sound of a rocket taking off. Combined, the two sounds measure 230 dB. How loud is a rocket taking off?

   Answer _____

Problem-Solving Applications

Write each number using words.

1. Scientists have seen creatures living 35,814 feet deep in the Pacific Ocean.

   Answer _____

2. About 281,421,900 people live in the United States.

   Answer _____

Write each number using digits.

3. The average mail carrier walks about one thousand, fifty-six miles every year.

   Answer _____

4. Your heart beats about one hundred thousand, eight hundred times a day.

   Answer _____

Compare. Write the greater number using words.

5. About 56,803 poodles and 56,946 beagles live in the United States.

   Answer _____

6. Americans eat about 4,400 tons of potato chips and 440 tons of pretzels every day.

   Answer _____

Solve.

7. Hot air balloons were invented in 1783. Airplanes were invented 120 years later. When were airplanes invented?

   Answer _____

8. The United States border with Canada runs 3,145 miles on land and 2,381 miles over water. How long is the entire border?

   Answer _____

9. Alaska's Mt. McKinley is the highest mountain in the United States at 20,320 feet. The tallest mountain in the world, Mount Everest, is 8,715 feet taller. How tall is Mount Everest?

   Answer _____

10. In a bag there are some red balls and twice as many green balls. The sum of the number of red ones and the number of green ones is 24. How many red balls are there?

   Answer _____

Estimate the sums or differences.

	a	b	c	d
1.	$289 \rightarrow$ $+126 \rightarrow$	$7{,}163 \rightarrow$ $+1{,}615 \rightarrow$	$716 \rightarrow$ $-225 \rightarrow$	$6{,}819 \rightarrow$ $-2{,}196 \rightarrow$

Add.

	a	b	c	d	e
2.	7 2 + 5	4 8 + 9	6 2 +1 6	5 8 +2 6	3 2 5 +1 6 4
3.	6 1 8 +1 2 9	5 4 2 +3 7 6	4 9 4 +2 5 8	7 0 9 +3 9 5	3,2 7 5 +6,9 4 8

Subtract.

	a	b	c	d	e
4.	2 9 − 6	6 8 −2 3	4 5 − 9	8 3 −2 6	1 2 4 − 6 8
5.	7 3 5 −2 1 2	6 5 2 −3 4 6	4 1 9 −1 2 5	8 2 3 −2 6 5	3,9 0 0 − 4 3 9

Solve.

6. A year on Neptune lasts 60,195 days. A year on Uranus has 30,685 days. How much longer is a year on Neptune than on Uranus?

7. When you add Joe's age to his brother's age, the sum is 38. When you subtract their ages, the difference is 2. What are the ages of the two brothers?

Answer _____

Answer _____

The Multiplication Facts

Shown below are some multiplication facts that you need to know very well. Practice multiplying until you have the facts memorized.

PRACTICE

Multiply.

	a	b	c	d	e	f	g	h	i	j
1.	5 ×1	4 ×6	7 ×0	1 ×2	9 ×1	4 ×7	3 ×4	2 ×0	5 ×6	3 ×0
2.	9 ×3	4 ×8	7 ×5	2 ×1	9 ×5	7 ×1	0 ×4	5 ×5	2 ×7	1 ×8
3.	7 ×7	2 ×5	7 ×6	3 ×8	2 ×6	6 ×4	3 ×6	2 ×9	4 ×3	8 ×4
4.	3 ×1	0 ×7	9 ×2	8 ×3	7 ×8	1 ×6	4 ×9	1 ×7	4 ×4	6 ×3
5.	7 ×2	8 ×9	9 ×4	7 ×3	8 ×6	9 ×8	6 ×5	8 ×8	9 ×7	7 ×4
6.	6 ×2	4 ×5	8 ×7	6 ×7	9 ×9	5 ×2	2 ×3	3 ×9	2 ×4	1 ×3
7.	9 ×6	7 ×9	6 ×9	3 ×7	4 ×1	1 ×9	6 ×6	4 ×2	3 ×5	8 ×5
8.	6 ×8	0 ×3	5 ×3	0 ×9	8 ×0	3 ×3	0 ×2	6 ×1	5 ×9	5 ×7
9.	5 ×8	2 ×8	1 ×5	1 ×1	3 ×2	5 ×4	1 ×4	8 ×1	2 ×2	8 ×2

Multiplying Larger Numbers

When multiplying larger numbers, use basic multiplication facts more than once. Always multiply the ones digits first. Multiply two **factors** to find a **product.**

Find: 2 × 34

Multiply the ones.	Multiply ones by tens.
2 × 4 ones = 8 ones	2 × 3 tens = 6 tens

```
  H | T | O              H | T | O
    | 3 | 4                | 3 | 4
  × |   | 2              × |   | 2
  -----------            -----------
    |   | 8                | 6 | 8
```

Find: 12 × 13

Multiply ones by ones. 2 × 3 ones = 6 ones	Multiply ones by tens. 2 × 1 ten = 2 tens	Multiply tens by ones. Use 0 as a placeholder. 1 ten × 3 = 3 tens	Multiply tens by tens. 1 ten × 1 ten = 1 hundred. Add the partial products.

```
 H | T | O       H | T | O       H | T | O         H | T | O
   | 1 | 3         | 1 | 3         | 1 | 3           | 1 | 3
 × | 1 | 2       × | 1 | 2       × | 1 | 2         × | 1 | 2
 -----------     -----------     -----------       -----------
   |   | 6         | 2 | 6         | 2 | 6           | 2 | 6
                                  | 3 | 0         + | 3 | 0
                                                  -----------
                                                  | 1 | 5 | 6
```

PRACTICE

Multiply.

	a	b	c	d	e
1.	1 2 × 4 ――― 4 8	3 2 × 3	2 1 × 7	5 2 × 4	2 4 × 2
2.	1 2 ×1 2	2 3 ×1 3	4 2 ×2 1	6 1 ×1 1	2 4 ×2 2
3.	1 6 ×1 1	2 1 ×4 1	1 1 ×1 1	3 3 ×2 2	3 2 ×2 3

Multiplying with Regrouping

Sometimes it is necessary to regroup a product when multiplying larger numbers. The regrouping is similar to what you did in addition.

Find: 4×58

Multiply the ones.	Multiply ones by tens.
$4 \times 8 = 32$ Regroup.	4×5 tens $= 20$ tens Add the 3 tens. 20 tens + 3 tens = 23 tens

```
  H | T | O
      3
      5   8
×         4
      ──────
          2
```

```
  H | T | O
      3
      5   8
×         4
  ──────────
      2   3   2
```

Find: 13×29

Multiply ones by ones.	Multiply tens by ones.
$3 \times 9 = 27$ Regroup. Multiply ones by tens. 3×2 tens $= 6$ tens Add the 2 tens. 6 tens + 2 tens = 8 tens	1 ten $\times 9 = 9$ tens Multiply tens by tens. 1 ten $\times 2$ tens $= 2$ hundreds Add the partial products. $87 + 290 = 377$

```
  H | T | O
      2
      2   9
×     1   3
  ──────────
      8   7
```

```
  H | T | O
      2
      2   9
×     1   3
  ──────────
      8   7
+ 2   9   0
  ──────────
  3   7   7
```

PRACTICE

Multiply.

    a   *b*   *c*   *d*

1.
```
  H | T | O
      3
      5   9
×         4
  ──────────
      2   3   6
```
```
  H | T | O
      2   8
×         3
```
```
  H | T | O
      2   7
×     1   3
```
```
  H | T | O
      3   4
×     2   3
```

    a   *b*   *c*   *d*   *e*

2.
```
  2 7
×   6
```
```
  2 5
×   4
```
```
  4 2
×   9
```
```
  3 6
×   3
```
```
  1 7
×   8
```

3.
```
  1 5 2
×     3
```
```
  2 5 2
×     3
```
```
  2 2 4
×     3
```
```
  3 2 5
×     3
```
```
  1 1 6
×     5
```

4.
```
  2 4
×3 2
```
```
  1 8
×1 2
```
```
  1 3
×4 3
```
```
  3 1
×2 1
```
```
  5 9
×1 7
```

More Multiplying with Regrouping

Sometimes it is necessary to regroup more than once when multiplying. Always start multiplying with the ones digits.

Find: 76 × 368

Multiply by the ones. 6 × 368 = 2,208	Multiply by the tens. 70 × 368 = 25,760	Add the partial products. 2,208 + 25,760 = 27,968
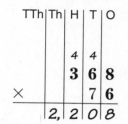		

Multiply by the ones.
6 × 368 = 2,208

```
  TTh Th  H  T  O
          4  4
          3  6  8
 ×           7  6
       2,  2  0  8
```

Multiply by the tens.
70 × 368 = 25,760

```
  TTh Th  H  T  O
          4  5
          4  4
          3  6  8
 ×           7  6
       2,  2  0  8
    2  5,  7  6  0
```

Add the partial products.
2,208 + 25,760 = 27,968

```
  TTh Th  H  T  O
          4  5
          4  4
          3  6  8
 ×           7  6
       2,  2  0  8
   + 2  5,  7  6  0
     2  7,  9  6  8
```

PRACTICE

Multiply.

1.

a
```
 Th  H  T  O
        2
        5
        4  7
 ×      3  8
     3  7  6
  +1,4  1  0
   1, 7  8  6
```

b
```
 Th  H  T  O
     3  5  6
 ×      2  4
```

c
```
 Th  H  T  O
     1  4  6
 ×      5  2
```

d
```
 Th  H  T  O
     4  3  7
 ×      3  8
```

2.

a	b	c	d	e
57 ×38	245 × 4	436 × 29	238 × 49	537 × 8

3.

a	b	c	d	e
86 ×64	209 × 35	784 × 9	98 ×75	514 × 46

4.

a	b	c	d	e
304 × 95	273 × 28	511 × 50	128 ×264	539 ×645

Multiplication Practice

PRACTICE

Multiply.

	a	b	c	d	e
1.	231 × 3	412 × 2	112 × 4	332 × 3	212 × 4
2.	769 × 8	825 × 6	892 × 8	483 × 9	536 × 7
3.	849 × 8	675 × 9	935 × 5	684 × 7	324 × 8
4.	18 ×70	56 ×20	49 ×30	37 ×50	25 ×10
5.	53 ×25	46 ×47	90 ×58	38 ×57	28 ×16
6.	456 × 13	308 × 18	764 × 46	354 × 55	418 × 23

Line up the digits. Then find the products.

           a   b   c

7. $597 \times 28 =$ _____ $936 \times 37 =$ _____ $284 \times 6 =$ _____

    597
  × 28

The Division Facts

If you know the multiplication facts, mastering the division facts should be easy. For example, $28 \div 7$ asks, "How many 7s are in 28?" Since you know that $4 \times 7 = 28$, then you know that the answer, or **quotient,** is 4.

PRACTICE

Complete the sentences.

a

b

1. Since $3 \times 9 = 27$, then $27 \div 9 =$ _____   Since $6 \times 4 = 24$, then $24 \div 4 =$ _____

2. Since $2 \times 8 = 16$, then $8\overline{)16} =$ _____   Since $5 \times 9 = 45$, then $9\overline{)45} =$ _____

Divide.

	a	b	c	d	e	f	g	h	i	j
3.	$1\overline{)5}$	$6\overline{)24}$	$7\overline{)0}$	$5\overline{)5}$	$1\overline{)9}$	$7\overline{)28}$	$4\overline{)12}$	$5\overline{)0}$	$6\overline{)30}$	$3\overline{)3}$
4.	$3\overline{)27}$	$8\overline{)32}$	$5\overline{)35}$	$1\overline{)2}$	$5\overline{)45}$	$7\overline{)7}$	$4\overline{)0}$	$5\overline{)25}$	$7\overline{)14}$	$8\overline{)8}$
5.	$7\overline{)49}$	$5\overline{)10}$	$6\overline{)42}$	$8\overline{)24}$	$6\overline{)12}$	$4\overline{)24}$	$6\overline{)18}$	$9\overline{)18}$	$3\overline{)12}$	$4\overline{)32}$
6.	$1\overline{)3}$	$8\overline{)0}$	$2\overline{)18}$	$3\overline{)24}$	$8\overline{)56}$	$6\overline{)6}$	$9\overline{)36}$	$1\overline{)6}$	$4\overline{)16}$	$3\overline{)18}$
7.	$2\overline{)14}$	$9\overline{)72}$	$4\overline{)36}$	$3\overline{)21}$	$6\overline{)48}$	$8\overline{)72}$	$5\overline{)30}$	$8\overline{)64}$	$7\overline{)63}$	$4\overline{)28}$
8.	$2\overline{)12}$	$5\overline{)20}$	$7\overline{)56}$	$7\overline{)42}$	$9\overline{)81}$	$2\overline{)10}$	$3\overline{)6}$	$9\overline{)27}$	$4\overline{)8}$	$6\overline{)0}$
9.	$6\overline{)54}$	$9\overline{)63}$	$9\overline{)54}$	$7\overline{)21}$	$1\overline{)4}$	$9\overline{)9}$	$6\overline{)36}$	$2\overline{)8}$	$5\overline{)15}$	$5\overline{)40}$
10.	$8\overline{)48}$	$3\overline{)0}$	$3\overline{)15}$	$9\overline{)0}$	$1\overline{)7}$	$3\overline{)9}$	$2\overline{)2}$	$1\overline{)0}$	$9\overline{)45}$	$7\overline{)35}$
11.	$8\overline{)40}$	$8\overline{)16}$	$2\overline{)0}$	$1\overline{)1}$	$2\overline{)6}$	$4\overline{)20}$	$4\overline{)4}$	$1\overline{)8}$	$2\overline{)4}$	$2\overline{)16}$

Division with 1-digit Divisors

To divide by a 1-digit **divisor**, first decide on a **trial quotient.**
Then multiply and subtract. Write the **remainder** in the quotient.

Remember, if your trial quotient is too large or too small, try
another number.

Find: 430 ÷ 4

Begin at the left side of the dividend. Divide 4 by 4. Write 1 in the quotient. Multiply and subtract. Then bring down the next digit.	4 does not go into 3. Write a zero in the quotient. Multiply and subtract. Then bring down the last digit.	Divide 30 by 4. Write 7 in the quotient. Multiply and subtract. The difference is the remainder.	Check: Multiply the quotient by the divisor. Add the remainder.

$$
\begin{array}{r}
1 \\
4\overline{)4\ 3\ 0} \\
-4 \\
\hline
0\ 3
\end{array}
$$

$4\overline{)4}$ is 1.

Quotient →
Divisor →

$4\overline{)30}$ is about 7.

Check:

$$
\begin{array}{r}
107 \\
\times\ \ 4 \\
\hline
428 \\
+\ \ 2 \\
\hline
430
\end{array}
$$

GUIDED PRACTICE

Divide. Check.

a   b   c   d

1.

$$
\begin{array}{r}
1\ 5\ R1 \\
5\overline{)7\ 6} \\
-5 \\
\hline
2\ 6 \\
-2\ 5 \\
\hline
1
\end{array}
$$

b. $3\overline{)8\ 6}$

c. $7\overline{)9\ 0}$

d. $5\overline{)6\ 8}$

2.

$$
\begin{array}{r}
3\ 8\ R3 \\
9\overline{)3\ 4\ 5} \\
-2\ 7 \\
\hline
7\ 5 \\
-7\ 2 \\
\hline
3
\end{array}
$$

b. $2\overline{)1\ 2\ 0}$

c. $7\overline{)7\ 2\ 1}$

d. $4\overline{)1\ 0\ 5}$

PRACTICE

Divide.

	a	*b*	*c*	*d*	*e*
1.	3)6 9	4)8 7	5)5 4	9)9 2	6)5 9
2.	4)5 6 8	6)7 2 6	7)8 0 0	3)4 3 4	9)3 0 8
3.	5)1 4 8	8)1 6 0	8)2 5 3	4)7 4 3	3)5 3 4
4.	6)1 0 0	9)9 0 7	5)6 1 9	7)4 4 0	4)6 5 2

Set up the problems. Then find the quotients.

         a   *b*   *c*

5. $128 \div 2 =$ _____ $57 \div 9 =$ _____ $283 \div 4 =$ _____

    2)128

MIXED PRACTICE

Find each answer.

	a	*b*	*c*	*d*
1.	3 8 1 2 9 5 + 3 2	6,1 8 3 −1,7 6 6	4 3,9 2 5 + 9,0 1 4	3 0,0 0 0 −1 0,9 2 1
2.	3 7 5 × 8	1 0 7 × 9	4 5 1 × 3 2	8 7 6 × 5 7

Division Practice

Here are two hints to help you know if your trial quotient is correct.

If the remainder is more than the divisor, then your trial quotient is not enough.

$$\begin{array}{r} 5 \\ 4\overline{)2\ 6\ 4} \\ -2\ 0 \\ \hline 6 \end{array}$$ ← **Not enough**

Just right →

$$\begin{array}{r} 6 \\ 4\overline{)2\ 6\ 4} \\ -2\ 4 \\ \hline 2 \end{array}$$

If you cannot subtract after multiplying the trial quotient and the divisor, then your trial quotient is too much.

$$\begin{array}{r} 7 \\ 4\overline{)2\ 7\ 6} \\ -2\ 8 \\ \hline \end{array}$$ ← **Too much**

Just right →

$$\begin{array}{r} 6 \\ 4\overline{)2\ 7\ 6} \\ -2\ 4 \\ \hline 3 \end{array}$$

PRACTICE

Divide. Check.

        a   **b**   **c**   **d**

1.

	T	O
	4	2 R1
2)8	5	
−8		
	0	5
−		4
		1

T	O
3)6	8

T	O
4)8	9

T	O
5)9	5

2.

H	T	O
2)1	2	3

H	T	O
3)1	5	5

H	T	O
5)3	5	8

H	T	O
2)5	1	7

3.

H	T	O
4)8	3	6

H	T	O
7)4	3	0

H	T	O
6)1	8	9

H	T	O
3)9	4	6

Division with 2-digit Divisors

To divide by a 2-digit divisor, decide on a trial quotient. Multiply and subtract. Then write the remainder in the quotient.

Find: 748 ÷ 35

Divide.		Multiply and subtract.		Multiply and subtract.
H T O 35)7 4 8	**Think:** 3)7 is about 2. So, 35)74	H T O $\quad$ 2 35)7 4 8 $-7\ 0$ ↓ $\quad\quad$ 4 8	**Think:** 3)4 is about 1. So, 35)48	H T O $\quad$ 2 1 R 13 35)7 4 8 $-7\ 0$ ↓ $\quad\quad$ 4 8 $\quad -3\ 5$ $\quad\quad$ 1 3

PRACTICE

Divide.

	a	b	c	d
1.	H T O $\quad$ 2 2 R 3 12)2 6 7 $-2\ 4$ ↓ $\quad$ 2 7 $-2\ 4$ $\quad\quad$ 3	H T O 25)5 3 2	H T O 31)6 3 0	H T O 2)4 0 8
2.	H T O $\quad\quad$ 9 R 5 30)2 7 5 $-2\ 7\ 0$ $\quad\quad$ 5	H T O 40)9 0 0	H T O 60)2 6 4	H T O 90)7 7 5
3.	Th H T O $\quad\quad$ 5 2 R 1 42)2,1 8 5 $-2\ 1\ 0$ ↓ $\quad\quad$ 8 5 $\quad -8\ 4$ $\quad\quad\quad$ 1	Th H T O 57)6,4 8 0	Th H T O 89)2,7 9 0	Th H T O 73)5,1 1 1

Division Practice

Sometimes when you divide, your trial quotient may not be great
enough or it may be too great. Here is how you can tell.

If the remainder is more than the divisor, then your trial quotient is not enough.	If you cannot subtract after multiplying the quotient and the divisor, then your trial quotient is too great.
$\begin{array}{r} 7 \leftarrow \textbf{Not} \\ 46\overline{)3\ 8\ 0} \\ -3\ 2\ 2 \\ \hline 5\ 8 \end{array}$ **enough** Just → **right** $\begin{array}{r} 8\ \text{R}\ 12 \\ 46\overline{)3\ 8\ 0} \\ -3\ 6\ 8 \\ \hline 1\ 2 \end{array}$	$\begin{array}{r} 7 \leftarrow \textbf{Too} \\ 33\overline{)2\ 2\ 5} \\ -2\ 3\ 1 \end{array}$ **much** Just → **right** $\begin{array}{r} 6\ \text{R}\ 27 \\ 33\overline{)2\ 2\ 5} \\ -1\ 9\ 8 \\ \hline 2\ 7 \end{array}$

PRACTICE

Divide.

	a	b	c	d
1.	$\begin{array}{r} 3\ \text{R}\ 27 \\ 73\overline{)2\ 4\ 6} \\ -2\ 1\ 9 \\ \hline 2\ 7 \end{array}$	$47\overline{)2\ 3\ 0}$	$33\overline{)1\ 7\ 5}$	$47\overline{)2\ 4\ 0}$
2.	$76\overline{)5\ 4\ 1}$	$52\overline{)4\ 1\ 2}$	$41\overline{)2\ 8\ 3}$	$28\overline{)1\ 9\ 4}$
3.	$84\overline{)3\ 3\ 1}$	$31\overline{)2\ 4\ 5}$	$57\overline{)2\ 9\ 1}$	$36\overline{)2\ 2\ 0}$
4.	$18\overline{)1\ 3\ 2}$	$38\overline{)2\ 7\ 4}$	$32\overline{)2\ 8\ 8}$	$89\overline{)5\ 8\ 2}$
5.	$92\overline{)5\ 5\ 0}$	$27\overline{)1\ 7\ 1}$	$69\overline{)3\ 5\ 6}$	$26\overline{)1\ 6\ 2}$

Unit 2 Whole Numbers

Dividing Larger Numbers

To divide greater numbers by a 2-digit divisor, decide on a
trial quotient. Multiply and subtract. Check to make sure the
quotient is great enough and not too great. Write the remainder
after the quotient.

Find: 96,446 ÷ 26

Divide.
Multiply. Subtract.

```
         3,
26)9 6,4 4 6
  -7 8 ↓
   1 8 4
```

Divide.
Multiply. Subtract.

```
          3, 7
26)9 6,4 4 6
  -7 8
   1 8 4
  -1 8 2 ↓
       2 4
```

Divide.
Multiply. Subtract.

```
          3, 7 0
26)9 6,4 4 6
  -7 8
   1 8 4
  -1 8 2
       2 4 
     -  0 ↓
       2 4 6
```

Divide.
Multiply. Subtract.

```
          3, 7 0 9 R 12
26)9 6,4 4 6
  -7 8
   1 8 4
  -1 8 2
       2 4
     -  0
       2 4 6
     -2 3 4
         1 2
```

PRACTICE

Divide.

       a   b   c   d

1.
```
         3 1 4
75)2 3,5 5 0
  -2 2 5 ↓
     1 0 5
    -  7 5 ↓
         3 0 0
        -3 0 0
             0
```

   42)5 4,3 6 4

   62)6 0,2 0 2

   89)9 5,7 2 0

2.
   92)7 7,7 7 7

   28)1 4,4 4 8

   39)6 7,6 1 2

   59)1 0,8 3 0

Dividing by Hundreds

When you divide by hundreds, look at the first 3 or 4 digits of the **dividend** to determine your first trial quotient. From that point on, use the same steps: divide, multiply, and subtract.

Find: 52,386 ÷ 388

Divide.
Multiply. Subtract.

```
        1
388)5 2, 3 8 6
   -3 8 8 ↓
   1, 3 5 8
```

Divide.
Multiply. Subtract.

```
        1 3
388)5 2, 3 8 6
   -3 8 8
   1, 3 5 8
  -1, 1 6 4 ↓
   1, 9 4 6
```

Divide.
Multiply. Subtract.

```
        1 3 5 R 6
388)5 2, 3 8 6
   -3 8 8
   1, 3 5 8
  -1, 1 6 4
   1, 9 4 6
  -1, 9 4 0
          6
```

PRACTICE

Divide.

       a   b   c   d

1.
```
            2 3 3 R 107
341)7 9, 5 6 0
   -6 8 2 ↓
    1, 1 3 6
   -1, 0 2 3 ↓
     1, 1 3 0
    -1, 0 2 3
         1 0 7
```

453)1 8, 3 2 7

236)3, 3 1 7

426)3, 9 6 6

2.

863)6 3, 0 4 3

904)7 5, 0 0 0

506)4 3 5, 1 6 0

246)1 2 3, 4 5 6

Multiplication and Division Practice

Multiply.

	a	b	c	d
1.	7 2 × 4	3 1 9 × 3	1,7 2 8 × 9	5 0,8 0 0 × 4
2.	3 7 ×2 4	7 8 ×5 6	4 8 5 × 9 2	6,9 4 8 × 8 9
3.	9,9 6 7 × 3 6	4 5,8 4 7 × 6 5	5 9 2 ×2 3 1	6,3 4 2 × 3 5 8

Divide.

	a	b	c	d
4.	63)8 3 4	9)8,4 5 2	4)2,5 6 3	7)3 6,5 3 3
5.	24)9 6	27)5,7 7 6	14)1,0 3 2	26)8,1 7 4
6.	85)7 1,9 9 5	60)2 8,9 8 8	57)3 4,6 7 6	357)4 4,9 8 2

Estimation of Products

To estimate products, round each factor. Then multiply the rounded factors.

Estimate: 37 × 54

Round each factor to the greatest place. Multiply.

$$\begin{array}{r} 3\ 7 \rightarrow\quad 40 \\ \times 5\ 4 \rightarrow \times\ 50 \\ \hline 2,000 \end{array}$$

Estimate: 25 × 211

Round each factor to the greatest place. Multiply.

$$\begin{array}{r} 2\ 1\ 1 \rightarrow\quad 200 \\ \times\ \ 2\ 5 \rightarrow \times\ \ 30 \\ \hline 6,000 \end{array}$$

PRACTICE

Estimate the products.

a	b	c	d

1.
$$\begin{array}{r} 42 \rightarrow\quad 40 \\ \times 82 \rightarrow \times\ 80 \\ \hline 3,200 \end{array}$$
$$\begin{array}{r} 27 \rightarrow \\ \times 14 \rightarrow \\ \hline \end{array}$$
$$\begin{array}{r} 58 \rightarrow \\ \times 33 \rightarrow \\ \hline \end{array}$$
$$\begin{array}{r} 76 \rightarrow \\ \times 30 \rightarrow \\ \hline \end{array}$$

2.
$$\begin{array}{r} 83 \rightarrow \\ \times 26 \rightarrow \\ \hline \end{array}$$
$$\begin{array}{r} 77 \rightarrow \\ \times 55 \rightarrow \\ \hline \end{array}$$
$$\begin{array}{r} 49 \rightarrow \\ \times 37 \rightarrow \\ \hline \end{array}$$
$$\begin{array}{r} 31 \rightarrow \\ \times 94 \rightarrow \\ \hline \end{array}$$

3.
$$\begin{array}{r} 193 \rightarrow \\ \times\ 41 \rightarrow \\ \hline \end{array}$$
$$\begin{array}{r} 788 \rightarrow \\ \times\ 29 \rightarrow \\ \hline \end{array}$$
$$\begin{array}{r} 572 \rightarrow \\ \times\ 15 \rightarrow \\ \hline \end{array}$$
$$\begin{array}{r} 299 \rightarrow \\ \times\ 38 \rightarrow \\ \hline \end{array}$$

4.
$$\begin{array}{r} 746 \rightarrow\quad 700 \\ \times 526 \rightarrow \times\ 500 \\ \hline 350,000 \end{array}$$
$$\begin{array}{r} 892 \rightarrow \\ \times 175 \rightarrow \\ \hline \end{array}$$
$$\begin{array}{r} 632 \rightarrow \\ \times 362 \rightarrow \\ \hline \end{array}$$
$$\begin{array}{r} 719 \rightarrow \\ \times 428 \rightarrow \\ \hline \end{array}$$

Estimate the products.

a	b	c

5. 38 × 66 _____   945 × 13 _____   211 × 747 _____

$$\begin{array}{r} 66 \rightarrow \\ \times 38 \rightarrow \\ \hline \end{array}$$

6. 756 × 912 _____   61 × 183 _____   22 × 59 _____

Estimation of Quotients

To estimate quotients, round the numbers to use basic facts.

Estimate: 424 ÷ 6

Round the dividend to use a basic fact. Divide.

$6\overline{)424}$ **424 ÷ 6**   **Think:** 424 is close to 420.

       ↓   ↓

       420 ÷ 6 = 70

Estimate: 928 ÷ 29

Round the dividend and the divisor to use a basic fact. Divide.

$29\overline{)928}$ **928 ÷ 29**   **Think:** 928 is close to 900 and 29 is

       ↓   ↓

       900 ÷ 30 = 30   close to 30.

PRACTICE

Round the dividends to estimate the quotients.

       a   *b*   *c*

1. $4\overline{)362} \rightarrow 4\overline{)360}$ (90) $7\overline{)558} \rightarrow$ $8\overline{)404} \rightarrow$

2. $5\overline{)3,005} \rightarrow 5\overline{)3,000}$ (600) $9\overline{)7,222} \rightarrow$ $6\overline{)2,432} \rightarrow$

Round the dividends and the divisors to estimate the quotients.

       a   *b*   *c*

3. $26\overline{)598} \rightarrow 30\overline{)600}$ (20) $38\overline{)812} \rightarrow$ $19\overline{)589} \rightarrow$

4. $12\overline{)664} \rightarrow$ $34\overline{)648} \rightarrow$ $42\overline{)630} \rightarrow$

5. $61\overline{)632} \rightarrow$ $52\overline{)936} \rightarrow$ $54\overline{)756} \rightarrow$

Problem-Solving Strategy: Choose an Operation

Recycling one ton of paper saves 17 trees. Suppose people in a country recycle about 77,163 tons of paper every day. How many trees would be saved by recycling each day?

Understand the problem.

- **What do you want to know?**
  the number of trees that are saved by recycling paper each day

- **What information is given?**
  One ton of recycled paper saves 17 trees.
  About 77,163 tons of paper are recycled every day.

Plan how to solve it.

- **What strategy can you use?**
  You can choose the operation needed to solve it.

Add to combine groups.	**Multiply** to combine equal groups.
Subtract to separate into groups.	**Divide** to separate into equal groups.

Solve it.

- **How can you use this strategy to solve the problem?**
  Since you need to combine 17 equal groups of 77,163, you should multiply.

- **What is the answer?**
  About 1,311,771 trees are saved by recycling paper every day.

$$\begin{array}{r} 77{,}163 \\ \times\quad 17 \\ \hline 540\ 141 \\ +771\ 63 \\ \hline 1{,}311{,}771 \end{array}$$

Look back and check your answer.

- **Is your answer reasonable?**
  Use an estimate to check multiplication.
  77,163 → 80,000 and 17 → 20
  20 × 80,000 = 1,600,000
  The answer is reasonable.

Choose an operation to solve each problem. Then solve the problem.

1. The distance from Chicago, Illinois, to Butte, Montana, is 1,522 miles. Seattle, Washington, is 567 miles beyond Butte. How far is it from Chicago to Seattle?

   Operation _____

   Answer _____

2. Each member of the hiking club contributed 15 hours of service. How many hours did the 27 members contribute in all?

   Operation _____

   Answer _____

3. Jupiter and Pluto are the largest and smallest planets in our solar system. Jupiter's diameter is 88,846 miles, and Pluto's diameter is 1,419 miles. How much larger is Jupiter than Pluto?

   Operation _____

   Answer _____

4. Nolan Ryan tops the list for the most career strikeouts with 5,714 strikeouts. Steve Carlton is second with 4,136 strikeouts. How many more strikeouts did Nolan Ryan have than Steve Carlton?

   Operation _____

   Answer _____

5. Killer whales can swim 35 miles per hour. How far can a killer whale swim in 8 hours?

   Operation _____

   Answer _____

6. There are 180 school days each year for most schools in the United States. How many school days are there in 4 years?

   Operation _____

   Answer _____

7. Halley's Comet returns to Earth every 76 years. It was last seen in 1986. When should the comet return?

   Operation _____

   Answer _____

8. Camels can drink about 420 pints of water in one hour. How much water can camels drink in 1 minute? (1 hour = 60 minutes)

   Operation _____

   Answer _____

Problem-Solving Applications

Solve.

1. Miami is 665 miles from Atlanta. Rita's car gets 35 miles per gallon of gasoline. How much gasoline will she use to drive from Miami to Atlanta?

Answer _____

2. Each car on a commuter train can seat 54 passengers. The train has 8 cars. How many people can be seated on the train at one time?

Answer _____

3. Peter's yearly salary is $24,000. Latasha earns $36,000 a year. How much more does Latasha earn each month than Peter? (1 year = 12 months)

Answer _____

4. Cricket frogs can jump 36 times their body length. Taylor is 6 feet tall. If he could jump like a cricket frog, how far could he go?

Answer _____

5. Ms. Kwan jogs the same trail every morning. She jogs 21 miles a week. How many miles does she jog each day? How many miles does she jog in 4 weeks?

Answer _____

6. A department store sold 6 television sets for a total of $3,120. Each set sold for the same price. What was the price for each television set?

Answer _____

7. A total of 224 people signed up for the volleyball tournament. Each team will have 8 players. How many teams will compete in the tournament?

Answer _____

8. The Smith family's last water bill from the city showed a daily usage of 31 gallons per day. Estimate how many gallons of water the Smith family uses each year. (1 year = 365 days)

Answer _____

Estimate the answers.

	a	b	c	d
1.	$37 \rightarrow$ $\times 12 \rightarrow$	$48 \rightarrow$ $\times 39 \rightarrow$	$5\overline{)463} \rightarrow$	$39\overline{)1,645} \rightarrow$

Multiply.

	a	b	c	d
2.	425 $\times \quad 6$	$2,307$ $\times \qquad 4$	62 $\times 23$	58 $\times 46$
3.	674 $\times \quad 20$	908 $\times \quad 63$	$2,587$ $\times \qquad 49$	452 $\times 378$

Divide.

	a	b	c	d
4.	$5\overline{)865}$	$8\overline{)3,572}$	$3\overline{)12,654}$	$42\overline{)139}$
5.	$32\overline{)7,455}$	$48\overline{)5,624}$	$40\overline{)92,571}$	$62\overline{)19,576}$

Solve.

6. During their vacation, the Anderson family drove an average of 324 miles a day. If their vacation was 7 days long, how many miles in all did they drive?

Answer _____

7. During their vacation, Mr. and Mrs. Cortez flew on an international jet liner that traveled 6,375 miles in 15 hours. What was the jet's average speed per hour?

Answer _____

Proper Fractions

A **fraction** names part of a whole. This circle has four equal parts. Each part is $\frac{1}{4}$ of the circle.

One of the four equal parts is shaded.

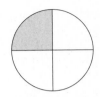

numerator

$$\frac{1}{4} \begin{array}{l} \text{— one shaded part} \\ \text{— four parts in all} \end{array}$$

denominator

We read $\frac{1}{4}$ as one fourth.

A fraction also names part of a group. Three of the four triangles are shaded.

$$\frac{3}{4} \begin{array}{l} \text{— three shaded} \\ \text{— four in all} \end{array}$$

Three fourths are shaded.

PRACTICE

Write the fraction and the word name for the part that is shaded.

             a   *b*   *c*

1.
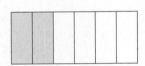
                           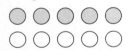
                                         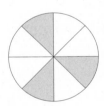

$\frac{2}{6}$ or ___two sixths___   _____ or _____   _____ or _____

Write the fraction for the word name.

             a   *b*   *c*

2. three fifths ___$\frac{3}{5}$___   two thirds _____   five eighths _____

3. one sixth _____   nine ninths _____   four sevenths _____

4. seven tenths _____   one eighth _____   one half _____

Write the word name for the fraction.

             a   *b*   *c*

5. $\frac{2}{7}$ ___two sevenths___ $\frac{6}{6}$ _____ $\frac{3}{10}$ _____

6. $\frac{8}{9}$ _____ $\frac{4}{5}$ _____ $\frac{7}{8}$ _____

7. $\frac{1}{5}$ _____ $\frac{3}{7}$ _____ $\frac{1}{3}$ _____

Improper Fractions and Mixed Numbers

An **improper fraction** is a fraction with a numerator that is greater than or equal to the denominator.

$\frac{5}{5}$, $\frac{15}{5}$, and $\frac{13}{5}$ are improper fractions.

An improper fraction can be written as a whole number or a mixed number.

A **mixed number** is a whole number and a fraction.

$1\frac{5}{12}$ is a mixed number.

A mixed number can be written as an improper fraction.

Write $\frac{5}{5}$ and $\frac{15}{5}$ as whole numbers.

> Divide the numerator by the denominator.
>
> $5\overline{)5}$ with quotient 1 $\frac{5}{5} = 1$
>
> $5\overline{)15}$ with quotient 3 $\frac{15}{5} = 3$

Write $\frac{13}{5}$ as a mixed number.

> Divide the numerator by the denominator. Write the remainder as a fraction.
>
> $5\overline{)13}$ quotient $2\frac{3}{5}$, -10, remainder 3 $\frac{13}{5} = 2\frac{3}{5}$

Write $1\frac{5}{12}$ as an improper fraction.

> Multiply the whole number and the denominator. Add this product to the numerator. Then write the sum over the denominator.
>
> $1\frac{5}{12} = \frac{12 \times 1 + 5}{12} = \frac{17}{12}$
>
> So, $1\frac{5}{12} = \frac{17}{12}$.

PRACTICE

Write as a mixed number or a whole number.

	a	b	c	d
1.	$\frac{24}{6} = \underline{\quad 4 \quad}$	$\frac{27}{9} = \underline{\qquad}$	$\frac{30}{15} = \underline{\qquad}$	$\frac{12}{12} = \underline{\qquad}$
2.	$\frac{13}{12} = \underline{\quad 1\frac{1}{12} \quad}$	$\frac{3}{2} = \underline{\qquad}$	$\frac{4}{3} = \underline{\qquad}$	$\frac{5}{4} = \underline{\qquad}$
3.	$\frac{11}{8} = \underline{\qquad}$	$\frac{36}{6} = \underline{\qquad}$	$\frac{7}{4} = \underline{\qquad}$	$\frac{9}{3} = \underline{\qquad}$
4.	$\frac{64}{4} = \underline{\qquad}$	$\frac{11}{5} = \underline{\qquad}$	$\frac{16}{8} = \underline{\qquad}$	$\frac{25}{6} = \underline{\qquad}$

Write as an improper fraction.

	a	b	c	d
5.	$4\frac{1}{2} = \underline{\quad \frac{9}{2} \quad}$	$5\frac{4}{5} = \underline{\qquad}$	$6\frac{2}{3} = \underline{\qquad}$	$7\frac{1}{4} = \underline{\qquad}$
6.	$2\frac{7}{10} = \underline{\qquad}$	$8\frac{2}{9} = \underline{\qquad}$	$17\frac{3}{5} = \underline{\qquad}$	$9\frac{5}{8} = \underline{\qquad}$

Equivalent Fractions

You can change a fraction to an **equivalent fraction**, or a fraction that has the same value.

To change a fraction to an equivalent fraction in **higher terms**, multiply the numerator and the denominator by the same nonzero number. This is the same as multiplying the fraction by 1.

Rewrite $\frac{2}{3}$ with 12 as the denominator.

Compare the denominators. $\frac{2}{3} = \frac{}{12}$ **Think:** $3 \times 4 = 12$	Multiply both the numerator and the denominator by 4. $\frac{2}{3} = \frac{2 \times 4}{3 \times 4} = \frac{8}{12}$

You can also use the **least common denominator (LCD)** to write equivalent fractions.

Use the LCD to write equivalent fractions for $\frac{2}{3}$ and $\frac{1}{4}$.

List several multiples of each denominator. Multiples of 3: 3 6 9 12 15 Multiples of 4: 4 8 12 16 20	Find the LCD. It is the smallest number that appears on both lists. The LCD of $\frac{2}{3}$ and $\frac{1}{4}$ is 12.	Write equivalent fractions. $\frac{2}{3} = \frac{2 \times 4}{3 \times 4} = \frac{8}{12}$ $\frac{1}{4} = \frac{1 \times 3}{4 \times 3} = \frac{3}{12}$

PRACTICE

Rewrite each fraction as an equivalent fraction in higher terms.

	a	b	c	d
1.	$\frac{2}{3} = \frac{2 \times 3}{3 \times 3} = \frac{6}{9}$	$\frac{1}{2} = \frac{}{30}$	$\frac{3}{4} = \frac{}{12}$	$\frac{2}{5} = \frac{}{15}$
2.	$\frac{1}{2} = \frac{}{14}$	$\frac{5}{6} = \frac{}{18}$	$\frac{4}{5} = \frac{}{10}$	$\frac{3}{8} = \frac{}{16}$

Use the LCD to write equivalent fractions.

	a	b	c	d
3.	$\frac{3}{4} = \frac{3 \times 3}{4 \times 3} = \frac{9}{12}$	$\frac{1}{3} =$	$\frac{2}{5} =$	$\frac{5}{6} =$
	$\frac{1}{6} = \frac{1 \times 2}{6 \times 2} = \frac{2}{12}$	$\frac{4}{5} =$	$\frac{1}{4} =$	$\frac{7}{8} =$
4.	$\frac{2}{3} =$	$\frac{9}{10} =$	$\frac{1}{2} =$	$\frac{1}{3} =$
	$\frac{5}{7} =$	$\frac{3}{4} =$	$\frac{3}{5} =$	$\frac{1}{2} =$

Unit 3 The Meaning and Use of Fractions

Simplifying Fractions

Sometimes you might need to change a fraction to an equivalent fraction in **simplest terms**. To **simplify** a fraction, divide both the numerator and the denominator by the same greatest number possible. This is the same as dividing by 1.

Simplify: $\frac{8}{10}$

Consider the numerator and the denominator.

$\frac{8}{10} =$ **Think:** 10 can be divided by 5 but 8 cannot.
8 can be divided by 4 but 10 cannot.
Both 10 and 8 can be divided by 2.

Divide the numerator and the denominator by 2.

$$\frac{8}{10} = \frac{8 \div 2}{10 \div 2} = \frac{4}{5}$$

A fraction is in simplest terms when 1 is the only number that divides both the numerator and denominator evenly. The fraction $\frac{4}{5}$ is in simplest terms.

PRACTICE

Simplify.

	a	b	c	d
1.	$\frac{6}{8} = \frac{3}{4}$	$\frac{10}{20} =$	$\frac{3}{9} =$	$\frac{9}{12} =$
2.	$\frac{10}{12} =$	$\frac{8}{20} =$	$\frac{2}{8} =$	$\frac{4}{6} =$
3.	$\frac{5}{15} =$	$\frac{14}{16} =$	$\frac{7}{14} =$	$\frac{10}{25} =$
4.	$\frac{2}{4} =$	$\frac{6}{9} =$	$\frac{2}{6} =$	$\frac{3}{15} =$
5.	$\frac{12}{18} =$	$\frac{4}{12} =$	$\frac{2}{10} =$	$\frac{9}{21} =$
6.	$\frac{8}{14} =$	$\frac{2}{12} =$	$\frac{9}{15} =$	$\frac{15}{45} =$

Addition and Subtraction of Fractions with Like Denominators

To add or subtract fractions with like denominators, add or subtract the numerators. Use the same denominator. Simplify the answer.

Remember,

- to simplify an improper fraction, write it as a whole number or mixed number.
- to simplify a proper fraction, write it in simplest terms.

Find: $\frac{2}{7} + \frac{5}{7}$

Add the numerators.	Use the same denominator.
$\frac{2}{7}$ $+\frac{5}{7}$ $\overline{\frac{}{7}}$	$\frac{2}{7}$ $+\frac{5}{7}$ $\overline{\frac{7}{7}=1}$ Simplify the answer.

Find: $\frac{7}{8} - \frac{3}{8}$

Subtract the numerators.	Use the same denominator.
$\frac{7}{8}$ $-\frac{3}{8}$ $\overline{\frac{4}{}}$	$\frac{7}{8}$ $-\frac{3}{8}$ $\overline{\frac{4}{8}=\frac{1}{2}}$ Simplify the answer.

PRACTICE

Add. Simplify.

	a	b	c	d	e
1.	$\frac{1}{8}$ $+\frac{3}{8}$ $\overline{\frac{4}{8}=\frac{1}{2}}$	$\frac{1}{5}$ $+\frac{2}{5}$	$\frac{2}{9}$ $+\frac{1}{9}$	$\frac{3}{4}$ $+\frac{1}{4}$	$\frac{7}{10}$ $+\frac{1}{10}$
2.	$\frac{9}{10}$ $+\frac{3}{10}$ $\overline{\frac{12}{10}=1\frac{2}{10}=1\frac{1}{5}}$	$\frac{9}{16}$ $+\frac{5}{16}$	$\frac{11}{12}$ $+\frac{5}{12}$	$\frac{5}{9}$ $+\frac{4}{9}$	$\frac{6}{11}$ $+\frac{4}{11}$

Subtract. Simplify.

	a	b	c	d	e
3.	$\frac{7}{12}$ $-\frac{1}{12}$	$\frac{5}{10}$ $-\frac{3}{10}$	$\frac{7}{15}$ $-\frac{4}{15}$	$\frac{15}{16}$ $-\frac{7}{16}$	$\frac{9}{10}$ $-\frac{1}{10}$

Addition of Fractions with Different Denominators

To add fractions with different denominators, first rewrite the fractions as equivalent fractions with like denominators. Then add the numerators and simplify the answer.

Find: $\frac{1}{4} + \frac{8}{16}$

Write equivalent fractions with like denominators.

$\frac{1}{4} = \frac{4}{16}$

Remember:

$+\frac{8}{16} = \frac{8}{16}$ $\frac{1}{4} = \frac{1 \times 4}{4 \times 4} = \frac{4}{16}$

Add the numerators. Use the same denominator.

$\frac{1}{4} = \frac{4}{16}$

$+\frac{8}{16} = \frac{8}{16}$

$\frac{12}{16} = \frac{3}{4}$ Simplify the answer.

PRACTICE

Add. Simplify.

        a   *b*   *c*   *d*

1. $\frac{5}{6} = \frac{5}{6}$ $\frac{3}{8}$ $\frac{1}{8}$ $\frac{5}{8}$

    $+\frac{1}{2} = \frac{3}{6}$ $+\frac{1}{2}$ $+\frac{3}{4}$ $+\frac{1}{2}$

         $\frac{8}{6} = 1\frac{2}{6} = 1\frac{1}{3}$

2. $\frac{7}{9}$ $\frac{5}{9}$ $\frac{3}{10}$ $\frac{2}{3}$

    $+\frac{2}{3}$ $+\frac{1}{3}$ $+\frac{1}{5}$ $+\frac{4}{21}$

3. $\frac{2}{3}$ $\frac{2}{5}$ $\frac{3}{7}$ $\frac{1}{20}$

    $+\frac{7}{15}$ $+\frac{9}{15}$ $+\frac{5}{14}$ $+\frac{7}{10}$

Set up the problems. Then find the sums. Simplify.

               a   *b*   *c*

4. $\frac{7}{10} + \frac{2}{5} =$ _____ $\frac{9}{16} + \frac{7}{8} =$ _____ $\frac{2}{21} + \frac{4}{7} =$ _____

    $\frac{7}{10}$

    $+\frac{2}{5}$

Addition of Fractions Using the Least Common Denominator

Find: $\frac{2}{3} + \frac{1}{5}$

Write equivalent fractions with like denominators. Use the LCD.

$$\frac{2}{3} = \frac{2 \times 5}{3 \times 5} = \frac{10}{15}$$
$$+\frac{1}{5} = \frac{1 \times 3}{5 \times 3} = \frac{3}{15}$$

Add the numerators.
Use the same denominator.

$$\frac{2}{3} = \frac{10}{15}$$
$$+\frac{1}{5} = \frac{3}{15}$$
$$\frac{13}{15}$$

PRACTICE

Add. Simplify.

	a	b	c	d
1.	$\frac{1}{2} = \frac{9}{18}$ $+\frac{7}{9} = \frac{14}{18}$ $\overline{\frac{23}{18}} = 1\frac{5}{18}$	$\frac{4}{5}$ $+\frac{2}{3}$	$\frac{1}{3}$ $+\frac{3}{10}$	$\frac{3}{7}$ $+\frac{1}{2}$
2.	$\frac{2}{3}$ $+\frac{3}{4}$	$\frac{5}{6}$ $+\frac{3}{5}$	$\frac{3}{7}$ $+\frac{1}{4}$	$\frac{1}{2}$ $+\frac{2}{8}$
3.	$\frac{2}{5}$ $+\frac{7}{9}$	$\frac{4}{5}$ $+\frac{7}{11}$	$\frac{2}{3}$ $+\frac{7}{8}$	$\frac{1}{7}$ $+\frac{3}{8}$

Set up the problems. Then find the sums. Simplify.

	a	b	c
4.	$\frac{3}{8} + \frac{5}{6} =$ _____ $\frac{3}{8}$ $+\frac{5}{6}$	$\frac{5}{6} + \frac{3}{4} =$ _____	$\frac{2}{7} + \frac{2}{3} =$ _____

Adding Mixed Numbers, Whole Numbers, and Fractions

To add mixed numbers, whole numbers, and fractions, first check for unlike denominators. Write mixed numbers and fractions as equivalent fractions with like denominators. Add the equivalent fractions. Then add the whole numbers and simplify.

Find: $3\frac{1}{6} + \frac{3}{4}$

Write the fractions with like denominators.	Add the fractions.	Add the whole numbers.
$3\frac{1}{6} = 3\frac{2}{12}$ $+ \;\frac{3}{4} = \;\frac{9}{12}$	$3\frac{1}{6} = 3\frac{2}{12}$ $+ \;\frac{3}{4} = \;\frac{9}{12}$ $\frac{11}{12}$	$3\frac{1}{6} = 3\frac{2}{12}$ $+ \;\frac{3}{4} = \;\frac{9}{12}$ $3\frac{11}{12}$

PRACTICE

Add. Simplify.

               a   b   c   d

1.

$5\frac{1}{3} = 5\frac{2}{6}$ $\frac{2}{5}$ $3\frac{1}{7}$ $\frac{1}{6}$

$+ \;\frac{1}{6} = \;\frac{1}{6}$ $+2\frac{1}{10}$ $+ \;\frac{3}{14}$ $+9\frac{1}{2}$

$5\frac{3}{6} = 5\frac{1}{2}$

2.

$11\frac{4}{9} = 11\frac{4}{9}$ $2\frac{1}{4}$ $1\frac{1}{2}$ $6\frac{4}{15}$

$+ \;4\frac{1}{3} = 4\frac{3}{9}$ $+3\frac{1}{8}$ $+4\frac{3}{8}$ $+3\frac{1}{3}$

$15\frac{7}{9}$

3.

$6\frac{1}{8}$ $1\frac{1}{4}$ $3\frac{1}{2}$ $12\frac{1}{5}$

$+2\frac{4}{7}$ $+5\frac{1}{3}$ $+6\frac{2}{5}$ $+ \;7\frac{3}{4}$

4. $5 + \frac{1}{10} + 2\frac{1}{2} = $ _____ $\frac{1}{4} + 3\frac{2}{3} + 1 = $ _____ $4\frac{1}{6} + 6 + \frac{3}{8} = $ _____ $7 + \frac{1}{2} + 8\frac{2}{5} = $ _____

Problem-Solving Strategy: Complete a Pattern

Oak trees are sometimes over 100 feet tall, but they grow very slowly. To study a young oak tree's growth, a forest ranger measures and records the tree's height every week. If the tree continues to grow at the same rate, how tall will it be at the end of Week 5?

Week 1	Week 2	Week 3	Week 4	Week 5
$10\frac{1}{5}$ inches	$10\frac{3}{5}$ inches	11 inches	$11\frac{2}{5}$ inches	?

Understand the problem.

- **What do you want to know?**
  how tall the oak tree will be at the end of Week 5

- **What information is given?**
  measurements for 4 weeks

Plan how to solve it.

- **What strategy can you use?**
  You can find and complete a pattern.

Solve it.

- **How can you use this strategy to solve the problem?**
  Look for a pattern between each week's height. Find how many inches the tree grew each week. Then add the same number of inches to Week 4's height to complete the pattern. The number pattern is **add $\frac{2}{5}$.**

$$10\frac{1}{5} \overset{+\frac{2}{5}}{\frown} 10\frac{3}{5} \overset{+\frac{2}{5}}{\frown} 10\frac{5}{5} = 11 \overset{+\frac{2}{5}}{\frown} 11\frac{2}{5} \overset{+\frac{2}{5}}{\frown} 11\frac{4}{5}$$

The number pattern is add $\frac{2}{5}$.

- **What is the answer?**
  The oak tree will be $11\frac{4}{5}$ inches tall at the end of Week 5.

Look back and check your answer.

- **Is your answer reasonable?**
  You can check the pattern by adding a different way.

$$\frac{2}{5} + \frac{2}{5} + \frac{2}{5} + \frac{2}{5} = \frac{8}{5} = 1\frac{3}{5} \leftarrow \text{4 weeks of growth}$$

Add this to Week 1's height.

$$10\frac{1}{5} + 1\frac{3}{5} = 11\frac{4}{5}$$

The sum matches the growth pattern.
The answer is reasonable.

Unit 3 The Meaning and Use of Fractions

Complete a pattern to solve each problem. Simplify.

1. The Acme Corporation stock has gone up in value for the past three months. How much will the stock be worth next month if the trend continues?

Month 1	Month 2	Month 3	Month 4
$51\frac{3}{8}$	$54\frac{3}{4}$	$58\frac{1}{8}$	?

Answer _____

2. The table below tells how many kilometers a high-speed train can travel for the first three hours. How many kilometers can it travel in 4 hours?

Hour 1	Hour 2	Hour 3	Hour 4
515 km	1,030 km	1,545 km	?

Answer _____

Write the number pattern. Then answer the question.

3. What is the next number in this pattern?

$8\frac{2}{3}$, 10, $11\frac{1}{3}$, $12\frac{2}{3}$, . . .

Pattern _____

Answer _____

4. What are the next two numbers in this pattern?

5, 15, 45, 135, . . .

Pattern _____

Answer _____

5. What is the missing number in this pattern?

$2\frac{1}{4}$, $2\frac{7}{8}$, _____, $4\frac{1}{8}$

Pattern _____

Answer _____

6. What is the missing number in this pattern?

1,280, 320, _____, 20

Pattern _____

Answer _____

7. Mr. Rivera's salary increased last year from $38,260 to $40,040. His present salary is $41,820. At this rate, what will his salary be at the end of next year?

Pattern _____

Answer _____

8. Fran measured the height of her tomato plant for the science fair and recorded the results. If the same pattern continued, what would be the next height?

$3\frac{3}{4}$ inches, 4 inches, $4\frac{1}{4}$ inches, _____

Pattern _____

Answer _____

Practice with Improper Fractions

When adding mixed numbers, whole numbers, and fractions, your sum might contain an improper fraction. To regroup a sum that contains an improper fraction, first write the improper fraction as a mixed number. Then add and simplify.

Find: $8\frac{2}{3} + 2\frac{5}{6}$

Write the fractions with like denominators. Add the mixed numbers.

$$8\frac{2}{3} = 8\frac{4}{6}$$
$$+2\frac{5}{6} = 2\frac{5}{6}$$
$$\overline{\phantom{+2\frac{5}{6} = } 10\frac{9}{6}}$$

The sum, **$10\frac{9}{6}$**, contains an improper fraction. To regroup, write the improper fraction as a mixed number.

$$\frac{9}{6} = 1\frac{3}{6} = 1\frac{1}{2}$$

Then add the whole numbers.

$$10\frac{9}{6} = 10 + 1\frac{1}{2} = 11\frac{1}{2}$$

PRACTICE

Add. Regroup. Simplify.

         a   *b*   *c*

1. $\quad 3\frac{11}{12} = 3\frac{11}{12}$ $\qquad\qquad\qquad \frac{5}{6}$ $\qquad\qquad\qquad\qquad 2\frac{9}{11}$

$\quad + \ \frac{1}{2} = \ \frac{6}{12}$ $\qquad\qquad\quad +9\frac{3}{4}$ $\qquad\qquad\qquad\quad + \ \frac{5}{8}$

$\qquad\qquad \overline{3\frac{17}{12} = 3 + 1\frac{5}{12} = 4\frac{5}{12}}$

2. $\quad 1\frac{3}{7}$ $\qquad\qquad\qquad\qquad\quad 6\frac{5}{6}$ $\qquad\qquad\qquad\qquad 7\frac{8}{9}$

$\quad +8\frac{7}{8}$ $\qquad\qquad\qquad\qquad +4\frac{1}{2}$ $\qquad\qquad\qquad\quad +3\frac{2}{3}$

3. $5 + \frac{1}{2} + \frac{2}{3} =$ _____ $\qquad \frac{5}{9} + 8 + \frac{1}{2} =$ _____ $\qquad \frac{3}{4} + \frac{2}{3} + 7 =$ _____

4. $1\frac{1}{2} + 3\frac{5}{8} + \frac{3}{8} =$ _____ $\qquad 9\frac{7}{10} + \frac{3}{10} + 4\frac{4}{5} =$ _____ $\qquad \frac{2}{3} + 6\frac{5}{12} + 2\frac{1}{3} =$ _____

Unit 3 The Meaning and Use of Fractions

Problem-Solving Applications

Solve. Simplify.

1. About one third of a town's residents has the newspaper delivered. What fraction of the town's residents does not have the newspaper delivered?

   Answer _____

2. Ann lives $\frac{3}{10}$ mile from school. Carlos lives only $\frac{1}{10}$ mile from school. How much farther from school does Ann live than Carlos?

   Answer _____

3. Antoine roped off a square section of the park for a picnic. Each side used $15\frac{1}{2}$ feet of rope. How much rope did Antoine use in all?

   Answer _____

4. The two prize-winning fish in the annual fresh-water tournament weighed $11\frac{1}{2}$ pounds and $12\frac{1}{16}$ pounds. How much did they weigh altogether?

   Answer _____

5. Sewing Stuff sold $9\frac{1}{3}$ yards from a bolt of fabric containing $53\frac{2}{3}$ yards. How much of the fabric was left?

   Answer _____

6. Tamara bought two bottles of perfume. One bottle contains $\frac{1}{2}$ ounce. The other bottle holds $1\frac{3}{4}$ ounces. How much perfume did Tamara buy in all?

   Answer _____

7. Two of the wettest cities in the Northern Hemisphere get about $65\frac{7}{10}$ inches and about $62\frac{1}{4}$ inches of rain per year. How much rain do the two cities receive each year in all?

   Answer _____

8. Donna's upper arm bone (humerus) is $36\frac{1}{2}$ centimeters (cm) long. The large bone in her lower arm (ulna) is $28\frac{1}{5}$ cm long. What is the combined length of these two bones?

   Answer _____

Subtraction of Fractions with Different Denominators

To subtract fractions with different denominators, first rewrite the fractions as equivalent fractions with like denominators. Then subtract and simplify the answer.

Find: $\frac{5}{6} - \frac{3}{8}$

Write equivalent fractions with like denominators. Use the LCD.

$$\frac{5}{6} = \frac{5 \times 4}{6 \times 4} = \frac{20}{24}$$
$$-\frac{3}{8} = \frac{3 \times 3}{8 \times 3} = \frac{9}{24}$$

Subtract the numerators. Use the same denominator.

$$\frac{5}{6} = \frac{20}{24}$$
$$-\frac{3}{8} = \frac{9}{24}$$
$$\frac{11}{24}$$

GUIDED PRACTICE

Subtract. Simplify.

	a	b	c	d
1.	$\frac{1}{2} = \frac{5}{10}$ $-\frac{3}{10} = \frac{3}{10}$ $\frac{2}{10} = \frac{1}{5}$	$\frac{1}{3} = \frac{}{6}$ $-\frac{1}{6} = \frac{}{6}$	$\frac{5}{8} = \frac{}{16}$ $-\frac{5}{16} = \frac{}{16}$	$\frac{1}{4} = \frac{}{20}$ $-\frac{1}{5} = \frac{}{20}$
2.	$\frac{7}{10} = \frac{}{70}$ $-\frac{3}{7} = \frac{}{70}$	$\frac{1}{3} = \frac{}{12}$ $-\frac{1}{4} = \frac{}{12}$	$\frac{3}{10} = \frac{}{10}$ $-\frac{1}{5} = \frac{}{10}$	$\frac{1}{2} = \frac{}{12}$ $-\frac{1}{12} = \frac{}{12}$
3.	$\frac{3}{5} = \frac{}{35}$ $-\frac{2}{7} = \frac{}{35}$	$\frac{7}{8} = \frac{}{40}$ $-\frac{3}{10} = \frac{}{40}$	$\frac{5}{6} = \frac{}{12}$ $-\frac{3}{4} = \frac{}{12}$	$\frac{3}{4} = \frac{}{8}$ $-\frac{1}{8} = \frac{}{8}$
4.	$\frac{2}{3} = \frac{}{24}$ $-\frac{3}{8} = \frac{}{24}$	$\frac{5}{6} = \frac{}{6}$ $-\frac{1}{3} = \frac{}{6}$	$\frac{4}{5} = \frac{}{15}$ $-\frac{2}{3} = \frac{}{15}$	$\frac{4}{5} = \frac{}{10}$ $-\frac{7}{10} = \frac{}{10}$

PRACTICE

Subtract. Simplify.

	a	*b*	*c*	*d*
1.	$\dfrac{11}{12}$ $-\dfrac{7}{8}$	$\dfrac{7}{9}$ $-\dfrac{1}{4}$	$\dfrac{5}{6}$ $-\dfrac{3}{8}$	$\dfrac{9}{11}$ $-\dfrac{3}{5}$
2.	$\dfrac{1}{2}$ $-\dfrac{1}{5}$	$\dfrac{8}{9}$ $-\dfrac{3}{8}$	$\dfrac{4}{5}$ $-\dfrac{3}{10}$	$\dfrac{14}{15}$ $-\dfrac{1}{3}$
3.	$\dfrac{11}{12}$ $-\dfrac{1}{3}$	$\dfrac{5}{6}$ $-\dfrac{5}{9}$	$\dfrac{5}{7}$ $-\dfrac{1}{2}$	$\dfrac{3}{4}$ $-\dfrac{3}{8}$

Set up the problems. Then find the differences. Simplify.

     a   *b*   *c*

4. $\dfrac{11}{12} - \dfrac{3}{8} =$ _____ $\dfrac{7}{8} - \dfrac{1}{4} =$ _____ $\dfrac{4}{5} - \dfrac{1}{2} =$ _____

$\dfrac{11}{12}$
$-\dfrac{3}{8}$

MIXED PRACTICE

Find each answer.

	a	*b*	*c*	*d*
1.	$\begin{array}{r} 1,2\ 4\ 9 \\ 6\ 3\ 4 \\ 2,9\ 1\ 7 \\ +6,2\ 3\ 6 \\ \hline \end{array}$	$\begin{array}{r} 2\ 4,1\ 0\ 2 \\ 1,9\ 0\ 8 \\ 4,7\ 3\ 9 \\ +\ \ \ \ 6\ 4\ 2 \\ \hline \end{array}$	$\begin{array}{r} 5\ \frac{1}{3} \\ +8\ \frac{1}{12} \\ \hline \end{array}$	$\begin{array}{r} 4\ \frac{3}{5} \\ +6\ \frac{1}{10} \\ \hline \end{array}$
2.	$\begin{array}{r} 1\ 9 \\ \times 3\ 9 \\ \hline \end{array}$	$\begin{array}{r} 3\ 1\ 8 \\ \times\ \ 2\ 3 \\ \hline \end{array}$	$5\ 2\overline{)5\ 7,7\ 2\ 0}$	$2\ 6\overline{)2,0\ 7\ 5}$

Subtraction of Fractions and Mixed Numbers from Whole Numbers

Sometimes you will need to subtract a fraction from a whole number. To subtract from a whole number, write the whole number as a mixed number with a like denominator. Then subtract the fractions. Subtract the whole numbers.

Find: $6 - 4\frac{1}{4}$

To subtract, you need two fractions with like denominators. 6 $-4\frac{1}{4}$	Write 6 as a mixed number with 4 as the denominator. $6 = 5 + \frac{4}{4} = 5\frac{4}{4}$ **Remember:** $\frac{4}{4} = 1$	Subtract the fractions. $6 = 5\frac{4}{4}$ $-4\frac{1}{4} = 4\frac{1}{4}$ $\overline{\frac{3}{4}}$	Subtract the whole numbers. $6 = 5\frac{4}{4}$ $-4\frac{1}{4} = 4\frac{1}{4}$ $\overline{1\frac{3}{4}}$

GUIDED PRACTICE

Write each whole number as a mixed number.

	a	b	c	d
1.	$12 = 11 + \frac{2}{2} = 11\frac{2}{2}$	$3 = 2 + \frac{}{9} =$	$21 = 20 + \frac{}{10} =$	$42 = 41 + \frac{}{24} =$
2.	$7 = 6 + \frac{}{5} =$	$14 = 13 + \frac{}{7} =$	$16 = 15 + \frac{}{11} =$	$35 = 34 + \frac{}{6} =$

Subtract.

	a	b	c	d
3.	$9 = 8\frac{5}{5}$ $-1\frac{2}{5} = 1\frac{2}{5}$ $\overline{7\frac{3}{5}}$	$7 = 6\frac{}{4}$ $-2\frac{3}{4} = 2\frac{3}{4}$	$11 = 10\frac{}{6}$ $-8\frac{5}{6} = 8\frac{5}{6}$	$4 = 3\frac{}{3}$ $-2\frac{1}{3} = 2\frac{1}{3}$
4.	$10 = 9\frac{11}{11}$ $-2\frac{5}{11} = 2\frac{5}{11}$ $\overline{7\frac{6}{11}}$	$6 =$ $-4\frac{2}{3} =$	$9 =$ $-1\frac{2}{7} =$	$12 =$ $-6\frac{5}{6} =$
5.	$8 = 7\frac{3}{3}$ $-\frac{1}{3} = \frac{1}{3}$ $\overline{7\frac{2}{3}}$	$2 =$ $-\frac{3}{5} =$	$5 =$ $-\frac{1}{2} =$	$3 =$ $-\frac{1}{4} =$

PRACTICE

Subtract.

	a	*b*	*c*	*d*
1.	10 $-\ 4\frac{5}{6}$	2 $-\ \frac{2}{7}$	8 $-1\frac{1}{6}$	25 $-12\frac{5}{7}$
2.	6 $-2\frac{4}{9}$	5 $-1\frac{1}{4}$	21 $-\ 3\frac{1}{9}$	3 $-\ \frac{9}{16}$
3.	19 $-13\frac{5}{6}$	12 $-\ \frac{1}{3}$	5 $-3\frac{3}{8}$	14 $-11\frac{2}{5}$
4.	3 $-2\frac{7}{10}$	10 $-\ 7\frac{1}{5}$	8 $-\ \frac{3}{5}$	18 $-13\frac{5}{8}$

Set up the problems. Then find the differences.

a

5. $10 - \frac{3}{4} =$ _____

10
$-\ \frac{3}{4}$

b

$6 - \frac{1}{5} =$ _____

c

$11 - 4\frac{7}{12} =$ _____

6. $12 - 9\frac{5}{9} =$ _____ $7 - 5\frac{1}{2} =$ _____ $9 - \frac{3}{10} =$ _____

MIXED PRACTICE

Find each answer.

	a	*b*	*c*	*d*
1.	$4\ 5\overline{)4,7\ 0\ 0}$	$2,4\ 0\ 7$ $\times\quad 9\ 0\ 8$	$3\ 8\overline{)9,7\ 2\ 8}$	$9\ 8\ 3,4\ 5\ 1$ $8\ 0,1\ 6\ 9$ $+6\ 1\ 9,2\ 4\ 2$

Subtraction of Mixed Numbers with Regrouping

When subtracting mixed numbers, it may be necessary to regroup first. To regroup a mixed number for subtraction, write the whole number part as a mixed number. Add the mixed number and the fraction. Then subtract and simplify.

Find: $5\frac{1}{8} - 3\frac{3}{4}$

Write the fractions with like denominators. Compare the numerators.	$\frac{6}{8}$ is greater than $\frac{1}{8}$.	Add the mixed number and the fraction.	Now you can subtract.
$5\frac{1}{8} = 5\frac{1}{8}$ $-3\frac{3}{4} = 3\frac{6}{8}$	You can't subtract the fractions. To regroup $5\frac{1}{8}$, write 5 as a mixed number. $5 = 4\frac{8}{8}$	$5\frac{1}{8} = 4\frac{8}{8} + \frac{1}{8} = 4\frac{9}{8}$ **Remember:** $\frac{9}{8}$ is an improper fraction.	$5\frac{1}{8} = 4\frac{9}{8}$ $-3\frac{3}{4} = 3\frac{6}{8}$ $\overline{\qquad 1\frac{3}{8}}$

GUIDED PRACTICE

Regroup each mixed number.

	a	b	c
1.	$9\frac{1}{4} = 8\frac{4}{4} + \frac{1}{4} = 8\frac{5}{4}$	$3\frac{2}{5} =$	$12\frac{1}{8} =$
2.	$5\frac{1}{3} =$	$6\frac{3}{7} =$	$7\frac{5}{6} =$

Subtract. Simplify.

a

3. $\quad 7\frac{1}{4} = 6\frac{5}{4}$
$\quad -3\frac{3}{4} = 3\frac{3}{4}$
$\quad\qquad\overline{\qquad 3\frac{2}{4} = 3\frac{1}{2}}$

b

$3\frac{1}{3} = 2\frac{}{3}$
$-\frac{2}{3} = \frac{2}{3}$

c

$5\frac{3}{10} = 4\frac{}{10}$
$-2\frac{7}{10} = 2\frac{7}{10}$

4. $\quad 6\frac{1}{9} = 6\frac{1}{9} = 5\frac{10}{9}$
$\quad -\frac{2}{3} = \frac{6}{9} = \frac{6}{9}$
$\quad\qquad\overline{\qquad\qquad 5\frac{4}{9}}$

$7\frac{1}{8} = 7\frac{1}{8} =$
$-5\frac{1}{2} = 5\frac{4}{8} =$

$10\frac{1}{6} = 10\frac{2}{12} =$
$-4\frac{5}{12} = 4\frac{5}{12} =$

5. $\quad 8\frac{1}{12} = 8\frac{3}{36} = 7\frac{39}{36}$
$\quad -4\frac{8}{9} = 4\frac{32}{36} = 4\frac{32}{36}$
$\quad\qquad\overline{\qquad\qquad 3\frac{7}{36}}$

$15\frac{1}{6} = 15\frac{2}{12} =$
$-12\frac{3}{4} = 12\frac{9}{12} =$

$5\frac{1}{6} = 5\frac{4}{24} =$
$-\frac{7}{8} = \frac{21}{24} =$

Subtract. Simplify.

a	b	c
1. $6\frac{1}{10}$ $-4\frac{7}{10}$	$5\frac{1}{3}$ $-3\frac{2}{3}$	$7\frac{1}{10}$ $-\ \ \frac{1}{5}$
2. $12\frac{1}{8}$ $-\ 9\frac{5}{8}$	$9\frac{1}{6}$ $-6\frac{3}{4}$	$11\frac{1}{4}$ $-\ 5\frac{3}{7}$
3. $8\frac{1}{8}$ $-4\frac{9}{20}$	$2\frac{1}{3}$ $-\ \ \frac{2}{3}$	$15\frac{1}{8}$ $-\ \ \frac{3}{4}$

Set up the problems. Then find the differences. Simplify.

a	b	c
4. $15\frac{1}{8} - 2\frac{1}{4} =$ $15\frac{1}{8}$ $-\ 2\frac{1}{4}$	$6\frac{3}{8} - \frac{1}{2} =$	$12\frac{1}{2} - 5\frac{4}{9} =$

5. $2\frac{1}{8} - \frac{7}{8} =$ $5\frac{1}{12} - 2\frac{11}{12} =$ $16\frac{1}{5} - 10\frac{5}{8} =$

MIXED PRACTICE

Estimate each sum or difference.

a	b	c	d
1. $5\ 8\ 1 \rightarrow$ $+4\ 8\ 7 \rightarrow$	$5,1\ 7\ 6 \rightarrow$ $+1\ 7,4\ 6\ 4 \rightarrow$	$2\ 1,8\ 7\ 5 \rightarrow$ $-\ \ \ \ 7\ 9\ 9 \rightarrow$	$6,5\ 0\ 8 \rightarrow$ $-\ \ \ 5\ 0\ 2 \rightarrow$

Problem-Solving Strategy: Make a Drawing

Bill is $\frac{1}{2}$ foot taller than Amy. Tameeka is $\frac{2}{3}$ foot shorter than Bill. Tameeka is $5\frac{1}{3}$ feet tall. How tall are Amy and Bill?

Understand the problem.

- **What do you want to know?**
  Amy's height and Bill's height

- **What information is given?**
  Fact 1: Tameeka is $5\frac{1}{3}$ feet tall.
  Fact 2: Tameeka is $\frac{2}{3}$ foot shorter than Bill.
  Fact 3: Bill is $\frac{1}{2}$ foot taller than Amy.

Plan how to solve it.

- **What strategy can you use?**
  You can make a drawing to model their heights.

Solve it.

- **How can you use this strategy to solve the problem?**
  Make drawings to help organize the facts. Then use the information to solve the problem.

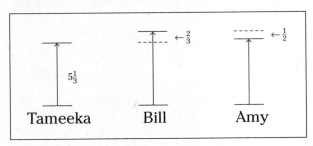

Tameeka's height $+ \frac{2}{3}$ foot = Bill's height

Bill's height $- \frac{1}{2}$ foot = Amy's height

- **What is the answer?**
  Bill is 6 feet tall. Amy is $5\frac{1}{2}$ feet tall.

Look back and check your answer.

- **Is your answer reasonable?**
  You can check your answer with addition and subtraction.

Bill's Height

$ 5\frac{1}{3} \leftarrow$ Tameeka's height
$+ \frac{2}{3}$
$\overline{ 5\frac{3}{3}} = \mathbf{6}$ feet

Amy's Height

$6 = 5\frac{2}{2} \leftarrow$ Bill's height
$- \frac{1}{2} = \frac{1}{2}$
$\overline{ 5\frac{1}{2}}$ feet

The sum and difference match the drawings.
The answer is reasonable.

Make a drawing to solve each problem.

1. The first-place finisher in the long jump event at a high school track meet recorded a jump of $18\frac{3}{4}$ feet. The second place jump was $\frac{1}{2}$ foot less than that. How long was the second place jump?

   Answer _____

2. Shawna is taller than Ted but shorter than Carlos. David is taller than Ted but shorter than Shawna. Ellen is taller than Shawna but shorter than Carlos. List their names from shortest to tallest.

   Answer _____

3. Brothers Rick and Sam operate an apple orchard. Rick begins picking apples at 7:00 A.M., picking at the rate of $1\frac{1}{2}$ bushels per hour. Sam begins at 8:00 A.M., picking at the rate of $2\frac{1}{4}$ bushels per hour. Which brother will have picked more apples at 11:00 A.M.?

   Answer _____

4. A mountain peak is 14,410 feet above sea level. A cloud is 1,470 feet above the peak. An eagle flies 7,516 feet above sea level. How far below the cloud is the eagle?

   Answer _____

5. Lou rode his bike 15 miles north from his house and got a flat tire. He walked $\frac{3}{4}$ mile west to a phone booth to call Pat. She lives 15 miles south of the phone booth. How far from Lou's house is Pat's house?

   Answer _____

6. For the science fair, Jenna measured a snail's movements in a maze. It crawled $5\frac{3}{4}$ inches north, $2\frac{1}{2}$ inches east, $6\frac{1}{2}$ inches south, $4\frac{1}{4}$ inches west, and $\frac{3}{4}$ inch north. How far was the snail from its starting point in the maze?

   Answer _____

Unit 3 The Meaning and Use of Fractions

Problem-Solving Applications

Solve.

1. The results of a survey showed that seven tenths of the households surveyed used a computer. What fraction of the households surveyed did not use a computer?

   Answer _____

2. A standard sheet of paper is $8\frac{1}{2}$ inches wide and 11 inches long. How much longer is the paper than it is wide?

   Answer _____

3. A share of Maxiflex stock costs $8\frac{7}{8}$ dollars. A share of Bentley stock sells for $8\frac{1}{2}$ dollars. Which stock costs less? How much less?

   Answer _____

4. For Thanksgiving dinner, Joe cooked a $17\frac{1}{2}$-pound turkey. His sister, Diana, cooked a $22\frac{1}{4}$-pound turkey. How much more did Diana's turkey weigh?

   Answer _____

5. The Jubilee Diamond is considered the world's most perfectly-cut diamond. It weighs $245\frac{1}{3}$ carats. The famous Hope Diamond weighs $45\frac{1}{2}$ carats. What is the difference in their weights?

   Answer _____

6. Sam, Laura, and Geena live outside town. Sam lives 5 miles from town. Laura lives $\frac{3}{4}$ mile closer than Sam. Geena lives $\frac{1}{2}$ mile closer than Laura. How far from town does Geena live?

   Answer _____

7. The Jones farm received $7\frac{7}{10}$ inches of rain one year and $4\frac{1}{2}$ inches less the following year. How much rain did the farm receive in that following year?

   Answer _____

8. Sue needs to fill in a 46-inch space with wood molding. She has two pieces to use which are $28\frac{1}{2}$ inches long and $23\frac{3}{4}$ inches long. What length must be cut from one of the pieces so that she will have the correct fit?

   Answer _____

Unit 3 The Meaning and Use of Fractions

Write as improper fractions.

a	b	c	d
1. $4\frac{1}{3}$ = _____	$5\frac{2}{3}$ = _____	$6\frac{2}{5}$ = _____	$8\frac{5}{8}$ = _____

Write as mixed numbers or whole numbers. Simplify.

a	b	c	d
2. $\frac{17}{3}$ = _____	$\frac{19}{4}$ = _____	$\frac{31}{5}$ = _____	$\frac{47}{9}$ = _____
3. $\frac{45}{15}$ = _____	$\frac{40}{18}$ = _____	$\frac{135}{45}$ = _____	$\frac{52}{10}$ = _____

Write each fraction as an equivalent fraction in higher terms.

a	b	c	d
4. $\frac{2}{3} = \frac{}{9}$	$\frac{3}{4} = \frac{}{16}$	$\frac{4}{5} = \frac{}{35}$	$\frac{7}{10} = \frac{}{20}$

Add or subtract. Simplify.

a	b	c	d
5. $\begin{array}{r} \frac{2}{3} \\ +\frac{1}{3} \\ \hline \end{array}$	$\begin{array}{r} \frac{1}{2} \\ +\frac{1}{2} \\ \hline \end{array}$	$\begin{array}{r} \frac{4}{5} \\ +\frac{3}{5} \\ \hline \end{array}$	$\begin{array}{r} \frac{5}{6} \\ +\frac{5}{6} \\ \hline \end{array}$
6. $\begin{array}{r} \frac{9}{10} \\ +\frac{2}{3} \\ \hline \end{array}$	$\begin{array}{r} 5\frac{3}{5} \\ +3\frac{3}{4} \\ \hline \end{array}$	$\begin{array}{r} \frac{3}{5} \\ -\frac{1}{5} \\ \hline \end{array}$	$\begin{array}{r} 12 \\ -\ 2\frac{2}{5} \\ \hline \end{array}$
7. $\begin{array}{r} \frac{7}{8} \\ +\frac{1}{2} \\ \hline \end{array}$	$\begin{array}{r} 8\frac{1}{3} \\ -2\frac{2}{5} \\ \hline \end{array}$	$\begin{array}{r} \frac{15}{16} \\ -\frac{3}{16} \\ \hline \end{array}$	$\begin{array}{r} \frac{2}{5} \\ +6\frac{1}{4} \\ \hline \end{array}$

Solve.

8. Mary needs $2\frac{2}{3}$ yards of cloth to sew a dress. She has $3\frac{3}{4}$ yards. How much cloth will she have left over?

9. Leroy ran $2\frac{1}{4}$ miles on Monday. He ran 3 miles on Tuesday and $3\frac{2}{5}$ miles on Wednesday. How many miles did he run in all?

Answer _____

Answer _____

Multiplication of Fractions

To multiply fractions, multiply the numerators and multiply the denominators. Simplify the answer.

Find: $\frac{1}{7} \times \frac{4}{5}$

Multiply the numerators.

$\frac{1}{7} \times \frac{4}{5} = \frac{1 \times 4}{} = \frac{4}{}$

Multiply the denominators.

$\frac{1}{7} \times \frac{4}{5} = \frac{1 \times 4}{7 \times 5} = \frac{4}{35}$

Find: $\frac{2}{3} \times \frac{3}{8}$

Multiply the numerators.

$\frac{2}{3} \times \frac{3}{8} = \frac{2 \times 3}{} = \frac{6}{}$

Multiply the denominators. Simplify.

$\frac{2}{3} \times \frac{3}{8} = \frac{2 \times 3}{3 \times 8} = \frac{6}{24} = \frac{1}{4}$

PRACTICE

Multiply. Simplify.

a

1. $\frac{2}{3} \times \frac{4}{5} = \frac{2 \times 4}{3 \times 5} = \frac{8}{15}$

2. $\frac{1}{2} \times \frac{1}{3} =$

3. $\frac{3}{4} \times \frac{7}{8} =$

4. $\frac{3}{5} \times \frac{2}{3} =$

5. $\frac{2}{3} \times \frac{1}{2} =$

6. $\frac{3}{7} \times \frac{2}{3} =$

7. $\frac{2}{3} \times \frac{1}{4} =$

b

$\frac{4}{5} \times \frac{2}{7} =$

$\frac{2}{3} \times \frac{1}{5} =$

$\frac{4}{9} \times \frac{4}{5} =$

$\frac{3}{10} \times \frac{5}{8} =$

$\frac{3}{5} \times \frac{2}{9} =$

$\frac{5}{6} \times \frac{2}{5} =$

$\frac{5}{8} \times \frac{2}{5} =$

Multiplication of Fractions Using Cancellation

Instead of simplifying fractions after they have been multiplied, it may be possible to use **cancellation** before multiplying. To cancel, find a **common factor** of a numerator and a denominator. Divide both the numerator and the denominator by the common factor. Then multiply, using the new numerator and denominator.

Find: $\frac{3}{10} \times \frac{1}{9}$

Find a common factor.	Cancel.	Multiply the numerators and denominators.
$\frac{3}{10} \times \frac{1}{9}$ The common factor of 3 and 9 is 3.	$\frac{\overset{1}{\cancel{3}}}{10} \times \frac{1}{\underset{3}{\cancel{9}}}$ Divide both the 3 and the 9 by 3.	$\frac{1 \times 1}{10 \times 3} = \frac{1}{30}$

PRACTICE

Multiply using cancellation.

           a   *b*

1. $\frac{1}{10} \times \frac{4}{7} = \frac{1}{\underset{5}{\cancel{10}}} \times \frac{\overset{2}{\cancel{4}}}{7} = \frac{1 \times 2}{5 \times 7} = \frac{2}{35}$ $\frac{3}{35} \times \frac{5}{8} =$

2. $\frac{3}{4} \times \frac{4}{5} =$ $\frac{2}{3} \times \frac{6}{7} =$

3. $\frac{5}{11} \times \frac{7}{10} =$ $\frac{1}{4} \times \frac{2}{5} =$

4. $\frac{1}{3} \times \frac{3}{7} =$ $\frac{3}{5} \times \frac{10}{13} =$

5. $\frac{7}{8} \times \frac{4}{21} = \frac{\overset{1}{\cancel{7}}}{\underset{2}{\cancel{8}}} \times \frac{\overset{1}{\cancel{4}}}{\underset{3}{\cancel{21}}} = \frac{1 \times 1}{2 \times 3} = \frac{1}{6}$ $\frac{3}{4} \times \frac{8}{9} =$

6. $\frac{5}{9} \times \frac{3}{10} =$ $\frac{7}{8} \times \frac{2}{7} =$

7. $\frac{5}{12} \times \frac{4}{15} =$ $\frac{3}{7} \times \frac{7}{9} =$

8. $\frac{3}{8} \times \frac{4}{9} =$ $\frac{5}{8} \times \frac{2}{5} =$

Multiplication of Whole Numbers by Fractions

To multiply a whole number by a fraction, first write the whole number as an improper fraction. Use cancellation if possible. Multiply the numerators and denominators. Simplify.

Find: $\frac{4}{9} \times 3$

Write the whole number as an improper fraction.	Cancel.	Multiply the numerators and denominators.	Simplify.
$\frac{4}{9} \times 3 = \frac{4}{9} \times \frac{3}{1}$	$\frac{4}{\underset{3}{9}} \times \frac{\overset{1}{3}}{1}$	$\frac{4 \times 1}{3 \times 1} = \frac{4}{3}$	$\frac{4}{3} = 1\frac{1}{3}$

GUIDED PRACTICE

Write each whole number as an improper fraction.

	a	b	c	d
1.	$1 = \frac{1}{1}$	$27 = \underline{\hspace{1cm}}$	$19 = \underline{\hspace{1cm}}$	$52 = \underline{\hspace{1cm}}$
2.	$7 = \underline{\hspace{1cm}}$	$36 = \underline{\hspace{1cm}}$	$125 = \underline{\hspace{1cm}}$	$11 = \underline{\hspace{1cm}}$

Multiply using cancellation. Simplify.

a

3. $\frac{5}{6} \times 18 = \frac{5}{\underset{1}{6}} \times \frac{\overset{3}{18}}{1} = \frac{5 \times 3}{1 \times 1} = \frac{15}{1} = 15$

b

$\frac{2}{5} \times 20 = \frac{2}{5} \times \frac{20}{1} =$

4. $\frac{2}{3} \times 15 = \frac{2}{3} \times \frac{15}{1} =$ $\frac{2}{3} \times 4 = \frac{2}{3} \times \frac{4}{1} =$

5. $\frac{2}{5} \times 125 = \frac{2}{5} \times \frac{125}{1} =$ $\frac{3}{10} \times 50 = \frac{3}{10} \times \frac{50}{1} =$

6. $12 \times \frac{3}{4} = \frac{12}{1} \times \frac{3}{4} =$ $18 \times \frac{3}{4} = \frac{18}{1} \times \frac{3}{4} =$

7. $25 \times \frac{3}{15} = \frac{25}{1} \times \frac{3}{15} =$ $21 \times \frac{3}{7} = \frac{21}{1} \times \frac{3}{7} =$

8. $9 \times \frac{3}{4} = \frac{9}{1} \times \frac{3}{4} =$ $18 \times \frac{2}{9} = \frac{18}{1} \times \frac{2}{9} =$

PRACTICE

Multiply using cancellation. Simplify.

        a   *b*

1. $6 \times \frac{4}{5} =$ $\frac{1}{3} \times 21 =$

2. $24 \times \frac{5}{8} =$ $7 \times \frac{1}{2} =$

3. $75 \times \frac{2}{5} =$ $10 \times \frac{3}{5} =$

4. $\frac{2}{3} \times 4 =$ $24 \times \frac{5}{8} =$

5. $33 \times \frac{1}{3} =$ $15 \times \frac{1}{5} =$

6. $40 \times \frac{5}{8} =$ $\frac{5}{6} \times 30 =$

7. $2 \times \frac{2}{7} =$ $32 \times \frac{3}{8} =$

8. $\frac{5}{12} \times 36 =$ $\frac{1}{5} \times 45 =$

MIXED PRACTICE

Find each answer.

	a	*b*	*c*	*d*
1.	$\begin{array}{r} 3,7\,9\,2 \\ +1,8\,6\,4 \end{array}$	$\begin{array}{r} 7\,0\,5 \\ -2\,3\,9 \end{array}$	$\begin{array}{r} 1\,5,3\,1\,7 \\ +8\,9\,2 \end{array}$	$\begin{array}{r} 7,3\,6\,3 \\ -1,4\,9\,7 \end{array}$
2.	$\begin{array}{r} 4\,3\,7 \\ \times2\,9 \end{array}$	$3\,6\overline{)1,4\,7\,6}$	$\begin{array}{r} 2\,4\,7 \\ \times1\,2\,9 \end{array}$	$\begin{array}{r} 2,3\,1\,6 \\ 4,2\,1\,9 \\ 1,6\,5\,7 \\ +7\,0\,2 \end{array}$

Multiplication of Mixed Numbers by Whole Numbers

To multiply a mixed number by a whole number, write the mixed number and the whole number as improper fractions. Use cancellation if possible. Multiply the new numerators and denominators. Simplify the answer.

Find: $1\frac{3}{5} \times 15$

Write the whole number and the mixed number as improper fractions.	Cancel.	Multiply the new numerators and denominators. Simplify.
$1\frac{3}{5} \times 15 = \frac{8}{5} \times \frac{15}{1}$	$\overset{}{\underset{1}{\frac{8}{5}}} \times \overset{3}{\frac{15}{1}}$	$\frac{8 \times 3}{1 \times 1} = \frac{24}{1} = 24$

PRACTICE

Multiply. Use cancellation if possible. Simplify.

  a

  b

1. $1\frac{1}{2} \times 4 = \frac{3}{\underset{1}{2}} \times \frac{\overset{2}{4}}{1} = \frac{3 \times 2}{1 \times 1} = \frac{6}{1} = 6$ $4\frac{3}{4} \times 3 =$

2. $2\frac{1}{3} \times 9 =$ $1\frac{4}{5} \times 5 =$

3. $3\frac{14}{15} \times 2 =$ $9\frac{1}{10} \times 11 =$

4. $12\frac{1}{10} \times 20 =$ $4\frac{5}{6} \times 9 =$

5. $1\frac{2}{3} \times 6 =$ $4\frac{5}{21} \times 6 =$

6. $4\frac{9}{10} \times 1 =$ $2\frac{3}{10} \times 7 =$

7. $1\frac{3}{8} \times 14 =$ $5\frac{1}{6} \times 2 =$

8. $2\frac{3}{4} \times 10 =$ $1\frac{5}{6} \times 3 =$

Multiplication of Mixed Numbers by Fractions

To multiply a mixed number by a fraction, first write the mixed number as an improper fraction. Use cancellation if possible. Multiply the new numerators and denominators. Simplify.

Find: $\frac{2}{3} \times 5\frac{1}{4}$

Write the mixed number as an improper fraction.	Cancel.	Multiply the new numerators and denominators. Simplify.
$\frac{2}{3} \times 5\frac{1}{4} = \frac{2}{3} \times \frac{21}{4}$	$\overset{1}{\underset{1}{\cancel{\frac{2}{3}}}} \times \overset{7}{\underset{2}{\cancel{\frac{21}{4}}}}$	$\frac{1 \times 7}{1 \times 2} = \frac{7}{2} = 3\frac{1}{2}$

PRACTICE

Multiply. Use cancellation if possible. Simplify.

      a   *b*

1. $\frac{1}{2} \times 3\frac{1}{2} = \frac{1}{2} \times \frac{7}{2} = \frac{1 \times 7}{2 \times 2} = \frac{7}{4} = 1\frac{3}{4}$ $\frac{3}{5} \times 3\frac{1}{3} =$

2. $\frac{2}{3} \times 5\frac{1}{4} =$ $\frac{2}{9} \times 4\frac{1}{2} =$

3. $\frac{1}{2} \times 1\frac{3}{5} =$ $\frac{1}{2} \times 3\frac{1}{2} =$

4. $\frac{12}{23} \times 5\frac{3}{4} =$ $\frac{9}{16} \times 2\frac{2}{3} =$

5. $3\frac{1}{2} \times \frac{3}{8} =$ $1\frac{7}{8} \times \frac{4}{15} =$

6. $7\frac{2}{3} \times \frac{1}{2} =$ $4\frac{2}{3} \times \frac{3}{7} =$

7. $2\frac{1}{2} \times \frac{1}{3} =$ $9\frac{1}{2} \times \frac{1}{8} =$

8. $2\frac{1}{3} \times \frac{6}{7} =$ $3\frac{3}{4} \times \frac{7}{12} =$

Multiplication of Mixed Numbers by Mixed Numbers

To multiply a mixed number by a mixed number, write both mixed numbers as improper fractions. Use cancellation if possible. Then multiply the new numerators and denominators. Simplify.

Find: $1\frac{2}{3} \times 4\frac{1}{2}$

Write the mixed numbers as improper fractions.	Cancel.	Multiply the new numerators and denominators. Simplify.
$1\frac{2}{3} \times 4\frac{1}{2} = \frac{5}{3} \times \frac{9}{2}$	$\frac{5}{\overset{}{\underset{1}{3}}} \times \frac{\overset{3}{9}}{2}$	$\frac{5 \times 3}{1 \times 2} = \frac{15}{2} = 7\frac{1}{2}$

PRACTICE

Multiply. Use cancellation if possible. Simplify.

      a   *b*

1. $2\frac{3}{8} \times 2\frac{1}{3} = \frac{19}{8} \times \frac{7}{3} = \frac{19 \times 7}{8 \times 3} = \frac{133}{24} = 5\frac{13}{24}$ $1\frac{1}{3} \times 2\frac{1}{2} =$

2. $2\frac{2}{5} \times 4\frac{1}{2} =$ $2\frac{1}{5} \times 2\frac{1}{4} =$

3. $1\frac{1}{14} \times 1\frac{3}{4} =$ $3\frac{3}{4} \times 2\frac{2}{3} =$

4. $3\frac{4}{7} \times 2\frac{4}{5} =$ $2\frac{3}{4} \times 5\frac{1}{4} =$

5. $8\frac{3}{9} \times 1\frac{2}{25} =$ $6\frac{1}{2} \times 1\frac{1}{3} =$

6. $2\frac{1}{3} \times 5\frac{1}{5} =$ $2\frac{1}{12} \times 3\frac{6}{25} =$

7. $1\frac{4}{5} \times 1\frac{2}{9} =$ $2\frac{5}{6} \times 3\frac{3}{4} =$

8. $2\frac{2}{7} \times 1\frac{2}{5} =$ $4\frac{3}{5} \times 2\frac{1}{3} =$

                                                Unit 4 Multiplication and Division of Fractions

Problem-Solving Applications

Solve.

1. Mr. Yanaga's car has a gas tank that holds 16 gallons. He used $\frac{3}{4}$ of a tank of gas. How many gallons of gas did he use?

   Answer _____

2. To make one bowl of a party punch, $4\frac{3}{4}$ cups of soda is used. How many cups of soda would you need to make 3 bowls of the party punch?

   Answer _____

3. Terry lives $\frac{5}{8}$ mile from town. Maria lives halfway between Terry and town. How far from town does Maria live?

   Answer _____

4. Each lap around the school track is $\frac{1}{4}$ mile. After soccer practice, the team runs 6 times around the track. How many miles do they run?

   Answer _____

5. Kevin made five shirts. Each shirt used $\frac{2}{3}$ yard of cloth. How many yards did he need in all?

   Answer _____

6. Will lives $\frac{9}{16}$ mile from his office. Latasha lives only one third as far from her office. How far is it to Latasha's office?

   Answer _____

7. Tanisha bought $25\frac{1}{2}$ feet of wood at 4 dollars a foot. How much did she pay for all of it?

   Answer _____

8. The Thompson family's new deck is $19\frac{2}{5}$ feet long. There are 12 inches in 1 foot. What is the length of the deck in inches?

   Answer _____

Problem-Solving Strategy: Write a Number Sentence

The top swimming speed per second for a certain species of fish is ten times its length. How fast can a fish of this type swim if it is $6\frac{1}{2}$ inches long?

Understand the problem.

- **What do you want to know?**
  how fast the fish can swim

- **What information is given?**
  The fish is $6\frac{1}{2}$ inches long.
  Its top swimming speed per second is ten times its length.

Plan how to solve it.

- **What strategy can you use?**
  You can write a number sentence to model the problem.

- **How can you use this strategy to solve the problem?**
  You want to combine 10 equal groups of $6\frac{1}{2}$ inches.
  So, write a multiplication number sentence.

$$6\frac{1}{2} \quad \times \quad 10 \quad = \quad \underline{\hspace{2cm}}$$

↑	↑	↑
fish's length	ten groups	top speed per second

- **What is the answer?**

$$6\frac{1}{2} \times 10 = \frac{13}{\overset{}{\underset{1}{2}}} \times \frac{\overset{5}{10}}{1} = \frac{65}{1} = 65$$

The fish can swim 65 inches per second.

Look back and check your answer.

- **Is your answer reasonable?**
  You can check multiplication with addition.

$$6\frac{1}{2} + 6\frac{1}{2} + 6\frac{1}{2} + 6\frac{1}{2} + 6\frac{1}{2} + 6\frac{1}{2} + 6\frac{1}{2} + 6\frac{1}{2} + 6\frac{1}{2} + 6\frac{1}{2} = 65$$

The sum matches the product.
The answer is reasonable.

Write a number sentence to solve each problem.

1. Jim works in the gift-wrapping department of a store. On average, he needs $2\frac{1}{2}$ feet of ribbon per package. What length of ribbon will he need for 12 packages?

Answer _____

2. Tyrone drinks $3\frac{1}{2}$ cups of milk every day. How much milk is that each week? (1 week = 7 days)

Answer _____

3. Ms. Finch's wading pool holds 400 gallons of water. If she makes it $\frac{5}{8}$ full, how many gallons has she put into it?

Answer _____

4. The $3\frac{1}{5}$-mile long Pharr Bridge linking the United States and Mexico is the longest border crossing in the world. If there are 10 cars per mile in the slow traffic lane on this bridge, how many cars are in this lane on the entire bridge?

Answer _____

5. The tallest tree ever measured was a eucalyptus tree measuring 459 feet. The tallest tree now standing is a sequoia tree measuring 385 feet. How much taller was the eucalyptus tree?

Answer _____

6. Will lives $\frac{3}{4}$ of a mile from the library. Fay lives halfway between Will and the library. How far does Fay live from the library?

Answer _____

7. Jill runs at the rate of one mile every $7\frac{1}{2}$ minutes. At this rate, how long will it take her to run $1\frac{1}{3}$ miles?

Answer _____

8. Sonya is helping her teacher by stacking books on shelves. If each book is $1\frac{1}{4}$ inches thick, how much space is taken up by 8 books?

Answer _____

Division of Fractions by Fractions

To divide a fraction by a fraction, multiply by the **reciprocal** of the second fraction. To find the reciprocal, **invert**, or switch, the second fraction. For example, the reciprocal of $\frac{3}{4}$ is $\frac{4}{3}$. Simplify your answer, if needed. Remember, only the second fraction is inverted.

Find: $\frac{2}{3} \div \frac{5}{12}$

Multiply by the reciprocal of the second fraction.	Cancel.	Multiply the numerators and denominators. Simplify.
$\frac{2}{3} \div \frac{5}{12} = \frac{2}{3} \times \frac{12}{5}$	$\frac{2}{3} \times \frac{\overset{4}{\cancel{12}}}{5}$ $\underset{1}{}$	$\frac{2 \times 4}{1 \times 5} = \frac{8}{5} = 1\frac{3}{5}$

GUIDED PRACTICE

Write the reciprocal.

	a	*b*	*c*	*d*	*e*
1.	$\frac{2}{9}$ _____	$\frac{3}{4}$ _____	$\frac{5}{6}$ _____	$\frac{7}{10}$ _____	$\frac{1}{8}$ _____
2.	$\frac{8}{9}$ _____	$\frac{1}{7}$ _____	$\frac{1}{2}$ _____	$\frac{2}{5}$ _____	$\frac{5}{11}$ _____

Divide. Simplify.

         a   *b*

3. $\frac{4}{9} \div \frac{8}{9} = \frac{\overset{1}{\cancel{4}}}{\underset{1}{\cancel{9}}} \times \frac{\overset{1}{\cancel{9}}}{\underset{2}{\cancel{8}}} = \frac{1 \times 1}{1 \times 2} = \frac{1}{2}$ $\frac{5}{6} \div \frac{3}{4} = \frac{5}{6} \times \frac{4}{3} =$

4. $\frac{5}{8} \div \frac{1}{2} = \frac{5}{8} \times \frac{2}{1} =$ $\frac{7}{12} \div \frac{7}{8} = \frac{7}{12} \times \frac{8}{7} =$

5. $\frac{2}{8} \div \frac{3}{8} = \frac{2}{8} \times \frac{8}{3} =$ $\frac{15}{16} \div \frac{2}{3} = \frac{15}{16} \times \frac{3}{2} =$

6. $\frac{1}{3} \div \frac{1}{16} = \frac{1}{3} \times \frac{16}{1} =$ $\frac{4}{5} \div \frac{8}{15} = \frac{4}{5} \times \frac{15}{8} =$

7. $\frac{2}{3} \div \frac{3}{8} = \frac{2}{3} \times \frac{8}{3} =$ $\frac{8}{11} \div \frac{1}{2} = \frac{8}{11} \times \frac{2}{1} =$

8. $\frac{3}{4} \div \frac{5}{8} = \frac{3}{4} \times \frac{8}{5} =$ $\frac{9}{16} \div \frac{3}{8} = \frac{9}{16} \times \frac{8}{3} =$

Unit 4 Multiplication and Division of Fractions

PRACTICE

Divide. Simplify.

      a   *b*

1. $\frac{1}{8} \div \frac{1}{3} =$ $\frac{5}{12} \div \frac{3}{4} =$

2. $\frac{9}{16} \div \frac{3}{8} =$ $\frac{1}{3} \div \frac{1}{7} =$

3. $\frac{7}{8} \div \frac{5}{12} =$ $\frac{4}{6} \div \frac{1}{10} =$

4. $\frac{1}{3} \div \frac{1}{3} =$ $\frac{10}{64} \div \frac{1}{4} =$

5. $\frac{2}{9} \div \frac{3}{4} =$ $\frac{3}{7} \div \frac{3}{14} =$

6. $\frac{3}{5} \div \frac{7}{8} =$ $\frac{4}{9} \div \frac{2}{3} =$

7. $\frac{5}{6} \div \frac{5}{8} =$ $\frac{1}{8} \div \frac{3}{16} =$

8. $\frac{5}{16} \div \frac{5}{32} =$ $\frac{1}{3} \div \frac{1}{5} =$

MIXED PRACTICE

Find each answer.

	a	*b*	*c*	*d*
1.	$\begin{array}{r} 3\,2,7\,0\,9 \\ +9\,3,8\,0\,4 \end{array}$	$\begin{array}{r} 3\,1\,8 \\ -2\,9\,6 \end{array}$	$\begin{array}{r} 9,7\,2\,2 \\ -8,7\,5\,6 \end{array}$	$\begin{array}{r} 2,5\,4\,6 \\ +8,3\,6\,9 \end{array}$
2.	$\begin{array}{r} 7\,3\,6 \\ \times\ \ 8\,4 \end{array}$	$1\,3\overline{)6,9\,0\,3}$	$\begin{array}{r} 9\,1\,2 \\ \times\ \ 6\,7 \end{array}$	$8\overline{)9\,4\,4}$

Division of Fractions by Whole Numbers

To divide a fraction by a whole number, multiply by the reciprocal of the whole number. The reciprocal of a whole number is 1 divided by that number. For example, the reciprocal of 3 is $\frac{1}{3}$. Simplify the quotient.

Find: $\frac{4}{7} \div 4$

Multiply by the reciprocal of the whole number.	Cancel.	Multiply.
$\frac{4}{7} \div 4 = \frac{4}{7} \times \frac{1}{4}$	$\overset{1}{\cancel{\frac{4}{7}}} \times \frac{1}{\underset{1}{\cancel{4}}}$	$\frac{1 \times 1}{7 \times 1} = \frac{1}{7}$

GUIDED PRACTICE

Write the reciprocal.

	a	*b*	*c*	*d*	*e*
1. 3	$\frac{1}{3}$	9 _____	7 _____	2 _____	16 _____
2. 10 _____		125 _____	36 _____	21 _____	48 _____

Divide. Simplify.

           a   *b*

3. $\frac{3}{4} \div 3 = \overset{1}{\cancel{\frac{3}{4}}} \times \frac{1}{\underset{1}{\cancel{3}}} = \frac{1 \times 1}{4 \times 1} = \frac{1}{4}$ $\frac{6}{7} \div 3 = \frac{6}{7} \times \frac{1}{3} =$

4. $\frac{5}{6} \div 7 = \frac{5}{6} \times \frac{1}{7} =$ $\frac{8}{15} \div 4 = \frac{8}{15} \times \frac{1}{4} =$

5. $\frac{9}{10} \div 9 = \frac{9}{10} \times \frac{1}{9} =$ $\frac{12}{25} \div 5 = \frac{12}{25} \times \frac{1}{5} =$

6. $\frac{2}{3} \div 6 = \frac{2}{3} \times$ $\frac{4}{5} \div 10 = \frac{4}{5} \times$

7. $\frac{1}{6} \div 2 = \frac{1}{6} \times$ $\frac{4}{9} \div 2 = \frac{4}{9} \times$

8. $\frac{11}{12} \div 7 = \frac{11}{12} \times$ $\frac{15}{16} \div 10 = \frac{15}{16} \times$

                                                    Unit 4 Multiplication and Division of Fractions

Divide. Simplify.

a	b
1. $\frac{7}{8} \div 14 =$	$\frac{5}{6} \div 9 =$
2. $\frac{2}{5} \div 10 =$	$\frac{13}{16} \div 4 =$
3. $\frac{4}{7} \div 2 =$	$\frac{9}{16} \div 9 =$
4. $\frac{3}{4} \div 12 =$	$\frac{11}{12} \div 3 =$
5. $\frac{1}{7} \div 4 =$	$\frac{3}{10} \div 6 =$
6. $\frac{1}{3} \div 15 =$	$\frac{15}{16} \div 5 =$

MIXED PRACTICE

Find each answer.

a	b	c	d
1. $\begin{array}{r} 8\ 3\ 7 \\ +9\ 0\ 5 \\ \hline \end{array}$	$\begin{array}{r} 7\ 9\ 2 \\ -1\ 9\ 9 \\ \hline \end{array}$	$\begin{array}{r} 1\ 3,7\ 0\ 2 \\ +6\ 9,8\ 4\ 9 \\ \hline \end{array}$	$\begin{array}{r} 5\ 0,0\ 0\ 0 \\ -2\ 9,8\ 0\ 6 \\ \hline \end{array}$
2. $\begin{array}{r} 3\ 2\ 9 \\ \times\quad 7 \\ \hline \end{array}$	$\begin{array}{r} 4\ 8\ 2 \\ \times\quad 4 \\ \hline \end{array}$	$\begin{array}{r} 8\ 7\ 1 \\ \times\ 2\ 6 \\ \hline \end{array}$	$\begin{array}{r} 4\ 2\ 3 \\ \times\ 9\ 5 \\ \hline \end{array}$
3. $4\ 1\overline{)9\ 8\ 4}$	$1\ 7\overline{)9\ 5\ 2}$	$8\overline{)2\ 5\ 6}$	$9\ 4\overline{)1,0\ 3\ 4}$

Division of Whole Numbers by Fractions

To divide a whole number by a fraction, write the whole number as an improper fraction. Multiply by the reciprocal of the second fraction. Simplify the answer.

Find: $6 \div \frac{2}{5}$

Write the whole number as an improper fraction.	Multiply by the reciprocal of the second fraction.	Cancel.	Multiply. Simplify.
$6 \div \frac{2}{5} = \frac{6}{1} \div \frac{2}{5}$	$\frac{6}{1} \times \frac{5}{2}$	$\overset{3}{\cancel{\frac{6}{1}}} \times \frac{5}{\underset{1}{\cancel{2}}}$	$\frac{3 \times 5}{1 \times 1} = \frac{15}{1} = 15$

PRACTICE

Divide. Simplify.

a

1. $1 \div \frac{1}{2} = \frac{1}{1} \div \frac{1}{2} = \frac{1}{1} \times \frac{2}{1} = \frac{1 \times 2}{1 \times 1} = \frac{2}{1} = 2$

2. $7 \div \frac{7}{8} =$

3. $8 \div \frac{2}{5} =$

4. $15 \div \frac{5}{6} =$

5. $21 \div \frac{7}{20} =$

6. $10 \div \frac{5}{18} =$

7. $2 \div \frac{1}{3} =$

8. $6 \div \frac{1}{2} =$

b

$6 \div \frac{3}{4} =$

$14 \div \frac{7}{8} =$

$9 \div \frac{3}{16} =$

$2 \div \frac{4}{9} =$

$4 \div \frac{1}{12} =$

$8 \div \frac{6}{7} =$

$3 \div \frac{9}{10} =$

$1 \div \frac{5}{6} =$

Unit 4 Multiplication and Division of Fractions

Division of Mixed Numbers by Whole Numbers

To divide a mixed number by a whole number, write the mixed number as an improper fraction. Multiply by the reciprocal of the whole number. Simplify the answer.

Find: $2\frac{5}{8} \div 3$

Write the mixed number as an improper fraction.	Multiply by the reciprocal of the whole number.	Cancel.	Multiply.
$2\frac{5}{8} \div 3 = \frac{21}{8} \div 3$	$\frac{21}{8} \times \frac{1}{3}$	$\frac{\overset{7}{\cancel{21}}}{8} \times \frac{1}{\underset{1}{\cancel{3}}}$	$\frac{7 \times 1}{8 \times 1} = \frac{7}{8}$

PRACTICE

Divide. Simplify.

a

1. $3\frac{1}{2} \div 7 = \frac{7}{2} \div 7 = \frac{\overset{1}{\cancel{7}}}{2} \times \frac{1}{\underset{1}{\cancel{7}}} = \frac{1 \times 1}{2 \times 1} = \frac{1}{2}$

2. $4\frac{1}{2} \div 3 =$

3. $3\frac{1}{7} \div 2 =$

4. $3\frac{1}{3} \div 5 =$

5. $6\frac{2}{3} \div 2 =$

6. $3\frac{3}{4} \div 12 =$

7. $3\frac{1}{9} \div 14 =$

8. $8\frac{1}{4} \div 11 =$

b

$1\frac{2}{3} \div 5 =$

$7\frac{1}{2} \div 10 =$

$4\frac{1}{8} \div 3 =$

$5\frac{4}{7} \div 13 =$

$2\frac{2}{3} \div 4 =$

$1\frac{1}{3} \div 2 =$

$4\frac{2}{5} \div 2 =$

$2\frac{1}{4} \div 6 =$

Division of Mixed Numbers by Fractions

To divide a mixed number by a fraction, write the mixed number as an improper fraction. Multiply by the reciprocal of the second fraction. Simplify the answer.

Find: $6\frac{5}{6} \div \frac{5}{6}$

Write the mixed number as an improper fraction.	Multiply by the reciprocal of the second fraction.	Cancel.	Multiply. Simplify.
$6\frac{5}{6} \div \frac{5}{6} = \frac{41}{6} \div \frac{5}{6}$	$\frac{41}{6} \times \frac{6}{5}$	$\frac{41}{\cancel{6}_1} \times \frac{\cancel{6}^1}{5}$	$\frac{41 \times 1}{1 \times 5} = \frac{41}{5} = 8\frac{1}{5}$

PRACTICE

Divide. Simplify.

a

1. $2\frac{1}{3} \div \frac{1}{6} = \frac{7}{3} \div \frac{1}{6} = \frac{7}{\cancel{3}_1} \times \frac{\cancel{6}^2}{1} = \frac{7 \times 2}{1 \times 1} = \frac{14}{1} = 14$

2. $1\frac{7}{12} \div \frac{3}{4} =$

3. $5\frac{1}{2} \div \frac{1}{2} =$

4. $1\frac{1}{2} \div \frac{3}{4} =$

5. $2\frac{1}{5} \div \frac{4}{5} =$

6. $1\frac{4}{5} \div \frac{2}{3} =$

7. $5\frac{1}{4} \div \frac{1}{3} =$

8. $3\frac{3}{4} \div \frac{5}{8} =$

b

$1\frac{1}{3} \div \frac{2}{3} =$

$3\frac{3}{4} \div \frac{1}{2} =$

$3\frac{1}{10} \div \frac{2}{5} =$

$1\frac{1}{5} \div \frac{4}{5} =$

$2\frac{2}{9} \div \frac{4}{5} =$

$1\frac{4}{7} \div \frac{1}{7} =$

$3\frac{2}{3} \div \frac{11}{12} =$

$5\frac{2}{5} \div \frac{3}{5} =$

Division of Mixed Numbers by Mixed Numbers

To divide a mixed number by a mixed number, write the mixed numbers as improper fractions. Multiply by the reciprocal of the second fraction. Simplify the answer.

Find: $2\frac{1}{4} \div 3\frac{3}{8}$

Write the mixed numbers as improper fractions.	Multiply by the reciprocal of the second fraction.	Cancel.	Multiply.
$2\frac{1}{4} \div 3\frac{3}{8} = \frac{9}{4} \div \frac{27}{8}$	$\frac{9}{4} \times \frac{8}{27}$	$\overset{1}{\underset{1}{\cancel{\frac{9}{4}}}} \times \overset{2}{\underset{3}{\cancel{\frac{8}{27}}}}$	$\frac{1 \times 2}{1 \times 3} = \frac{2}{3}$

PRACTICE

Divide. Simplify.

a

1. $4\frac{1}{4} \div 8\frac{1}{2} = \frac{17}{4} \div \frac{17}{2} = \overset{1}{\underset{2}{\cancel{\frac{17}{4}}}} \times \overset{1}{\underset{1}{\cancel{\frac{2}{17}}}} = \frac{1 \times 1}{2 \times 1} = \frac{1}{2}$

b

$7\frac{1}{2} \div 4\frac{3}{5} =$

2. $5\frac{1}{2} \div 1\frac{1}{2} =$
   $3\frac{1}{3} \div 1\frac{20}{21} =$

3. $8\frac{1}{4} \div 2\frac{1}{2} =$
   $2\frac{1}{3} \div 3\frac{1}{2} =$

4. $6\frac{2}{3} \div 2\frac{1}{5} =$
   $8\frac{2}{3} \div 1\frac{1}{3} =$

5. $8\frac{1}{2} \div 4\frac{1}{4} =$
   $6\frac{4}{5} \div 1\frac{1}{5} =$

6. $4\frac{1}{2} \div 1\frac{1}{4} =$
   $9\frac{7}{9} \div 1\frac{5}{6} =$

7. $2\frac{1}{2} \div 1\frac{1}{3} =$
   $1\frac{3}{8} \div 3\frac{2}{3} =$

8. $6\frac{2}{3} \div 2\frac{1}{4} =$
   $4\frac{2}{9} \div 1\frac{7}{12} =$

Problem-Solving Strategy: Identify Extra Information

Carlos brought 5 pounds of cole slaw and 3 pies to his uncle's 50th birthday party. How many $\frac{1}{4}$-pound servings of cole slaw were there?

Understand the problem.

- **What do you want to know?**
  how many $\frac{1}{4}$-pound servings of cole slaw there were

- **What information is given?**
  5 pounds, 3 pies, 50th birthday

Plan how to solve it.

- **What strategy can you use?**
  You can identify extra information that is not needed to solve the problem.

Solve it.

- **How can you use this strategy to solve the problem?**
  Reread the problem. Cross out any unnecessary facts. Then you can focus on the needed facts to solve the problem.

> Carlos brought 5 pounds of cole slaw ~~and 3 pies to his uncle's 50th birthday party.~~ How many $\frac{1}{4}$-pound servings of cole slaw were there?

- **What is the answer?**

  $5 \div \frac{1}{4} = \frac{5}{1} \div \frac{1}{4} = \frac{5}{1} \times \frac{4}{1} = \frac{20}{1} = 20$

  There were 20 servings of cole slaw.

Look back and check your answer.

- **Is your answer reasonable?**
  You can check division with multiplication.

  $20 \times \frac{1}{4} = \frac{20}{1} \times \frac{1}{4} = \frac{20}{4} = 5$

  The product matches the dividend.
  The answer is reasonable.

In each problem, cross out the extra information. Then solve the problem.

1. The computer Joel wants is on sale for $980. The original price of the computer is $1,125. The computer includes a printer and a mouse pad. How much will Joel save?

Answer _____

2. Mary needs 12 yards of fabric for a sewing project. The fabric comes in 5 different styles and will be available in 8 weeks. How much will the fabric cost at $6 per yard?

Answer _____

3. Angela is $5\frac{1}{2}$ feet tall. She is taller than her mother but shorter than her father. Angela's sister is 5 feet tall. How much taller is Angela than her sister?

Answer _____

4. The small intestine of an adult is about 25 feet long. There are 206 bones and 32 teeth in an adult body. The large intestine of an adult is about $\frac{1}{5}$ the length of the small intestine. What is the length of the large intestine?

Answer _____

5. Ted drove his new car for 260 miles. The trip took $4\frac{1}{2}$ hours. He used 6 gallons of fuel, which cost $2 per gallon. How much did he spend on the fuel?

Answer _____

6. Shawn bought a six-pack of water. Each bottle was 1 liter and had no calories. The six-pack cost $7. How much did each bottle of water cost?

Answer _____

7. The main span of a bridge is the distance between its supports. The longest bridge in the world is the Akashi Kaikyo Bridge in Japan. The main span of the bridge is 6,750 feet long. How many yards long is the main span?

Answer _____

8. Alaska is the largest state in the United States. The area of Alaska is 587,878 square miles. Quebec is the largest province in Canada. Quebec's area is 594,860 square miles. What is the difference between the two areas?

Answer _____

Problem-Solving Applications

Solve. Simplify.

1. There are 16 cups in one gallon. How many cups of juice can be served from a container that holds $2\frac{1}{2}$ gallons?

Answer _____

2. Anita has 20 yards of cloth to make T-shirts. Each shirt uses $\frac{3}{4}$ yard of cloth. How many T-shirts can she make?

Answer _____

3. A bundle of shingles is 12 inches high. If each shingle is $\frac{1}{4}$-inch thick, how many shingles are in each bundle?

Answer _____

4. A crew is paving a 22-mile road. They divided the road into $5\frac{1}{2}$-mile sections to pave each day. How long will it take them to pave the whole road?

Answer _____

5. A truck is hauling 4 cars that each weigh $2\frac{2}{3}$ tons. How many tons does the truck's load weigh?

Answer _____

6. Jeff cut a 6-foot piece of lumber into $1\frac{1}{2}$-foot pieces. How many pieces of wood did he cut?

Answer _____

7. A recipe for a batch of brownies uses $2\frac{1}{2}$ cups of sugar. One bag of sugar holds 20 cups. How many batches can you make with one bag of sugar?

Answer _____

8. Juan bought $24\frac{1}{2}$ yards of fabric to make curtains. Each window requires $3\frac{1}{2}$ yards. How many sets of curtains can Juan make?

Answer _____

Multiply or divide. Simplify.

  a   *b*

1. $\frac{2}{3} \times \frac{1}{5} =$ $\frac{7}{8} \div 7 =$

2. $1\frac{2}{5} \times \frac{5}{12} =$ $\frac{3}{5} \times \frac{5}{9} =$

3. $4\frac{4}{9} \times \frac{9}{10} =$ $1\frac{2}{5} \div \frac{7}{10} =$

4. $2\frac{6}{7} \div 3\frac{1}{14} =$ $\frac{1}{10} \div \frac{1}{20} =$

5. $5 \div \frac{3}{4} =$ $5 \times \frac{3}{4} =$

6. $6\frac{1}{8} \times \frac{3}{7} =$ $4\frac{1}{4} \div 1\frac{1}{8} =$

7. $15 \div \frac{7}{10} =$ $\frac{4}{15} \div \frac{1}{3} =$

8. $2\frac{7}{10} \times 2\frac{1}{5} =$ $\frac{7}{8} \div \frac{3}{4} =$

9. $9 \div \frac{2}{3} =$ $9 \div \frac{3}{5} =$

10. $8\frac{1}{8} \times 1\frac{3}{5} =$ $\frac{1}{10} \div \frac{1}{10} =$

Solve.

11. Tonia used metal spacers to separate two steel plates. Each spacer was $\frac{3}{16}$-inch thick. How many spacers did she need to separate the plates $1\frac{1}{2}$ inches?

12. From Mr. Chan's house to St. Louis is 222 miles. At an average of $55\frac{1}{2}$ miles per hour, how long does it take to drive from Mr. Chan's house to St. Louis?

Answer _____

Answer _____

Reading and Writing Decimals

To read a **decimal,** read it as a whole number. Then name the place value of the last digit.

Read and write 0.53 as fifty-three hundredths.

To read a decimal that also has a whole number part,

- read the whole number part
- read the **decimal point** as *and*
- read the decimal part as a whole number and then name the place value of the last digit.

Read and write 23.705 as twenty-three and seven hundred five thousandths.

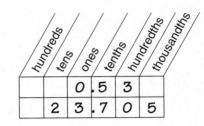

← whole number . decimal →

PRACTICE

Write as a decimal.

a   b

1. three tenths _____0.3_____   twenty-five hundredths _____

2. fifteen thousandths _____   one and five tenths _____

3. ten and four hundredths _____   five and fifty-five thousandths _____

4. one hundred seventy-five thousandths _____

Write each decimal in words.

5. 0.005 _____five thousandths_____

6. 39.374 _____

7. $1.23 _____

8. $14.08 _____

9. 0.06 _____

Write each money amount with a dollar sign and a decimal point.

a   b   c

10. nine dollars ___$9.00___   ninety cents _____   nine cents _____

11. sixty-six cents _____   eleven cents _____   forty-two dollars _____

12. one hundred ten dollars and seventy-four cents _____

13. two thousand, five dollars and three cents _____

14. one dollar and nineteen cents _____

Compare and Order Decimals

To compare two decimal numbers, begin at the left. Compare the digits in each place.

The symbol < means **is less than.**   4.2 < 4.6
The symbol > means **is greater than.**   2.7 > 2.3
The symbol = means **is equal to.**   3.4 = 3.40

Compare: 2.6 and 2.3

2 . 6
2 . 3

The ones digits are the same. Compare the tenths.

6 > 3, so 2.6 > 2.3

Compare: $0.08 and $0.25

$ 0 . 0 8
$ 0 . 2 5

The ones digits are the same. Compare the tenths.

0 < 2, so $0.08 < $0.25

Compare: 0.4 and 0.47

0 . 4 0
0 . 4 7

The ones and tenths digits are the same. Write a zero. Compare the hundredths.

0 < 7, so 0.4 < 0.47

PRACTICE

Compare. Write <, >, or =.

	a		b		c
1.	0.3 ___<___ 0.32 $\quad$ 0.30 $\quad$ 0.32		0.047 _____ 0.47		0.5 _____ 0.500
2.	0.125 _____ 13		0.15 _____ 0.115		9.5 _____ 9.50
3.	0.620 _____ 0.62		0.11 _____ 0.110		0.26 _____ 0.3
4.	5.561 _____ 5.56		0.95 _____ 0.905		2.65 _____ 2.60
5.	0.25 _____ 0.3		0.65 _____ 0.6		3.008 _____ 3.080
6.	4.50 _____ 4.500		0.78 _____ 0.789		2.001 _____ 2.1

Write in order from least to greatest.

	a		b
7.	67.5 $\quad$ 0.675 $\quad$ 60.80 _____		7.026 $\quad$ 7.260 $\quad$ 7.230 _____
8.	1.025 $\quad$ 1.20 $\quad$ 1.1 _____		0.34 $\quad$ 0.034 $\quad$ 0.304 _____

Fraction and Decimal Equivalents

Sometimes you will need to either change a decimal to a fraction or a fraction to a decimal.

To write a decimal as a fraction, identify the value of the last place in the decimal. Use this place value to write the denominator. Simplify if possible.

To write a fraction that has a denominator of 10, 100, or 1,000 as a decimal, write the digits from the numerator. Write the decimal point so that the number of decimal places is the same as the number of zeros in the denominator of the fraction. Write zeros as needed.

Decimal		Fraction or Mixed Number
0.9	=	$\frac{9}{10}$
0.01	=	$\frac{1}{100}$
0.045	=	$\frac{45}{1,000} = \frac{9}{200}$
1.74	=	$\frac{174}{100} = 1\frac{74}{100} = 1\frac{37}{50}$

Fraction or Mixed Number		Decimal
$\frac{3}{10}$	=	0.3
$\frac{15}{100}$	=	0.15
$\frac{6}{1,000}$	=	0.006
$\frac{59}{10}$ or $5\frac{9}{10}$	=	5.9

PRACTICE

Write each decimal as a fraction. Simplify.

a　　　　　　　　　b　　　　　　　　　c　　　　　　　　　d

1. $0.4 = \frac{4}{10} = \frac{2}{5}$　　0.6 = _____　　0.08 = _____　　0.002 = _____

2. $0.21 =$ _____　　0.083 = _____　　0.901 = _____　　0.018 = _____

Write each decimal as a mixed number. Simplify.

a　　　　　　　　　b　　　　　　　　　c　　　　　　　　　d

3. $4.5 = 4\frac{5}{10} = 4\frac{1}{2}$　　1.62 = _____　　10.1 = _____　　1.275 = _____

4. $9.07 =$ _____　　38.24 = _____　　5.46 = _____　　13.8 = _____

Write each fraction as a decimal.

a　　　　　　　　　b　　　　　　　　　c　　　　　　　　　d

5. $\frac{1}{10} = 0.1$　　$\frac{2}{10} =$ _____　　$\frac{5}{10} =$ _____　　$\frac{7}{10} =$ _____

6. $\frac{6}{100} =$ _____　　$\frac{80}{100} =$ _____　　$\frac{52}{1,000} =$ _____　　$\frac{416}{1,000} =$ _____

7. $\frac{56}{10} =$ _____　　$\frac{31}{10} =$ _____　　$\frac{76}{10} =$ _____　　$\frac{65}{100} =$ _____

8. $\frac{103}{100} =$ _____　　$\frac{509}{100} =$ _____　　$\frac{1,643}{1,000} =$ _____　　$\frac{2,051}{1,000} =$ _____

More Fraction and Decimal Equivalents

Not all fractions can be changed to decimal form easily. To write fractions that have denominators other than 10, 100, or 1,000 as decimals, first write an equivalent fraction that has a denominator of 10, 100, or 1,000. Then write the equivalent fraction as a decimal.

Some fractions do not have simple decimal equivalents.

Examples: $\frac{2}{3} = 0.666\ldots$ and $\frac{5}{6} = 0.833\ldots$

Write $\frac{1}{5}$ as a decimal.

Write $\frac{1}{5}$ with 10 as the denominator.	Write the fraction as a decimal.
$\frac{1}{5} = \frac{1 \times 2}{5 \times 2} = \frac{2}{10}$	$= 0.2$

Write $2\frac{3}{4}$ as a decimal.

Write $2\frac{3}{4}$ as an improper fraction.	Write the new fraction with 100 as the denominator.	Write the fraction as a decimal.
$2\frac{3}{4} = \frac{11}{4}$	$\frac{11}{4} = \frac{11 \times 25}{4 \times 25} = \frac{275}{100}$	$= 2.75$

PRACTICE

Write each fraction as a decimal.

	a	*b*	*c*
1.	$\frac{1}{8} = \frac{1 \times 125}{8 \times 125} = \frac{125}{1,000} = 0.125$	$\frac{2}{5} = $ _____	$\frac{3}{20} = $ _____
2.	$\frac{4}{5} = $ _____	$\frac{17}{50} = $ _____	$\frac{11}{25} = $ _____
3.	$\frac{7}{200} = $ _____	$\frac{8}{25} = $ _____	$\frac{3}{8} = $ _____
4.	$\frac{13}{2} = \frac{13 \times 5}{2 \times 5} = \frac{65}{10} = 6.5$	$\frac{43}{20} = $ _____	$\frac{37}{5} = $ _____
5.	$\frac{25}{4} = $ _____	$\frac{69}{50} = $ _____	$\frac{39}{25} = $ _____

Write each mixed number as a decimal.

	a	*b*
6.	$1\frac{9}{20} = \frac{29}{20} = \frac{29 \times 5}{20 \times 5} = \frac{145}{100} = 1.45$	$2\frac{21}{25} = $ _____
7.	$6\frac{3}{25} = $ _____	$13\frac{1}{50} = $ _____
8.	$19\frac{1}{2} = $ _____	$4\frac{7}{8} = $ _____

Addition of Decimals

To add decimals, line up the decimal points. Write zeros as needed. Then add as with whole numbers. Be sure to write a decimal point in the sum.

Find: 4.6 + 7.32

Write a zero.	Add the hundredths.	Add the tenths. Write a decimal point in the sum.	Add the ones.

T O Ts Hs
  4 .6 0 ↙
+ 7 .3 2
	T O Ts Hs
	  4 .6 **0**
	+ 7 .3 **2**
	         2
		T O Ts Hs
		  4 .6 0
		+ 7 .3 2
		    .9 2
			T O Ts Hs
			  4 .6 0
			+ 7 .3 2
			1 1 .9 2

GUIDED PRACTICE

Add. Write zeros as needed.

        a   *b*   *c*   *d*

1.

a	b	c	d
O Ts Hs 1 $3 .1 9 + 2 .2 2 $5 .4 1	O Ts Hs $0 .0 2 + 0 .5 7	T O Ts Hs $1 4 .9 0 + 1 .9 6	T O Ts Hs $4 2 .0 8 + 0 .1 6

2.

a	b	c	d
O Ts Hs Ths 0 .3 0 0 +0 .0 0 6 0 .3 0 6	T O Ts Hs Ths 2 2 .1 3 + 7 .0 9 8	H T O Ts 2 3 8 + 7 7 .3	T O Ts Hs 2 4 .1 5 +3 0 .1

3.

a	b	c	d

T O Ts Hs
1   1
$ 2 .1 0
  4 .0 8
+ 5 .2 5
$1 1 .4 3
	T O Ts Hs Ths
	1 4 .0 0 5
	1 6 .1 9 3
	+ 7 .3 2 7
		O Ts Hs Ths
		0 .3 5 6
		0 .4 3 0
		+0 .8 1 7
			T O Ts Hs Ths
			1 4 .0 0 5
			  0 .0 4 3
			+ 2 .6 8 9

4.

a	b	c	d

T O Ts Hs Ths
1 2 2
  4 .0 9 0
3 3 .9 8 4
1 0 .4 0 0
+2 3 .7 3 0
7 2 .2 0 4
	T O Ts Hs Ths
	9 .4 5 1
	0 .0 0 7
	7 .3
	+ 6 .5 3 6
		H T O Ts Hs
		$2 3 1 .2 4
		  6 1 .6
		1 4 2 .0 5
		+1 0 0 .1 1
			T O Ts Hs Ths
			5 6 .1 1 2
			  4 .2 2
			2 4 .7 3 6
			+1 4

PRACTICE

Add. Write zeros as needed.

	a	b	c	d
1.	5.9 +3.6 2	7.0 8 +3.2 6 5	1 4.0 7 6 + 8.4 6	1 7.0 5 + 3.3 5 1
2.	2 8.0 0 9 4.6 5 + 6.0 0 3	7 7.0 1 6 4.5 7 + 0.6 4 7	8 4.7 0.4 0 3 + 3.0 8	8.2 3 3 6.5 + 0.0 0 9
3.	$1 2.2 0 2.1 0 4.0 8 + 5.2 5	8.0 5 0 1 4.0 0 5 1 6.1 + 7.3 2	0.2 2 0.3 5 6 0.4 3 9 +0.8	6.1 2 6 1 4.0 0 5 0.0 4 + 2.6
4.	2.0 0 5 0.1 5 0.6 +3	0.0 0 9 0.1 4 0.6 +2.1 0	0.1 4 0.0 6 0 0.1 7 +8.5	0.7 0 2 0.0 0 5 0.0 3 4 +7.1 6

Line up the decimals. Then find the sums. Write zeros as needed.

a

5. 9 + 3.4 + 0.7 = _____

  9.0
  3.4
+0.7

b

$6.54 + $10 + $8.35 = _____

6. 6.9 + 12.7 + 38.6 = _____

37.5 + 5.3 + 8 + 3.273 = _____

MIXED PRACTICE

Multiply or divide.

	a	b	c	d
1.	2 3 4 × 1 5	3 1 5 × 2 8	3 5)7 7 0	1 8)4,0 5 0

Subtraction of Decimals

To subtract decimals, line up the decimal points. Write zeros as needed. Then subtract as with whole numbers. Be sure to write a decimal point in the difference.

Find: 34.3 − 17.94

Write a zero. Regroup to subtract the hundredths.	Regroup to subtract the tenths. Write a decimal point in the difference.	Regroup to subtract the ones.	Subtract the tens.
T O Ts Hs $\quad$ 2 10 3 4 .3 Ø − 1 7 .9 4 $\qquad$ 6	T O Ts Hs $\quad$ 12 3 2 10 3 4 .3 Ø − 1 7 .9 4 $\qquad$ .3 6	T O Ts Hs 13 12 2 3 2 10 3 4 .3 Ø − 1 7 .9 4 $\qquad$ 6 .3 6	T O Ts Hs 13 12 2 3 2 10 3 4 .3 Ø − 1 7 .9 4 1 6 .3 6

GUIDED PRACTICE

Subtract. Write zeros as needed.

$\qquad$ a $\qquad\qquad$ b $\qquad\qquad$ c $\qquad\qquad$ d

1.

a. O Ts Hs Ths
$\quad$ 5 .4 9 8
− 2 .3 6 2
3 .1 3 6

b. O Ts Hs
$\quad$ 7 .5 4
− 6 .3 8

c. T O Ts Hs Ths
1 5 .0 6 5
−$\quad$ 9 .4 6 6

d. T O Ts Hs
$4 7 .6 2
− 2 3 .8 5

2.

a. O Ts Hs Ths
6 10 4 10
7 .0 5 0
− 3 .1 3 5
3 .9 1 5

b. T O Ts Hs
1 2 .5 0
−$\quad$ 7 .7 5

c. O Ts Hs
8 .1 4
− 6 .1 0

d. O Ts Hs Ths
2 .8 7 7
− 0 .9 8 0

3.

a. O Ts Hs Ths
7 .5 8 9
− 3 .3 4 7

b. T O Ts Hs
2 4 .3 6
−$\quad$ 7 .1 6

c. O Ts Hs Ths
8 .1 1 3
− 7 .3 0 5

d. T O Ts Hs
$2 1 .0 9
− 1 6 .9 5

4.

a. O Ts Hs Ths
8 .0 9 0
− 4 .2 5 6

b. O Ts Hs Ths
1 .5 2 0
− 0 .4 0 8

c. T O Ts Hs
7 5 .1 6
− 5 2 .8 0

d. T O Ts Hs
4 0 .3 3
− 2 9 .7 0

PRACTICE

Subtract. Write zeros as needed.

	a	*b*	*c*	*d*
1.	8.3 2 5 −3.2 0 3	7.2 7 8 −5.1 2	9.0 6 8 −7.0 5 4	1 0.3 9 9 −1 0.2 3 9
2.	$3 4.9 5 − 2 7.9 9	$9 2.0 0 − 6 7.5 0	$9 4.7 8 − 1 5.0 0	$1 1,5 3 2.3 0 − 2,5 0 0.0 0
3.	6.2 −4.5 7 5	1.9 −0.6 7 4	1.3 5 4 −0.2 6 5	9 2.1 5 −8 4.7
4.	8.0 9 −4.2 5 6	9 4.7 8 −1 5	1 9.0 0 5 −1 4.5	1.5 2 −0.4 0 8

Line up the decimals. Then find the difference. Write zeros as needed.

         a   *b*   *c*

5. $7.05 - 3.035 =$ _____ $8.14 - 6.1 =$ _____ $75.06 - 52.8 =$ _____

        7.050
     −3.035

6. $92.15 - 84.7 =$ _____ $12.5 - 7.75 =$ _____ $1.354 - 0.265 =$ _____

MIXED PRACTICE

Write as a decimal.

	a		*b*
1.	six thousandths _____	twelve hundredths _____
2.	twenty thousandths _____	four hundredths _____
3.	nine tenths _____	forty thousandths _____
4.	three and three tenths _____	six and eight thousandths _____

Compare. Write <, >, or =.

	a	*b*	*c*	*d*
5.	2.10 ____ 2.1	0.456 ____ 4.56	7.09 ____ 7.009	8.110 ____ 8.11
6.	0.078 ____ 0.08	3.405 ____ 3.4	19.230 ____ 19.23	0.89 ____ 0.90

Problem-Solving Strategy: Work Backwards

Alan has $1,079.36 in his checking account. During the last two weeks, he withdrew $191.50, deposited $417.69, and wrote a check for $525.00 to pay his rent. How much money did Alan have in his account two weeks ago?

Understand the problem.

- **What do you want to know?**
  how much money was in his account two weeks ago

- **What information is given?**
  There is $1,079.36 in his account now.
  He withdrew $191.50, deposited $417.69, and wrote a check for $525.00.

Plan how to. solve it

- **What strategy can you use?**
  You can work backwards. Work from the money in the account now to find the money in the account two weeks ago.

Solve it.

- **How can you use this strategy to solve the problem?**
  Addition and subtraction are opposite operations. So, add the amounts taken out of the account and subtract the amounts added.

$$
\begin{array}{rl}
\$1,079.36 & \leftarrow \text{ amount in bank now} \\
+ \quad 191.50 & \leftarrow \text{ amount withdrawn} \\
\hline
\$1,270.86 & \\
- \quad 417.69 & \leftarrow \text{ amount deposited} \\
\hline
\$ \quad 853.17 & \\
+ \quad 525.00 & \leftarrow \text{ amount of check written} \\
\hline
\$1,378.17 &
\end{array}
$$

- **What is the answer?**
  Two weeks ago, Alan had $1,378.17 in his account.

Look back and check your answer.

- **Is your answer reasonable?**
  You can check by working forwards from the amount of money in the account two weeks ago.

$$
\begin{array}{r}
\$1,378.17 \\
- \quad 191.50 \\
\hline
\$1,186.67 \\
+ \quad 417.69 \\
\hline
\$1,604.36 \\
- \quad 525.00 \\
\hline
\$1,079.36
\end{array}
$$

The amounts in his account balance.
The answer is reasonable.

Work backwards to solve each problem.

1. Rita had $14.25 left after a day at the county fair. She had spent $12.75 for her ticket. Then she had bought lunch for $6.50 and souvenirs for $15.99. How much money had Rita brought to the fair?

   Answer _____

2. Deanne is writing invitations for her party. She will have 70 guests. When she writes twice as many as she has finished, she'll have only 10 more invitations to write. How many has she written so far?

   Answer _____

3. This week, Gretchen earned $20.50 mowing lawns and she spent $4.00 on lunch. She has $28.59 left. How much did Gretchen have at the beginning of the week?

   Answer _____

4. Mario is driving in the Indianapolis 500-mile race. When he has driven twice as far as he's gone already, he'll be 50 miles from the finish line. How far has he driven?

   Answer _____

5. Mei spends 50 minutes getting ready for work each day. After leaving the house, she walks 10 minutes to a diner, where she eats breakfast for 25 minutes. Then she walks 5 minutes to the bus stop for the 15-minute ride to work. What time must Mei wake up to reach her office by 9 A.M.?

   Answer _____

6. From 1990 to 1997, the price of a monthly commuter train ticket doubled. In 1998 the price dropped $4.00, and in 1999 it dropped $6.00 more. Then in 2000 it doubled again to $32.00. How much did a monthly train ticket cost in 1990?

   Answer _____

Problem-Solving Applications

Solve.

1. Canada and the United States are two of the largest countries in the world. Canada covers about 3.85 million square miles, and the U.S. covers about 3.68 million square miles. How many square miles do they cover in all?

   Answer _____

2. Rick had $4.40 remaining after a shopping trip. He had bought a CD for $11.95, a shirt for $15.50, and a belt for $12.00. How much money did he have before the shopping trip?

   Answer _____

3. A human's ribs are different sizes. If a woman's seventh rib is 9.45 inches long, and her eighth rib is 0.39 inch shorter, what is the length of her eighth rib?

   Answer _____

4. Isabel owns a coffee shop. At the end of a day, she had 10.5 pounds of her house blend. During that day, she had sold 6.25 pounds of the blend and had made 3.5 pounds of the blend. How much of the house blend did Isabel have at the start of the day?

   Answer _____

This table shows the distance in kilometers by rail from Chicago to New Orleans and other cities in between. Use it to solve problems 5–8.

0.0	Chicago, IL	850.3	Memphis, TN
204.1	Champaign, IL	1,010.2	Grenada, MS
580.9	Cairo, IL	1,173.7	Jackson, MS
652.9	Fulton, KY	1,399.7	Hammond, LA
786.9	Covington, KY	1,485.6	New Orleans, LA

5. How far is it from Chicago to Cairo?

   Answer _____

6. How far is it from Chicago to New Orleans?

   Answer _____

7. How far is Memphis from New Orleans?

   Answer _____

8. How far is it from Covington to New Orleans?

   Answer _____

Unit 5 Working with Decimals

Estimation of Decimal Sums and Differences

To estimate a decimal sum or difference, first round the decimals to the same place. Then add or subtract the rounded numbers.

Estimate: 7.69 + 4.19

Round each decimal to the nearest one. Add.

$$
\begin{array}{r}
7.69 \rightarrow\ \ 8 \\
+4.19 \rightarrow +\ 4 \\
\hline
12
\end{array}
$$

Estimate: 10.34 − 6.78

Round each decimal to the nearest tenth. Subtract.

$$
\begin{array}{r}
10.34 \rightarrow\ \ 10.3 \\
-\ 6.78 \rightarrow -\ 6.8 \\
\hline
3.5
\end{array}
$$

PRACTICE

Estimate each sum or difference by rounding to the nearest one.

	a	b	c	d

1.
$$
\begin{array}{r}
\$7.6\,5 \rightarrow\ \ 8 \\
+\ 5.3\,3 \rightarrow +5 \\
\hline
\$13
\end{array}
\qquad
\begin{array}{r}
\$1\,0.4\,5 \rightarrow \\
+\ 2\,3.5\,6 \rightarrow \\
\hline
\end{array}
\qquad
\begin{array}{r}
\$\ \ 9\,9.9\,0 \rightarrow \\
+\ 1\,2\,1.2\,5 \rightarrow \\
\hline
\end{array}
\qquad
\begin{array}{r}
2\,6.7\,6 \rightarrow \\
+\ \ 1.9\,8 \rightarrow \\
\hline
\end{array}
$$

2.
$$
\begin{array}{r}
9\,9.7\,6 \rightarrow\ \ 100 \\
-2\,0.3\,0 \rightarrow -\ 20 \\
\hline
80
\end{array}
\qquad
\begin{array}{r}
\$1\,0.4\,5 \rightarrow \\
-\ \ \ 9.2\,3 \rightarrow \\
\hline
\end{array}
\qquad
\begin{array}{r}
9.8\,7 \rightarrow \\
-5.5\,7 \rightarrow \\
\hline
\end{array}
\qquad
\begin{array}{r}
\$1\,3.4\,5 \rightarrow \\
-\ 1\,2.8\,9 \rightarrow \\
\hline
\end{array}
$$

3.
$$
\begin{array}{r}
\$8.5\,4 \rightarrow \\
-\ 4.5\,0 \rightarrow \\
\hline
\end{array}
\qquad
\begin{array}{r}
3\,0.6\,8 \rightarrow \\
+2\,4.1\,0 \rightarrow \\
\hline
\end{array}
\qquad
\begin{array}{r}
2\,3.0\,5 \rightarrow \\
+1\,0\,1.8\,6 \rightarrow \\
\hline
\end{array}
\qquad
\begin{array}{r}
2\,9.7\,0 \rightarrow \\
-\ \ 8.2\,9 \rightarrow \\
\hline
\end{array}
$$

Estimate the sum or difference by rounding to the nearest tenth.

	a	b	c

4. 12.35 − 2.17   5.08 + 3.07   19.18 − 9.28

$$
\begin{array}{r}
12.35 \rightarrow\ \ 12.4 \\
-\ 2.17 \rightarrow -\ 2.2 \\
\hline
10.2
\end{array}
$$

5. 10.67 + 9.33   4.75 − 0.66   300.31 + 25.32

6. 25.04 + 4.86   30.28 − 9.83   175.37 + 24.62

Practice Adding and Subtracting Decimals

Estimate the answer. Then add or subtract.
Use your estimate to check your answer.

PRACTICE

Add.

	a	b	c	d
1.	0.4 0.2 +0.3	0.0 2 0.0 5 +0.0 1	1.0 8 2.0 2 +0.4 5	4.5 7 2.9 3 +4.8 7
2.	3.0 6 4.0 9 2.0 8 +1.0 1	0.0 8 0.0 3 0.0 2 +0.0 6	0.1 5 0.0 8 0.4 3 +0.1 7	0.2 5 0.6 0.1 0 +0.0 5
3.	2.8 6 0.7 0.1 2 +0.0 8 1	4 0.0 5 1.6 +0.0 0 3	2.0 3 1 4.1 7 5 3.0 9 8 +1.0 0 6	1 5 0.4 8 2 5.9 8 1 6.5 0 +2 5 0.0 0

Subtract.

	a	b	c	d
4.	0.8 −0.2	1 4.6 − 5.4	0.6 7 −0.4 8	0.8 6 −0.7 9
5.	0.6 7 9 −0.3 9 8	1 5.8 − 3.9	6.5 0 4 −2.8	7.8 −1.2 6
6.	0.6 5 9 3 −0.4 2 7 1	1.8 5 3 1 −0.9 2 4 8	8 4.3 5 −3 6.9 5	8.0 0 0 −1.7 4 2

Line up the decimals. Then find the sum and differences.

a	b	c
7. 1.24 + 0.078 + 2.9 = _____	18.4957 − 2.36 = _____	324.6 − 75.908 = _____

Unit 5 Working with Decimals

More Practice Adding and Subtracting Decimals

After you find each answer, check with a calculator.

PRACTICE

Add.

	a	b	c	d
1.	1.4	8	7.0 5 3	1.3 8
	0.7	0.5 3	0.9 6	1 6.4 8
	0.2 9	2.1	8.5 2 4	9.2 7
	+2.4 5 6	+0.6 8	+1.8	+ 0.8 4

	a	b	c	d
2.	8.3 4 0 7	3.9 7	2 2.9 5	3 4 9.9 5
	0.0 0 3 8	0.9 5	5.5 0	6.5 0
	1.1 5 3	8.4 9	0.9 8	2 4.0 0
	+7.4 6 1 9	+3.1 6	+1 6.4 9	+ 9.9 9

Line up the decimals. Then find the sums.

             a   b

3. $3.3 + 0.07 + 6 + 2.63 + 0.174 =$ _____ $15.4 + 2.185 + 0.66 + 21.009 =$ _____

4. $0.74 + 1.6 + 0.99 + 4.88 + 0.04 =$ _____ $3.42 + 15.98 + 25 + 12.45 =$ _____

Subtract.

	a	b	c	d
5.	0.4 5	2 3.8 7	4.2	3.5 6
	−0.2 1 6	− 2.1	−0.3 7 2	−0.8

	a	b	c	d
6.	1 2	8.7 6 4 5	7.0 0 0 8	5 6
	− 0.7 4 3	−3	−2.5	− 2.0 0 3

Line up the decimals. Then find the differences.

         a   b   c

7. $12.54 − 1.054 =$ _____ $4 − 0.875 =$ _____ $15.42 − 9 =$ _____

8. $27 − 0.0067 =$ _____ $0.03 − 0.0034 =$ _____ $100 − 84.53 =$ _____

Multiplying Decimals by Whole Numbers

To multiply decimals by whole numbers, multiply the same way you would multiply whole numbers. Place the decimal point in the product by counting the total number of decimal places in the factors. The product will have the same number of decimal places.

Remember, sometimes you might need to write a zero in the product in order to place the decimal point correctly.

Find: 13 × 6.4

Multiply. Write the decimal point in the product.	

$$\begin{array}{r} 6.4 \\ \times\ 13 \\ \hline 192 \\ +640 \\ \hline 83.2 \end{array}$$

1 decimal place
+0 decimal places

1 decimal place

Find: 0.018 × 5

Multiply. Write the decimal point in the product.

$$\begin{array}{r} 0.018 \\ \times\quad 5 \\ \hline 0.090 \end{array}$$

3 decimal places
+0 decimal places
3 decimal places

⌐Write zeros.

GUIDED PRACTICE

Multiply. Write zeros as needed.

  a   b   c

1.
$$\begin{array}{r} \overset{2}{1}7 \\ \times0.3 \\ \hline 5.1 \end{array}$$
___1___ place

$$\begin{array}{r} 24 \\ \times0.09 \\ \hline \end{array}$$
___ places

$$\begin{array}{r} 0.707 \\ \times\quad 2 \\ \hline \end{array}$$
___ places

2.
$$\begin{array}{r} 2 \\ \times0.2 \\ \hline \end{array}$$
___ place

$$\begin{array}{r} 0.105 \\ \times\quad 8 \\ \hline \end{array}$$
___ places

$$\begin{array}{r} 0.19 \\ \times\quad 5 \\ \hline \end{array}$$
___ places

3.
$$\begin{array}{r} 0.0\overset{1}{0}3 \\ \times\quad 4 \\ \hline 0.012 \end{array}$$
___3___ places

$$\begin{array}{r} 2 \\ \times0.03 \\ \hline \end{array}$$
___ places

$$\begin{array}{r} 0.006 \\ \times\quad 9 \\ \hline \end{array}$$
___ places

4.
$$\begin{array}{r} 3.84 \\ \times\quad 35 \\ \hline 1920 \\ +11520 \\ \hline 134.40 \end{array}$$
___2___ places

$$\begin{array}{r} 0.135 \\ \times\quad 44 \\ \hline \end{array}$$
___ places

$$\begin{array}{r} 9.28 \\ \times230 \\ \hline \end{array}$$
___ places

5.
$$\begin{array}{r} 321 \\ \times1.46 \\ \hline \end{array}$$
___ places

$$\begin{array}{r} 4.53 \\ \times579 \\ \hline \end{array}$$
___ places

$$\begin{array}{r} 0.692 \\ \times\quad 168 \\ \hline \end{array}$$
___ places

PRACTICE

Multiply. Write zeros as needed.

	a	b	c	d
1.	0.8 6 2 × 2	0.0 8 4 × 3	1.6 3 × 6	2.3 4 × 5
2.	1 3.6 × 3	2 8.5 2 × 4	1.3 ×1 3	2 6 ×1.3
3.	8.2 ×1 2	6 2 ×0.3 5	7 0 ×5.0	0.9 0 × 5 5
4.	3.0 7 × 2 5	0.0 4 8 × 8 2	2 3 4 ×0.0 5 9	7 0 7 ×0.6 9 0

Line up the digits. Then find the products. Write zeros as needed.

a	b	c
5. 15.2 × 6 = _____	0.908 × 31 = _____	7.85 × 109 = _____

15.2
× 6

MIXED PRACTICE

Divide.

	a	b	c	d
1.	2 3)4, 5 7 7	1 8)3, 6 3 6	7 4)9, 0 8 8	6 9)4, 8 1 5
2.	1 2)1, 2 3 4	2 5)1, 9 3 0	5 0)8, 0 4 0	8 5)9, 6 9 6

Multiplying Decimals by Decimals

To multiply decimals by decimals, multiply the same way you would multiply whole numbers. Place the decimal point in the product by counting the total number of decimal places in the factors. The product will have the same number of decimal places. Write zeros as needed.

Find: 0.48 × 13.7

Multiply. Write the decimal point in the product.	
13.7	1 place
× 0.48	+2 places
1096	
+548	
6.576	3 places

Find: 0.008 × 0.137

Multiply. Write the decimal point in the product.	
0.137	3 places
×0.008	+3 places
0.001096	6 places
└── Write zeros.	

GUIDED PRACTICE

Multiply. Write zeros as needed.

	a		b		c	
1.	1.6 (2) × 0.4 0.6 4	1 place + 1 place 2 places	5.3 ×0.0 9	place + places places	0.7 6 × 0.5	places + place places
2.	0.1 2 (1) × 0.6 0.0 7 2	2 places + 1 place 3 places	0.0 9 × 0.3	places + place places	0.0 0 2 × 0.4	places + place places
3.	0.1 8 4 × 0.0 7	places + places places	2.0 4 × 0.2	places + place places	5.1 9 ×0.0 3	places + places places
4.	2.5 ×0.5 7	place + places places	3.4 7 × 1.4	places + place places	1 6.5 × 2.8	place + place places
5.	4 5.4 ×4.0 2	place + places places	1.5 4 ×1 0.6	places + place places	4.6 8 ×3.1 2	places + places places

PRACTICE

Multiply. Write zeros as needed.

	a	*b*	*c*	*d*
1.	$\begin{array}{r} 0.3 \\ \times 0.6 \\ \hline \end{array}$	$\begin{array}{r} 0.0\ 3 \\ \times\ \ \ 0.6 \\ \hline \end{array}$	$\begin{array}{r} 9.8 \\ \times 0.5 \\ \hline \end{array}$	$\begin{array}{r} 6.3 \\ \times 0.0\ 4 \\ \hline \end{array}$
2.	$\begin{array}{r} 0.0\ 8 \\ \times 0.0\ 4 \\ \hline \end{array}$	$\begin{array}{r} 0.0\ 0\ 6 \\ \times\ \ \ \ 0.4 \\ \hline \end{array}$	$\begin{array}{r} 1.3\ 7 \\ \times\ \ \ 0.8 \\ \hline \end{array}$	$\begin{array}{r} 1.3\ 7 \\ \times 0.0\ 0\ 8 \\ \hline \end{array}$
3.	$\begin{array}{r} 0.0\ 1\ 5 \\ \times\ \ \ 0.1\ 4 \\ \hline \end{array}$	$\begin{array}{r} 0.0\ 7\ 5 \\ \times\ \ \ 0.2\ 2 \\ \hline \end{array}$	$\begin{array}{r} 1\ 5.5 \\ \times 2.1\ 2 \\ \hline \end{array}$	$\begin{array}{r} 7.0\ 5 \\ \times 2.0\ 4 \\ \hline \end{array}$

Line up the digits. Then find the products. Write zeros as needed.

a	*b*	*c*
4. $0.43 \times 0.02 = $ _____	$0.206 \times 0.37 = $ _____	$8.79 \times 6.08 = $ _____
$\begin{array}{r} 0.43 \\ \times 0.02 \\ \hline \end{array}$		

MIXED PRACTICE

Find each answer.

	a	*b*	*c*	*d*
1.	$\begin{array}{r} 7.0\ 0\ 5 \\ 0.2\ 5 \\ 1\ 6 \\ +\ \ \ 3.1 \\ \hline \end{array}$	$\begin{array}{r} 1.0\ 9 \\ 0.0\ 3\ 6 \\ 0.1\ 7 \\ +2.4 \\ \hline \end{array}$	$\begin{array}{r} 1\ 7.6\ 4\ 9 \\ 3.0\ 5\ 4 \\ 0.0\ 1\ 6 \\ +\ \ \ 0.1\ 9 \\ \hline \end{array}$	$\begin{array}{r} 2.0\ 5\ 3 \\ 0.1\ 7\ 6 \\ 0.0\ 3\ 4 \\ +2.9\ 3\ 4 \\ \hline \end{array}$
2.	$\begin{array}{r} 1.9\ 4\ 3 \\ -0.8\ 4\ 9 \\ \hline \end{array}$	$\begin{array}{r} 0.7\ 3\ 4 \\ -0.2\ 7\ 5 \\ \hline \end{array}$	$\begin{array}{r} 1\ 9.0\ 6 \\ -\ \ 9.9\ 7 \\ \hline \end{array}$	$\begin{array}{r} 2\ 0\ 5 \\ -1\ 5\ 6.4 \\ \hline \end{array}$
3.	$\begin{array}{r} \$3\ 0\ 1.5\ 0 \\ -\ \ 1\ 9\ 6.4\ 8 \\ \hline \end{array}$	$\begin{array}{r} \$6\ 2\ 0.0\ 4 \\ -\ \ 1\ 4\ 8.9\ 9 \\ \hline \end{array}$	$\begin{array}{r} \$1,0\ 0\ 0.4\ 4 \\ -\ \ \ \ 9\ 0\ 9.7\ 5 \\ \hline \end{array}$	$\begin{array}{r} \$8\ 7\ 0.0\ 0 \\ -\ \ 6\ 7\ 0.9\ 9 \\ \hline \end{array}$
4.	$\begin{array}{r} 9\frac{5}{8} \\ -\ \frac{1}{2} \\ \hline \end{array}$	$\begin{array}{r} 1\ 6\frac{5}{6} \\ -\ \ \frac{1}{3} \\ \hline \end{array}$	$\begin{array}{r} 7\ 1\frac{1}{4} \\ -\ \ \frac{1}{2} \\ \hline \end{array}$	$\begin{array}{r} 7\frac{2}{7} \\ -\ \frac{2}{3} \\ \hline \end{array}$

Dividing Decimals by Whole Numbers

To divide a decimal by a whole number, write the decimal point in the quotient directly above the decimal point in the dividend. Then divide as with whole numbers.

Find: 9.92 ÷ 16

Write a decimal point in the quotient.	Divide.

$$16\overline{)9.92}$$

$$\begin{array}{r} 0.62 \\ 16\overline{)9.92} \\ -96\downarrow \\ \hline 32 \\ -32 \\ \hline 0 \end{array}$$

Find: $48.96 ÷ 24

Write a decimal point in the quotient.	Divide.

$$24\overline{)\$48.96}$$

$$\begin{array}{r} \$2.04 \\ 24\overline{)\$48.96} \\ -48\downarrow\downarrow \\ \hline 096 \\ -96 \\ \hline 0 \end{array}$$

PRACTICE

Divide.

	a	b	c	d
1.	$\begin{array}{r} 8.2 \\ 8\overline{)65.6} \\ -64\downarrow \\ \hline 16 \\ -16 \\ \hline 0 \end{array}$	$5\overline{)\$3.45}$	$3\overline{)8.28}$	$7\overline{)0.784}$
2.	$\begin{array}{r} 0.04 \\ 61\overline{)2.44} \\ -244 \\ \hline 0 \end{array}$	$39\overline{)\$58.50}$	$46\overline{)9.338}$	$14\overline{)\$43.96}$
3.	$7\overline{)29.12}$	$4\overline{)\$16.48}$	$71\overline{)1.278}$	$22\overline{)0.154}$

Set up each problem. Then find the quotient.

	a	b	c
4.	22.5 ÷ 15 = _____	$6.03 ÷ 9 = _____	114.8 ÷ 82 = _____

$15\overline{)22.5}$

Unit 5 Working with Decimals

Dividing Decimals by Decimals

To divide a decimal by a decimal, change the divisor to a whole number by moving the decimal point. Move the decimal point in the dividend the same number of places. Then divide.

Remember, write a decimal point in the quotient directly above the position of the new decimal point in the dividend.

Find: 4.34 ÷ 0.7

Move each decimal point 1 place.	Divide.
0.7)4.34	6.2 7)43.4 −42 ↓ 14 −14 0

Find: 0.0713 ÷ 0.23

Move each decimal point 2 places.	Divide.
0.23)0.0713	0.31 23)007.13 −6 9↓ 23 −23 0

PRACTICE

Divide.

        a   b   c   d

1.
```
        4.8
  1.7)8.1 6          0.5)2.6 4 5        4.6)0.0 1 3 8      3.9)$5 3.4 3
   −6 8 ↓
     1 3 6
   −1 3 6
         0
```

2.
```
         2 9.9
  0.16)4.7 8 4       0.24)1.4 8 8       0.08)$6.4 8        0.57)2.5 6 5
    −3 2 ↓
      1 5 8
    −1 4 4 ↓
        1 4 4
      −1 4 4
            0
```

Set up each problem. Then find the quotient.

        a   b   c

3. 1.854 ÷ 0.9 = _____   0.91 ÷ 1.3 = _____ $15.18 ÷ 0.33 = _____

0.9)1.854

Dividing Whole Numbers by Decimals

To divide a whole number by a decimal number, change the
divisor to a whole number by moving the decimal point. Move
the decimal point in the dividend the same number of places
by adding one or more zeros. Then divide.

Find: 102 ÷ 1.7

Move each decimal point 1 place.	Divide.
$1.7\overline{)102.0}$	$\begin{array}{r} 60 \\ 17\overline{)1020} \\ -102\downarrow \\ \hline 00 \end{array}$

Find: $230 ÷ 0.25

Move each decimal point 2 places.	Divide.
$0.25\overline{)\$230.00}$	$\begin{array}{r} \$920 \\ 025\overline{)\$23000} \\ -225\downarrow \\ \hline 50 \\ -50\downarrow \\ \hline 00 \end{array}$

PRACTICE

Divide. Write zeros as needed.

          a   *b*   *c*   *d*

1. $\begin{array}{r} 160 \\ 0.6\overline{)96.0} \\ -6\downarrow \\ \hline 36 \\ -36\downarrow \\ \hline 00 \end{array}$ $2.4\overline{)72}$ $1.8\overline{)9}$ $0.9\overline{)\$306}$

2. $\begin{array}{r} 150 \\ 0.34\overline{)51.00} \\ -34\downarrow \\ \hline 170 \\ -170\downarrow \\ \hline 00 \end{array}$ $0.17\overline{)85}$ $0.08\overline{)\$52}$ $0.32\overline{)128}$

3. $0.2\overline{)\$7}$ $0.5\overline{)13}$ $0.14\overline{)84}$ $1.6\overline{)\$224}$

Set up each problem. Then find the quotient. Write zeros as needed.

          a   *b*   *c*

4. $117 ÷ 7.8 = $ _____ $162 ÷ 1.5 = $ _____ $328 ÷ 0.4 = $ _____

$7.8\overline{)\$117}$

Decimal Quotients

Sometimes when you divide, the divisor will be greater than the dividend. To divide, add a decimal point and zeros as needed to the dividend. Continue to divide until the remainder is zero. In some cases, you may never have a remainder of zero. When dividing money, round the quotient to the nearest cent. Remember, zeros may be needed in the quotient also.

You can use this method to change some fractions to decimals by dividing the numerator by the denominator.

Find: $19 ÷ 300

Add a decimal point and zeros to the dividend.

$$300\overline{)\$19.00}$$

Divide. Place a zero in the quotient.

$$
\begin{array}{r}
\$0.0633 \\
300\overline{)\$19.0000} \\
-18\,00 \\
\hline
1\,000 \\
-900 \\
\hline
1000 \\
-900 \\
\hline
100
\end{array}
$$

Round $0.0633 to $0.06.

Change $\frac{8}{125}$ to a decimal.

Divide the numerator by the denominator. Add a decimal point and zeros to the dividend.

$$125\overline{)8.00}$$

Divide until the remainder is zero.

$$
\begin{array}{r}
0.064 \\
125\overline{)8.000} \\
-7\,50 \\
\hline
500 \\
-500 \\
\hline
0
\end{array}
$$

$$\frac{8}{125} = 0.064$$

PRACTICE

Divide. Write zeros as needed.

	a	b	c	d

1.

a.
$$
\begin{array}{r}
0.5 \\
40\overline{)2\,0.0} \\
-2\,0\,0 \\
\hline
0
\end{array}
$$

b. $100\overline{)\$3\,0}$ c. $5\overline{)2}$ d. $20\overline{)\$1\,5}$

2.

a. $50\overline{)1}$ b. $500\overline{)2\,5}$ c. $5\overline{)\$4}$ d. $20\overline{)1\,9}$

Use division to change each fraction to a decimal.

	a	b	c	d

3. $\frac{1}{4}$

$$
\begin{array}{r}
0.25 \\
4\overline{)1.00} \\
-8 \\
\hline
20 \\
-20 \\
\hline
0
\end{array}
$$

b. $\frac{1}{8}$ c. $\frac{1}{40}$ d. $\frac{3}{5}$

4. $\frac{6}{12}$ b. $\frac{6}{8}$ c. $\frac{2}{500}$ d. $\frac{15}{60}$

Multiplying and Dividing by Powers of 10

To multiply a decimal by a **power of ten,** move the decimal point to the *right* as many places as there are zeros in the **multiplier.**

Remember, sometimes you might need to write zeros in the product in order to move the decimal point the correct number of places.

Study these examples.

$10 \times 0.89 = 8.9$ $100 \times 0.73 = 73$ $1,000 \times 0.52 = 520$
$10 \times 8.9 = 89$ $100 \times 7.3 = 730$ $1,000 \times 5.2 = 5,200$

To divide a decimal by a power of ten, move the decimal point to the *left* as many places as there are zeros in the divisor.

Remember, sometimes you might need to write zeros in the quotient in order to correctly insert the decimal point.

Study these examples.

$0.89 \div 10 = 0.089$ $0.73 \div 100 = 0.0073$ $0.52 \div 1,000 = 0.00052$
$8.9 \div 10 = 0.89$ $7.3 \div 100 = 0.073$ $5.2 \div 1,000 = 0.0052$

PRACTICE

Multiply or divide. Write zeros as needed.

	a	b	c
1.	$7.5 \times 10 = \underline{\quad 75 \quad}$	$46 \times 10 = \underline{\qquad}$	$0.07 \times 10 = \underline{\qquad}$
2.	$100 \times 0.7 = \underline{\qquad}$	$100 \times 4.6 = \underline{\qquad}$	$0.075 \times 100 = \underline{\qquad}$
3.	$0.5 \div 10 = \underline{\quad 0.05 \quad}$	$8 \div 1,000 = \underline{\qquad}$	$1.25 \div 100 = \underline{\qquad}$
4.	$12.5 \div 100 = \underline{\qquad}$	$0.125 \div 1,000 = \underline{\qquad}$	$14.92 \div 100 = \underline{\qquad}$
5.	$6.2 \times 1,000 = \underline{\qquad}$	$642.15 \div 10 = \underline{\qquad}$	$642.15 \div 100 = \underline{\qquad}$
6.	$3.15 \times 1,000 = \underline{\qquad}$	$0.048 \times 100 = \underline{\qquad}$	$0.048 \div 100 = \underline{\qquad}$
7.	$0.375 \div 10 = \underline{\qquad}$	$3.75 \div 10 = \underline{\qquad}$	$37.5 \div 10 = \underline{\qquad}$
8.	$375 \div 10 = \underline{\qquad}$	$0.375 \times 1,000 = \underline{\qquad}$	$0.007 \times 1,000 = \underline{\qquad}$
9.	$719.35 \times 100 = \underline{\qquad}$	$16.147 \times 1,000 = \underline{\qquad}$	$14.92 \times 1,000 = \underline{\qquad}$
10.	$261.78 \div 100 = \underline{\qquad}$	$2.6178 \div 1,000 = \underline{\qquad}$	$2.6178 \times 1,000 = \underline{\qquad}$

Unit 5 Working with Decimals

Estimating Decimal Products and Quotients

To estimate decimal products or quotients, round each number
to the same place. Then multiply or divide the rounded numbers.

Estimate: 15.3 × 2.8

Round each number.	Multiply.
15.3 → 15	15
2.8 → 3	× 3
	45

Estimate: 360.41 ÷ 2.89

Round each number.	Divide.
360.41 → 360	120
2.89 → 3	3)360
	−3↓
	06	
	−6↓
	00

PRACTICE

Estimate each product.

a

1. $\begin{array}{r} 3\ 1.7\ 5 \to\ \ 3\ 2 \\ \times\quad\ \ 2.2 \to \times\ \ 2 \\ \hline 6\ 4 \end{array}$

b

$\begin{array}{r} 1\ 5.6 \to \\ \times\ \ 3.5 \to \\ \hline \end{array}$

c

$\begin{array}{r} 2\ 3.8 \to \\ \times\ \ 4.7 \to \\ \hline \end{array}$

2. $\begin{array}{r} 9.5 \to \\ \times 1\ 3.4\ 2 \to \\ \hline \end{array}$

$\begin{array}{r} 1.1\ 7 \to \\ \times\ \ 8.1 \to \\ \hline \end{array}$

$\begin{array}{r} 1\ 2.6\ 9 \to \\ \times\quad\ 6.2 \to \\ \hline \end{array}$

Estimate each quotient.

a

3. 4.9)1 9.9 5 → 5)2 0 (quotient 4)

b

6.2)1 2.1 7 →

c

9.95)1 0 9.5 →

4. 22.15)6 5.7 9 →

3.6)2 3.8 →

2.98)7 4.9 7 →

Estimate each product or quotient.

a

5. 45.8 × 9.3

$\begin{array}{r} 46 \\ \times\ 9 \\ \hline \end{array}$

b

30.27 ÷ 10.14

c

31.996 × 4.2

Practice Multiplying and Dividing Decimals

Estimate each answer. Then multiply or divide.
Use your estimate to check your answer.

PRACTICE

Multiply.

	a	b	c	d
1.	$\begin{array}{r} 0.3 \\ \times\ \ 8 \\ \hline \end{array}$	$\begin{array}{r} 4.3 \\ \times 0.2\ 4 \\ \hline \end{array}$	$\begin{array}{r} 0.3\ 5\ 1 \\ \times\ \ \ \ \ 8\ 6 \\ \hline \end{array}$	$\begin{array}{r} 0.6\ 7\ 3\ 9 \\ \times\ \ \ \ \ \ \ \ 7 \\ \hline \end{array}$
2.	$\begin{array}{r} 7\ 5 \\ \times 0.4\ 8 \\ \hline \end{array}$	$\begin{array}{r} 0.0\ 3 \\ \times\ \ \ \ 2 \\ \hline \end{array}$	$\begin{array}{r} 1\ 4 \\ \times 0.0\ 0\ 7 \\ \hline \end{array}$	$\begin{array}{r} 0.0\ 0\ 2 \\ \times\ \ \ \ \ \ 4 \\ \hline \end{array}$
3.	$\begin{array}{r} 3.1\ 4 \\ \times\ \ \ 1\ 8 \\ \hline \end{array}$	$\begin{array}{r} 0.6 \\ \times 0.3 \\ \hline \end{array}$	$\begin{array}{r} 0.3 \\ \times 0.2 \\ \hline \end{array}$	$\begin{array}{r} 0.5\ 8 \\ \times\ \ 0.6 \\ \hline \end{array}$

Divide.

4. $4\overline{)9.2}$ $0.3\overline{)2\ 4\ 7.8}$ $0.02\overline{)5\ 2\ 1.5\ 6}$ $0.006\overline{)7\ 4.8\ 9\ 8}$

5. $7\overline{)8.9\ 6}$ $0.5\overline{)9.2\ 5}$ $0.79\overline{)4.6\ 6\ 1}$ $0.018\overline{)0.4\ 5\ 5\ 4}$

6. $2\overline{)5.3\ 2\ 8}$ $0.8\overline{)0.8\ 9\ 6}$ $0.56\overline{)5.0\ 1\ 7\ 6}$ $0.007\overline{)6.5\ 3\ 9\ 1\ 2}$

More Practice Multiplying and Dividing Decimals

After you find an answer, check with a calculator.

PRACTICE

Multiply.

	a	b	c	d

1.
```
    1 5.3        2 8.7       1 2.6 1 5         8.7
  ×   8.1       ×0.2 4     ×        2 5     ×0.4 8
```

2.
```
    0.2 1        0.5 6        0.0 5          1 6.2
  ×   0.4       ×0.3 7      ×0.0 1        ×0.0 4 5
```

3.
```
   3 4.8 9       0.1 4 7      3.1 4 1 6       0.0 5 9
  ×0.8 7 5      ×   0.0 3    ×     0.7 5    ×0.0 6 4
```

Divide.

4.
```
  8)0.7 3 6    0.2)0.0 0 3 4    0.03)0.0 0 0 9    0.231)0.0 0 9 2 4
```

5.
```
  36)9 1.4 4    1.2)1 0 8.7 2    1.44)1 3 5.0 7 2    0.048)6 0
```

6.
```
  8)5.0 0 0    0.6)1 2.0    0.25)5 0    0.125)5 3.7 5
```

Problem-Solving Strategy: Use Estimation

During the summer of 2000, Maria visited the Netherlands, where the unit of currency is the guilder. At that time, one dollar could be exchanged for 1.88 guilders. The price of Maria's hotel room was 122 guilders per night. About how much was this in dollars?

Understand the problem.

- **What do you want to know?**
  about how much Maria's hotel room cost in dollars

- **What information is given?**
  Each dollar could be exchanged for 1.88 guilders.
  The cost of the room was 122 guilders.

Plan how to solve it.

- **What strategy can you use?**
  Since the problem is not asking for an exact answer,
  you can use estimation to find the cost.

Solve it.

- **How can you use this strategy to solve the problem?**
  Round both amounts, then divide.

$$
\begin{array}{ll}
1.88 \rightarrow 2 & \quad\quad 60 \\
122 \rightarrow 120 & 2)\overline{120}
\end{array}
$$

- **What is the answer?**
  The cost of the hotel room was about $60.

Look back and check your answer.

- **Is your answer reasonable?**
  You can check your estimate by finding how many guilders
  $60 was worth. Multiply.

$$
\begin{array}{r}
1.88 \\
\times \ \ 60 \\
\hline
112.80
\end{array}
$$

Since 112.8 is close to 122, the estimate is reasonable.

Use estimation to solve each problem.

1. One hundred quarters weigh about 1.25 pounds. About how many quarters are there in 20 pounds?

Answer _____

2. Pedro bought two hats for $7.65 each. He gave the clerk $20.00. About how much change should he get back?

Answer _____

3. Mel's driveway is 5.1 meters wide. His neighbor's driveway is 3.98 meters wide. About how much wider is Mel's driveway than his neighbor's?

Answer _____

4. Angela is using a craft kit to make jewelry. The directions say that each bracelet needs 11.95 cm of wire. Angela has 108.39 centimeters of wire. About how many bracelets can she make?

Answer _____

5. Charlie's paycheck each week is $309.15. His average workweek is 30.8 hours. About how much does he earn each hour? About how much does he make in one year? (1 year = 52 weeks)

Answer _____

6. Jose used 3.1 gallons of fuel during his drive to his vacation cabin. If his vehicle gets 29 miles per gallon, about how many miles did he drive to his cabin?

Answer _____

7. Jennifer earns $95.00 per month at her part-time job. About how much does Jennifer earn in one year? (1 year = 12 months)

Answer _____

8. Miguel ordered lunchmeat at the supermarket. The lunchmeat cost $3.98 per pound and weighed 2.02 pounds. About how much did the lunchmeat cost?

Answer _____

Problem-Solving Applications

Solve.

1. Paulo is paid $14.10 per hour and 1.5 times that rate for every hour worked more than 40 hours in a week. How much will he earn for working 42 hours in a week?

   Answer _____

2. Mary wanted to find the length of her average stride. She walked 100 strides and found that the distance she covered was 92 meters. What was the length of her average stride?

   Answer _____

3. Dan bought three books for $29.85. Each book was the same price. About how much did each book cost?

   Answer _____

4. Sam paid $41.97 for 3 CDs. Latoya paid $51.00 for 4 CDs. Who paid more for each of the CDs? How much more?

   Answer _____

5. Kim's family drove to Montréal yesterday. The trip took 8.5 hours, and their car averaged 75.4 kilometers per hour. How far did Kim's family drive to get to Montréal?

   Answer _____

6. Ms. Soto planted a tree that was 1.2 meters tall. She was told that it would grow at the rate of 0.15 meter per year. At that rate, what will be the tree's height after 12 years?

   Answer _____

7. Tavon bought 500 bricks for a patio project. If each brick weighs 2.2 pounds, what is the total weight of all the bricks?

   Answer _____

8. Tavon paid $85.00 for the 500 bricks. What was the cost per brick?

   Answer _____

Unit 5 Working with Decimals

Write each fraction as a decimal.

	a	b	c	d
1.	$\frac{1}{10} =$ _____	$\frac{3}{100} =$ _____	$\frac{1}{5} =$ _____	$\frac{3}{4} =$ _____

| 2. | $\frac{1}{8} =$ _____ | $\frac{5}{8} =$ _____ | $1\frac{1}{4} =$ _____ | $2\frac{3}{5} =$ _____ |

Write each decimal as a fraction or a mixed number.

	a	b	c	d
3.	$1.1 =$ _____	$1.5 =$ _____	$0.75 =$ _____	$5.50 =$ _____

Find each answer.

	a	b	c	d
4.	7.7 6 6.6 7 +4.3 9	1.9 2 3 2.7 4 9 +1.6 3 7	0.0 9 0.5 4 +0.9 7 8	0.0 1 8 0.2 0 9 +4 0.0 9
5.	7.9 4 −4.5 6	0.5 0 6 −0.1 8 9 2	3 0 6.0 9 − 4 6.4 5	7.4 7 6 3 −6.4 7 6 7
6.	1.2 5 ×0.0 4	3.0 8 × 1 2	3.5 ×2.4	2.0 7 5 × 0.0 8
7.	6)0.3 6	12)1.4 4	0.12)1 4 4	0.6)3.6

Line up the digits. Then find the products or quotients.

	a	b	c
8.	$2.25 \times 10 =$ _____	$0.225 \times 1,000 =$ _____	$22.5 \times 100 =$ _____
9.	$35.2 \div 10 =$ _____	$18.6 \div 100 =$ _____	$149.2 \times 100 =$ _____

Meaning of Percent

The symbol % is read as **percent.** Percent means *per hundred* or *out of one hundred.* Therefore, 35% means 35 per hundred, 35 out of 100, or 35 hundredths.

We can write a percent as a fraction or as a decimal.

To change a percent to a decimal, move the decimal point 2 places to the left and drop the percent sign (%). Write zeros as needed.

Examples:

$$35\% = 0.35 \qquad 6\% = 0.06 \qquad 480\% = 4.8$$

To change a percent to a fraction, place the percent over 100 and drop the % sign. Simplify.

Examples:

$$35\% = \frac{35}{100} = \frac{7}{20} \qquad 6\% = \frac{6}{100} = \frac{3}{50} \qquad 480\% = \frac{480}{100} = 4\frac{4}{5}$$

PRACTICE

Change each percent to a decimal and then to a fraction. Simplify.

a

1. 82% = $0.82 = \frac{82}{100} = \frac{41}{50}$ *b*   7% = _____

2. 1% = _____   142% = _____

3. 95% = _____   55% = _____

4. 109% = _____   73% = _____

5. 98% = _____   12% = _____

6. 4% = _____   44% = _____

7. 175% = _____   83% = _____

8. 26% = _____   137% = _____

Changing Decimals and Fractions to Percents

To change a decimal to a percent, move the decimal point 2 places to the right and write a percent symbol. Write zeros as needed.

To change a fraction to a percent, first change the fraction to a decimal by dividing the numerator by the denominator. Then rewrite the decimal quotient as a percent.

Examples:

$0.8\underset{\smile}{2}5 = 82.5\%$	$0.\underset{\smile}{4} = 40\%$

Write $\frac{3}{4}$ as a percent.

Divide.

$$\frac{0.75}{4)3.00} = 75\%$$

Write $\frac{3}{20}$ as a percent.

Divide.

$$\frac{0.15}{20)3.00} = 15\%$$

PRACTICE

Change each decimal to a percent.

	a	b	c
1.	$0.30 = \underline{\quad 30\% \quad}$	$0.08 = \underline{\qquad}$	$0.45 = \underline{\qquad}$
2.	$0.91 = \underline{\qquad}$	$0.56 = \underline{\qquad}$	$1.49 = \underline{\qquad}$
3.	$0.73 = \underline{\qquad}$	$0.672 = \underline{\qquad}$	$0.02 = \underline{\qquad}$
4.	$3.25 = \underline{\qquad}$	$0.09 = \underline{\qquad}$	$0.7 = \underline{\qquad}$
5.	$1.333 = \underline{\qquad}$	$0.54 = \underline{\qquad}$	$0.62 = \underline{\qquad}$

Change each fraction to a percent.

	a	b	c
6.	$\frac{3}{8} = \underline{\quad 37.5\% \quad}$	$\frac{2}{5} = \underline{\qquad}$	$\frac{7}{10} = \underline{\qquad}$
7.	$\frac{21}{100} = \underline{\qquad}$	$\frac{5}{16} = \underline{\qquad}$	$\frac{1}{4} = \underline{\qquad}$
8.	$\frac{3}{5} = \underline{\qquad}$	$\frac{7}{20} = \underline{\qquad}$	$\frac{5}{12} = \underline{\qquad}$

Interchanging Fractions, Decimals, and Percents

Fill in the blanks below as shown in the first example.

1. $\frac{6}{10}$ _____ = _____ 0.6 _____ = _____ 60% _____   — Work Space —

2. $\frac{1}{4}$ _____ = _____ 0.25 _____ = _____

3. _____ = _____ = _____ 20% _____

4. $\frac{17}{20}$ _____ = _____ = _____

5. _____ = _____ 0.5 _____ = _____

6. _____ = _____ = _____ 75% _____

Solve.

7. The Ortega family spends $37 out of every $100 earned on rent. What percent of their income does the Ortega family spend on rent?

    Answer _____

8. The sales tax in one state is $7\frac{1}{2}$%. Write $7\frac{1}{2}$% as a decimal.

    Answer _____

9. A suit is on sale for 10% off the regular price. Write the decimal you should use to figure the amount of the discount.

    Answer _____

10. At Super Subs, 8 out of the 25 employees work part-time. What percent of the employees work part-time?

    Answer _____

11. Lakita saves 15% of her salary. What fraction of her salary does Lakita save?

    Answer _____

12. For a class project, Chang polled his friends and found that five out of eight do some kind of exercise each week. Write this fraction as a decimal.

    Answer _____

Percents Greater Than 100%

To change a percent to a decimal, you always move the
decimal point 2 places to the left and drop the percent sign.
This also applies to percents greater than 100.

Examples:

$200\% = 2.00 = 2$ $375\% = 3.75$ $105\frac{3}{10}\% = 105.3\% = 1.053$

PRACTICE

Change each percent to a decimal.

	a	*b*	*c*
1.	$205\% = \underline{\ 2.05\ }$	$500\% = \underline{\hspace{2cm}}$	$175\% = \underline{\hspace{2cm}}$
2.	$999.9\% = \underline{\hspace{2cm}}$	$320\% = \underline{\hspace{2cm}}$	$101\frac{3}{10}\% = \underline{\hspace{2cm}}$
3.	$450\% = \underline{\hspace{2cm}}$	$609\% = \underline{\hspace{2cm}}$	$1{,}100\% = \underline{\hspace{2cm}}$
4.	$807\% = \underline{\hspace{2cm}}$	$725\frac{1}{2}\% = \underline{\hspace{2cm}}$	$198\% = \underline{\hspace{2cm}}$

Solve.

5. A clothing store has a 210% markup on
the price of their clothing. Write the
decimal used for the markup on the
price of their clothing.

Answer _____

6. Larry's test scores have improved 152%.
Write this percent as a decimal.

Answer _____

7. The profits for Fun Times, Inc., have
increased 333% since the company
started. Write this amount as a decimal.

Answer _____

8. Doreen's savings have increased by
135%. What decimal would you use to
calculate the amount of money in
Doreen's account?

Answer _____

Percents Less Than 1%

When working with a percent less than 1%, change the percent to
a decimal using the same method used with larger percents.

Examples:

$$0.1\% = 0.001 \qquad \frac{3}{4}\% = 0.75\% = \frac{0.75}{100} = 100\overline{)0.7500}^{\,0.0075}$$

PRACTICE

Change each percent to a decimal.

a	b	c

1. $0.5\% =$ ___0.005___ $0.33\% =$ _____ $0.25\% =$ _____

2. $0.4\% =$ _____ $0.41\% =$ _____ $0.05\% =$ _____

3. $\frac{1}{4}\% =$ _____ $\frac{1}{2}\% =$ _____ $\frac{2}{5}\% =$ _____

4. $\frac{4}{5}\% =$ _____ $\frac{5}{8}\% =$ _____ $\frac{7}{8}\% =$ _____

Solve.

5. The sales at a clothing store decreased
by 0.9% last month. Write this percent as
a decimal.

Answer _____

6. The interest rate on loans increased by
0.64%. What is this percent expressed as
a decimal?

Answer _____

7. A plant's height increased by 0.55%.
What is this percent as a decimal?

Answer _____

8. Which is greater, 0.45% or $\frac{3}{8}$%? Write
each as a decimal and compare.

Answer _____

Problem-Solving Applications

Solve.

1. The average household in the United States spends $0.20 of every dollar on housing costs. What percent is this amount?

   Answer _____

2. Three out of four students passed the exam. What percent of the students passed the exam?

   Answer _____

3. Real estate taxes in the city increased by 7.25%. What decimal number would you use to figure the new real estate taxes?

   Answer _____

4. In the last election, 36% of the people voted "Yes" on Proposition 6. What fraction of the people is this?

   Answer _____

5. The bank used 0.0975 to figure the interest charge on the McCalls' mortgage. What percent is this?

   Answer _____

6. For a research assignment, Selena found that 9 out of every 60 television viewing minutes were taken up by commercials. What percent of the viewing time was taken up by commercials?

   Answer _____

7. Sales tax in the state is $8\frac{1}{2}\%$. Write the number used to figure the sales tax on a purchase.

   Answer _____

8. Home improvement costs have increased by $\frac{4}{5}$ in the last few years. By what percent have home improvement costs increased?

   Answer _____

Problem-Solving Strategy: Use a Bar Graph

The manager of a frozen yogurt shop recorded the number of cups of frozen yogurt sold over the summer. What percent of the frozen yogurt sold was chocolate?

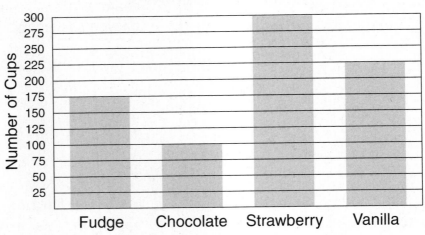

Cups of Frozen Yogurt Sold

Understand the problem.

- **What do you want to know?**
  the percent of frozen yogurt sold that was chocolate

- **What information is given?**
  a bar graph showing the number of cups of each flavor sold

Plan how to solve it.

- **What strategy can you use?**
  You can use the bar graph to find what percent of the total cups sold was chocolate.

Solve it.

- **How can you use this strategy to solve the problem?**
  Look at the bar graph to find the number of cups of chocolate frozen yogurt sold. Write that amount as a fraction of the total cups sold. Then change the fraction to a percent.

$$\frac{\text{cups of chocolate}}{\text{total cups}} = \frac{100}{800} = \frac{1}{8} = 0.125 = 12.5\%$$

- **What is the answer?**
  12.5% of the frozen yogurt sold was chocolate.

Look back and check your answer.

- **Is your answer reasonable?**
  You can check your answer by finding 12.5% of the total number of cups of frozen yogurt. The total number of cups is 800, and 12.5% of 800 is 100. There were 100 cups of chocolate sold. The answer is reasonable.

$$12.5\% = 0.125$$

$$\begin{array}{r} 800 \\ \times 0.125 \\ \hline 100 \end{array}$$

Use the bar graph below to solve each problem.

Company Fund Raiser

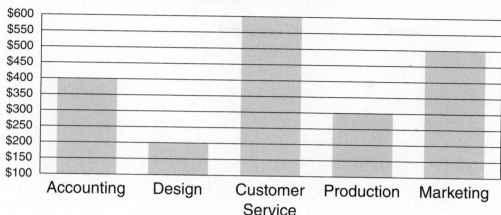

1. What percent of the total money was raised by Marketing?

   Answer _____

2. What fractional portion of the total money was raised by Production?

   Answer _____

3. Write the fractional portion of money raised by Customer Service as a decimal.

   Answer _____

4. Write the portion of the total raised by Design as a fraction, as a decimal, and as a percent.

   Answer _____

5. Write the portion of the total raised by Accounting as a fraction, as a decimal, and as a percent.

   Answer _____

6. Write the combined portion raised by Accounting and Customer Service as a decimal.

   Answer _____

7. What fractional portion of the total was raised by Production and Marketing combined?

   Answer _____

8. What percent of the total was raised by Accounting and Design combined?

   Answer _____

Using Decimals to Find a Percent of a Number

To find a percent of a number, write a percent sentence. Every percent sentence consists of three numbers: the **rate**, the **whole**, and the **part**.

$$20\% \text{ of } 48 = 9.6$$
$$\nearrow \qquad \uparrow \qquad \nwarrow$$
$$\text{rate} \quad \text{whole} \quad \text{part}$$

If the part is missing in a percent problem, solve by first changing the rate to a decimal. Then multiply the rate by the whole.

Remember, **of** means multiply.

Find: 25% of 84

$$25\% \times 84 = ? \qquad 0.25 \times 84 = 21$$

$$
\begin{array}{r}
84 \\
\times\ 0.25 \\
\hline
420 \\
+168 \\
\hline
21.00
\end{array}
$$

Find: 105% of 280

$$105\% \times 280 = ? \qquad 1.05 \times 280 = 294$$

$$
\begin{array}{r}
280 \\
\times\quad 1.05 \\
\hline
1400 \\
000 \\
+280 \\
\hline
294.00
\end{array}
$$

PRACTICE

Change each percent to a decimal. Solve.

	a	b
1.	50% of 90 $0.5 \times 90 = 45$	300% of 60
2.	80% of 120	75% of 80
3.	40% of 75	90% of 200
4.	250% of 100	99% of 55

Solve.

5. Rachel decided to save 15% of the money she earned. In one month, Rachel earned $1,584. How much money did she save?

6. Walter read an advertisement for a 30%-off sale on stereo equipment. How much money would Walter save if he bought a CD player that normally sold for $219?

Answer _____

Answer _____

Using Fractions to Find a Percent of a Number

Another way to find the missing part in a percent problem is to use fractions rather than decimals. Change the rate and the whole to fractions. Multiply the fractions. Simplify.

Find: 20% of 50

$$20\% \times 50 = ?$$

$$\frac{1}{\overset{}{\underset{1}{5}}} \times \frac{\overset{10}{50}}{1} = \frac{10}{1} = 10$$

Find: 75% of $1\frac{3}{4}$

$$75\% \times 1\frac{3}{4} = ?$$

$$\frac{3}{4} \times \frac{7}{4} = \frac{21}{16} = 1\frac{5}{16}$$

PRACTICE

Change each percent to a fraction. Solve. Simplify.

        a   *b*

1. 25% of 16   50% of $1\frac{1}{3}$

$$\frac{1}{\overset{}{\underset{1}{4}}} \times \frac{\overset{4}{16}}{1} = \frac{4}{1} = 4$$

2. 85% of 40   40% of $3\frac{1}{3}$

$$\frac{85}{\overset{}{\underset{5}{100}}} \times \frac{\overset{2}{40}}{1} = \frac{170}{5} = 34$$

3. 60% of 55   80% of $3\frac{3}{4}$

4. 6% of 20   70% of $6\frac{2}{3}$

Solve.

5. A sweater that normally sells for $66 was on sale for $33\frac{1}{3}\%$ off. How much would a customer save by paying the sale price? (Hint: $33\frac{1}{3}\% = \frac{1}{3}$.)

6. A survey of college students showed that $66\frac{2}{3}\%$ of the 600 students studied a foreign language. How many students studied a foreign language? (Hint: $66\frac{2}{3}\% = \frac{2}{3}$.)

Answer _____

Answer _____

Finding What Percent One Number Is of Another

To find the rate in a percent problem, write a percent sentence. Divide the part by the whole. Then write the decimal answer as a percent.

What percent of 75 is 60?

$? \% \times 75 = 60$

$? = 60 \div 75$
$0.8 = 60 \div 75$
$0.8 = 80\%$

What percent of 160 is 4?

$? \% \times 160 = 4$

$? = 4 \div 160$
$0.025 = 4 \div 160$
$0.025 = 2.5\%$

PRACTICE

Find each rate.

a

b

1. What percent of 8 is 40?

$?\% \times 8 = 40$
$? = 40 \div 8$
$5 = 40 \div 8$
$5 = 500\%$

What percent of 25 is 15?

2. What percent of 48 is 7.2?

What percent of 23 is 6.9?

3. What percent of 180 is 81?

What percent of $35 is $5.25?

4. What percent of 400 is 268?

What percent of 112 is 140?

Solve.

5. Jerry owes a friend $20 on a $50 loan. What percent of the loan does he owe?

Answer _____

6. A movie theater sold 500 tickets on Saturday. If 225 tickets were sold in the afternoon, what percent of the tickets were sold in the afternoon?

Answer _____

7. Every week the Garcias save $154 for their vacation. They have a combined income of $1,400 a week. What percent of their earnings do they save for vacation?

Answer _____

8. There are 640 students in the school, and 352 of them are boys. What percent of the students are boys?

Answer _____

Finding a Number When a Percent of It Is Known

To find the whole in a percent problem, write a percent sentence.
Change the rate to a decimal. Divide the part by the decimal.

12% of what number is 18?

$$12\% \times ? = 18$$
$$? = 18 \div 0.12$$
$$150 = 18 \div 0.12$$

30% of what number is 180?

$$30\% \times ? = 180$$
$$? = 180 \div 0.30$$
$$600 = 180 \div 0.30$$

PRACTICE

Change each percent to a decimal. Solve.

a

b

1. 25% of what number is 17?
$$25\% \times ? = 17$$
$$? = 17 \div 0.25$$
$$68 = 17 \div 0.25$$

32% of what number is 40?

2. 80% of what number is 64?

135% of what number is 270?

3. 60% of what number is 33?

45% of what number is 90?

4. 10% of what number is 73?

75% of what number is 120?

Solve.

5. Peter bought a sweater for $32. This was 80% of the original price. What was the original price?

   Answer _____

6. Katie got a 5% discount for paying cash for her furniture purchase. She paid $2,850 for the furniture. What would the price have been if she had charged her purchase?

   Answer _____

7. The distance by boat from New York City to San Francisco is 5,200 miles by way of the Panama Canal. This is 40% of the distance by way of the Strait of Magellan. How far is it by way of the Strait of Magellan?

   Answer _____

8. Adelena got a score of 90% on a true-false test. She answered 36 questions correctly. How many questions were on the test?

   Answer _____

Simple Interest

Interest is a charge that is paid for borrowed money. To find the **simple interest** on a loan, multiply the amount borrowed, or **principal,** times the annual rate of interest (a percent) times the number of years the loan is for. Change part of a year to a decimal.

Example:

Find the simple interest on a loan of $2,000 for 3 years at a rate of 6% per year.

$$\text{Interest} = \text{Principal} \times \text{Rate} \times \text{Time}$$
$$I = prt$$
$$I = \$2,000 \times 0.06 \times 3$$
$$I = \$360$$

GUIDED PRACTICE

Find the simple interest for each loan. Round to the nearest cent.

	a	*b*

1. $500 at 5.5% for $\frac{1}{2}$ year $225 at $6\frac{1}{2}$% for 1 year
$I = \$500 \times 0.055 \times 0.5$ $I = \$225 \times 0.065 \times 1$

$I = 500 \times 0.0275$
$I = \$13.75$

2. $800 at 18% for 1 year $1,000 at 5% for 2 years
$I = \$800 \times 0.18 \times 1$ $I = \$1,000 \times 0.05 \times 2$

3. $400 at 8.25% for 3 months $150 at 12% for 2 years
$I = \$400 \times 0.0825 \times 0.25$ $I = \$150 \times 0.12 \times 2$

4. $2,000 at 7% for 5 years $850 at 4% for 6 months
$I = \$2,000 \times 0.07 \times 5$ $I = \$850 \times 0.04 \times 0.5$

PRACTICE

Find the simple interest for each loan. Round to the nearest cent as needed.

                   a   *b*

1. $3,460 at 6.5% for 6 months $75 at 5.25% for 1 year
   (Hint: Change 6 months to 0.5 year.)

2. $225 at 4.75% for $1\frac{1}{4}$ years $3,210 at 6% for 3 years
   (Hint: Change $1\frac{1}{4}$ years to 1.25 years.)

3. $615 at 6.5% for 2 years $4,000 at $6\frac{7}{10}$% for 4 years

4. $3,750 at $6\frac{1}{4}$% for 3 months $525 at 5% for 15 months

5. $2,940 at 4.8% for 2.25 years $465 at 4.75% for $1\frac{1}{2}$ years

6. $3,500 at 5.75% for 6 years $11,500 at 8.25% for 3 years

MIXED PRACTICE

Find each answer.

a	*b*	*c*	*d*
1. 9 1.3 4 +5 2.9	$1.4 2 × 1 8 0	$2 7.0 0 − 1.9 9	3)1.8 9
2. 6 3 7 ×1 2 8	7 5 4 −6 9 9	2,8 1 3 +4 8,9 7 5	2 3)6,7 8 5

Percent of Increase

To find the **current value** or amount, first multiply the original amount by the **percent of increase.** Then add.

Example:

The rent for a 1-bedroom apartment was $425 per month. This year the rent went up 4%. For how much will the apartment rent each month this year?

original amount	$425		original amount	$425
percent of increase	×0.04		amount of increase	+$ 17
amount of increase	$17		current rent	$442

The apartment will rent for $442 this year.

Solve.

1. Rajeev's dog weighed 60 pounds 4 months ago. Since then his weight has increased by 6%. How much does Rajeev's dog weigh now?

    $$\begin{array}{r} 60 \\ \times 0.06 \\ \hline 3.6 \end{array} \qquad \begin{array}{r} 60.0 \\ + 3.6 \\ \hline 63.6 \end{array}$$

    Answer _____ 63.6 pounds _____

2. A local movie theater increased the price of admission by 20%. Tickets had sold for $6.50. What is the current ticket price?

    Answer _____

3. Lawrence bought his condominium for $100,900. During the past 2 years, its value increased 8%. What is the current value of Lawrence's condominium?

    Answer _____

4. A university's enrollment is up 4% from last year. That year's enrollment was 19,050 students. How many students are attending the university this year?

    Answer _____

5. The price of a mid-size car went up 7% from last year. The car sold for $22,000 last year. What is the price for the same car this year?

    Answer _____

6. The Steak House increased its menu prices by 10%. A complete dinner had been $22.50. What is the new price for the dinner?

    Answer _____

Percent of Decrease

To find the current value or amount, first multiply the original amount by the **percent of decrease.** Then subtract.

Example:

Last year's total sales figure for The Clothier Chain was $950,000. This year the total sales figure decreased by 3%. What is this year's sales figure?

original figure	$950,000	original figure	$950,000
percent of decrease	× 0.03	amount of decrease	− $ 28,500
amount of decrease	$ 28,500	new sales figure	$921,500

This year's total sales figure at The Clothier Chain is $921,500.

Solve.

1. A school had 500 students last year. This year the enrollment decreased by 5%. How many students are attending the school this year?

$$500 \times 0.05 = 25 \qquad 500 - 25 = 475$$

Answer ___475 students___

2. A store decreased the price of its best shirts by 20%. If the shirts normally sold for $30, what was the reduced price?

Answer _____

3. The value of a car that cost $16,000 decreased by 20% the first year. What was the value of the car after the first year?

Answer _____

4. The average number of points scored by the Ridgeview basketball team decreased by 8%. They had been averaging 75 points per game. What is their new average?

Answer _____

5. A city had a population of 560,000 in 2002. In 2003, its population had decreased by 2%. How many people were living in the city in 2003?

Answer _____

6. The Rinallis' average gas bill decreased by 4.5% after they moved. They had been spending about $125 per month for gas. How much are they now spending for gas? Round to the nearest cent.

Answer _____

Problem-Solving Strategy: Use a Circle Graph

Alecia's monthly income is $3,000. The circle graph shows how she divides her money each month. How much money does Alecia save each month?

Alecia's Budget

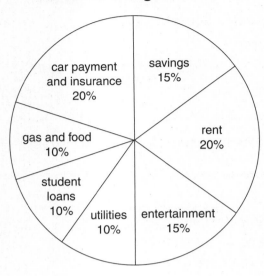

Understand the problem.

- **What do you want to know?**
  the amount of money Alecia saves each month

- **What information is given?**
  Alecia's monthly income is $3,000. The circle graph shows how she divides the money each month.

Plan how to solve it.

- **What strategy can you use?**
  You can use the circle graph and the given information to find how much money she saves each month.

Solve it.

- **How can you use this strategy to solve the problem?**
  Find what percent she saves each month. Then find that percent of her total monthly income.

  | 15% = 0.15
  | 0.15 × $3,000 = $450

- **What is the answer?**
  Alecia saves $450 each month.

Look back and check your answer.

- **Is your answer reasonable?**
  Note that 15% of Alecia's budget is savings, and 100% − 15% = 85%. This means that all the other categories make up 85% of her budget. Find 85% of $3,000, then add that amount to $450. The two amounts add up to $3,000. The answer is reasonable.

  85% = 0.85

  0.85 × $3,000 = $2,550

  $2,550
  +   450
  ⎯⎯⎯⎯⎯⎯
  $3,000

Solve. Use the circle graph below.

Profit Earned from Fall Fair

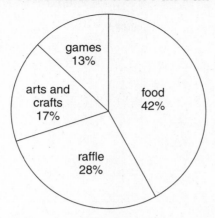

games 13%

arts and crafts 17%

food 42%

raffle 28%

---

1. If the total profit from the fair was $6,000, how much money was made from food sales?

   Answer _____

2. If the total profit from the fair was $7,500, how much money was made by arts and crafts?

   Answer _____

---

3. If the games brought in $910, what was the total profit made from the fair?

   Answer _____

4. If the raffle earned $1,008, what was the total profit made from the fair?

   Answer _____

---

5. If $8,000 was the total profit from the fair, how much money was earned by food sales and games combined?

   Answer _____

6. If raffle tickets and arts and crafts combined made $3,825, what was the total profit made from the fair?

   Answer _____

Problem-Solving Applications

Fill in the numbered circles to show the answers.

1. The selling price on athletic shoes is a 65% increase over the store's cost. Run-Fast running shoes cost the store $60. What is the selling price of the shoes?

⑨ ⑨
⑧ ⑧
⑦ ⑦
⑥ ⑥
⑤ ⑤
④ ④
③ ③
② ②
① ①
⓪ ⓪

2. A customer saved $135 by buying a dishwasher on sale for 30% off the regular price. What was the regular price?

⑨ ⑨ ⑨
⑧ ⑧ ⑧
⑦ ⑦ ⑦
⑥ ⑥ ⑥
⑤ ⑤ ⑤
④ ④ ④
③ ③ ③
② ② ②
① ① ①
⓪ ⓪ ⓪

3. A 300-seat theater has 25% of the seats reserved. How many seats are reserved?

⑨ ⑨
⑧ ⑧
⑦ ⑦
⑥ ⑥
⑤ ⑤
④ ④
③ ③
② ②
① ①
⓪ ⓪

4. Sonya's TV and Appliance requires a 20% down payment to hold a purchase. If a down payment is $172, what is the total cost of the item?

⑨ ⑨ ⑨
⑧ ⑧ ⑧
⑦ ⑦ ⑦
⑥ ⑥ ⑥
⑤ ⑤ ⑤
④ ④ ④
③ ③ ③
② ② ②
① ① ①
⓪ ⓪ ⓪

5. Several years ago, a desk sold for $120. Now the same desk sells for $150. What is the percent of increase in the price?

⑨ ⑨
⑧ ⑧
⑦ ⑦
⑥ ⑥
⑤ ⑤
④ ④
③ ③
② ②
① ①
⓪ ⓪

6. Lin bought a new television. The sales tax on the television was $16.00. The sales tax rate was 5%. What was the selling price of the television?

⑨ ⑨ ⑨
⑧ ⑧ ⑧
⑦ ⑦ ⑦
⑥ ⑥ ⑥
⑤ ⑤ ⑤
④ ④ ④
③ ③ ③
② ② ②
① ① ①
⓪ ⓪ ⓪

7. On an order of 60 lamps, 12 were broken when the clerk unpacked them. What percent of the lamps were broken?

⑨ ⑨
⑧ ⑧
⑦ ⑦
⑥ ⑥
⑤ ⑤
④ ④
③ ③
② ②
① ①
⓪ ⓪

8. A leather coat that regularly sells for $400 is on sale for 20% off. What is the sale price of the coat?

⑨ ⑨ ⑨
⑧ ⑧ ⑧
⑦ ⑦ ⑦
⑥ ⑥ ⑥
⑤ ⑤ ⑤
④ ④ ④
③ ③ ③
② ② ②
① ① ①
⓪ ⓪ ⓪

Change each percent to a decimal and then to a fraction. Simplify.

a   b

1. 26% = _____ = _____   0.2% = _____ = _____

2. 115% = _____ = _____   5% = _____ = _____

Fill in the blanks.

fraction	=	*decimal*	=	*percent*

3. $\frac{7}{20}$ _____ = _____ = _____

4. _____ = 0.81 _____ = _____

Find the percent or number.

a   b

5. 54% of 75   0.9% of 200

6. What percent of 60 is 9?   What percent of 18 is 36?

7. 70% of what number is 21?   34% of what number is 17?

Solve.

8. Shelly took out a loan for $1,600 from the bank. The loan was for 2 years at a rate of 6.25%. How much simple interest did Shelly pay on the loan?

Answer _____

9. Mr. and Mrs. Jones gave $420 to Bi-Rite Furniture to hold new furniture. The furniture cost $1,200. What percent of the price of the furniture did Mr. and Mrs. Jones give to hold the furniture?

Answer _____

10. The selling price on toys at Toy City is a 40% increase over the store's cost. What is the selling price of a doll that costs the store $16.50?

Answer _____

11. Last year the cost of a Quick-Calc computer was $1,200. This year the cost dropped by 15%. What is this year's cost of a Quick-Calc computer?

Answer _____

What is Algebra?

Study the following number sentences to find a pattern.

$1 \times 2 = 2$ $1 \times 29 = 29$ $1 \times 3.45 = 3.45$

You can write a general statement about the three number sentences: if a number is multiplied by 1, the product is the number. Here is a way to describe the pattern using a **variable.** Variables are letters or symbols used to represent numbers. The number is represented by the variable n.

$1 \times n = n$ where n represents any number

Algebra is the study of variables and operations with variables. Sometimes more than one variable is needed to describe a pattern.

EXAMPLE 1

Describe the pattern using two variables, a and b.

$3 + 5 = 5 + 3$
$10 + 12 = 12 + 10$
$9.8 + 3.4 = 3.4 + 9.8$

The pattern is $a + b = b + a$.

EXAMPLE 2

Write three number sentences that fit the pattern $\frac{p}{p} = 1$.

Choose any number for p. Here are three possible number sentences.

$\frac{2}{2} = 1$ $\frac{4.5}{4.5} = 1$ $\frac{78}{78} = 1$

PRACTICE

Describe each pattern using one or two variables.

	a	b	c	d
1.	$1 \times 4 = 4 \times 1$	$2 - 2 = 0$	$3 + 3 = 2 \times 3$	$0 \times 6 = 0$
	$3 \times 4 = 4 \times 3$	$46 - 46 = 0$	$10 + 10 = 2 \times 10$	$0 \times 8 = 0$
	$10 \times 4 = 4 \times 10$	$1.5 - 1.5 = 0$	$25 + 25 = 2 \times 25$	$0 \times 42 = 0$
	$\underline{a \times b = b \times a}$	_____	_____	_____

Write three number sentences that fit the pattern.

	a	b
2.	$0 + q = q$	$s \div 2 = t$

Sets of Numbers

Every number belongs to a **set** of numbers. Some numbers belong to more than one set.

Natural Numbers {1, 2, 3, 4, 5, 6...}

The set of **natural numbers** (or counting numbers) consists of numbers used to count. The least natural number is 1.

Whole Numbers {0, 1, 2, 3, 4, 5, 6, 7...}

The set of **whole numbers** consists of all the natural numbers and the number zero.

Integers

{..., $^-5$, $^-4$, $^-3$, $^-2$, $^-1$, 0, 1, 2, 3, 4, 5, 6, 7...}

    negative integers   positive integers

The set of **integers** consists of all the whole numbers and their **opposites.**

Rational Numbers is the set of numbers that can be written as fractions of the form $\frac{a}{b}$, where a and b are integers and $b \neq 0$.

$4 = \frac{4}{1}$; 4 is rational

$1\frac{1}{2} = \frac{3}{2}$; $1\frac{1}{2}$ is rational

$0.25 = \frac{1}{4}$; 0.25 is rational

Irrational Numbers is the set of numbers that **cannot** be written as fractions of the form $\frac{a}{b}$, where a and b are integers and $b \neq 0$. Non-terminating, non-repeating decimals such as 4.232521... are irrational numbers.

Real Numbers is the set containing rational and irrational numbers.

The examples below show how the sets of natural numbers, whole numbers, integers, and rational numbers are related.

5 is a natural number, whole number, integer, and rational number.	$^-$**3** is an integer and a rational number.	**0** is a whole number, integer, and rational number.	$3\frac{1}{2} = \frac{7}{2}$ $3\frac{1}{2}$ is a rational number.	**1.25** $= 1\frac{1}{4} = \frac{5}{4}$ 1.25 is a rational number.

PRACTICE

Write the name of the set or sets in which each number belongs.

	a	b	c
1. 18	*Natural, Whole, Integers, Rational*	$^-9$	$\frac{7}{10}$
2. $^-6.02$		0.12	$3\frac{3}{5}$

Understanding Numbers and Absolute Value

The **absolute value** of a number is its distance from 0 on a number line. Look at 2 and –2. They are both 2 units away from 0.

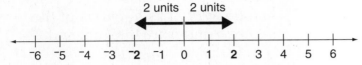

2 is 2 units from 0. The absolute value of 2 is 2.

⁻2 is 2 units from 0. The absolute value of ⁻2 is 2.

$|2| = 2$ is read as **the absolute value of 2 equals 2.**

$|⁻2| = 2$ is read as **the absolute value of ⁻2 equals 2.**

EXAMPLE 1	EXAMPLE 2	EXAMPLE 3	EXAMPLE 4
$|3| = 3$	$|⁻4| = 4$	$|1| = 1$	$|⁻5| = 5$

PRACTICE

Find the absolute value of each number.

	a	b	c	d
1.	$|6| = $ 6	$|⁻9| = $	$|⁻8| = $	$|⁻13| = $
2.	$|18| = $	$|⁻3| = $	$|10| = $	$|⁻15| = $
3.	$|⁻7| = $	$|0| = $	$|⁻17| = $	$|22| = $
4.	$|⁻12| = $	$|⁻19| = $	$|⁻11| = $	$|26| = $

Name the two numbers that have the given absolute value.

5. 30 30, ⁻30	14	32	29
6. 21	23	42	99

Unit 7 Algebra: Expressions and Equations

Comparing and Ordering Integers

To compare integers, think about their positions on a number line. An integer is less than any integer to its right. An integer is greater than any integer to its left.

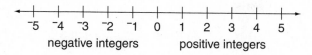

negative integers   positive integers

EXAMPLE 1

4 is to the right of 2.

$2 < 4$ and $4 > 2$

$^-1$ is to the right of $^-2$.

$^-2 < ^-1$ and $^-1 > ^-2$

EXAMPLE 2

3 is to the left of 5.

$5 > 3$ and $3 < 5$

$^-4$ is to the left of $^-3$.

$^-3 > ^-4$ and $^-4 < ^-3$

PRACTICE

Compare. Write <, >, or =.

	a		b		c	
1.	4 $\underline{\quad<\quad}$ 5	$^-2$ $\underline{\qquad}$ 9	4 $\underline{\qquad}$ $^-4$
2.	6 $\underline{\qquad}$ $^-3$	0 $\underline{\qquad}$ 0	$^-8$ $\underline{\qquad}$ $^-1$
3.	$^-2$ $\underline{\qquad}$ $^-6$	$^-7$ $\underline{\qquad}$ 3	10 $\underline{\qquad}$ $^-15$
4.	$^-10$ $\underline{\qquad}$ 1	$^-14$ $\underline{\qquad}$ $^-12$	$^-4$ $\underline{\qquad}$ $^-9$
5.	14 $\underline{\qquad}$ 14	7 $\underline{\qquad}$ $^-5$	$^-6$ $\underline{\qquad}$ $^-6$
6.	1 $\underline{\qquad}$ $^-2$	0 $\underline{\qquad}$ $^-3$	$^-9$ $\underline{\qquad}$ 5
7.	$^-7$ $\underline{\qquad}$ $^-9$	16 $\underline{\qquad}$ 16	$^-5$ $\underline{\qquad}$ $^-8$
8.	$^-15$ $\underline{\qquad}$ $^-11$	$^-8$ $\underline{\qquad}$ 5	$^-4$ $\underline{\qquad}$ $^-5$

Write in order from least to greatest.

a	b
9. 0, 7, $^-6$ $\underline{\quad ^-6 < 0 < 7 \quad}$	$^-5$, $^-9$, 7 $\underline{\qquad}$
10. 1, $^-1$, 11 $\underline{\qquad}$	27, 12, $^-21$ $\underline{\qquad}$
11. 8, 3, $^-2$ $\underline{\qquad}$	$^-3$, $^-13$, 0 $\underline{\qquad}$
12. 5, 4, $^-11$ $\underline{\qquad}$	$^-20$, $^-16$, 19 $\underline{\qquad}$

Adding and Subtracting Integers

To add integers, use the absolute value of the numbers.

Adding Integers with the Same Sign

$(^-3) + (^-4)$

Find the absolute value of each integer.

$|^-3| = 3$ $|^-4| = 4$

Add the absolute values.

$3 + 4 = 7$

Use the sign of the addends for the sum.

$(^-3) + (^-4) = ^-7$

Adding Integers with Different Signs

$^-6 + 2$

Find the absolute value of each integer.

$|^-6| = 6$ $|2| = 2$

Subtract the lesser absolute value from the greater absolute value.

$6 - 2 = 4$

Use the sign of the addend with the greater absolute value for the sum.

$^-6 + 2 = ^-4$

Subtracting an integer is the same as adding its opposite.

EXAMPLE 1

Subtract: $5 - 2$

The opposite of 2 is $^-2$.

$5 - 2 = 5 + (^-2) = 3$

EXAMPLE 2

Subtract: $6 - (^-3)$

The opposite of $^-3$ is 3.

$6 - (^-3) = 6 + 3 = 9$

EXAMPLE 3

Subtract: $^-4 - 1$

The opposite of 1 is $^-1$.

$-4 - 1 = ^-4 + (^-1) = ^-5$

PRACTICE

Add.

	a	b	c	d
1.	$5 + ^-3 =$ 2	$^-4 + ^-6 =$	$3 + ^-1 =$	$^-7 + 3 =$
2.	$^-9 + ^-3 =$	$8 + ^-1 =$	$4 + ^-11 =$	$^-8 + ^-10 =$
3.	$^-1 + ^-2 =$	$^-10 + 2 =$	$12 + ^-3 =$	$^-2 + 15 =$

Rewrite the subtraction problems as addition. Use addition rules to find the answer.

4. $5 - ^-3 = 5 + 3 = 8$	$^-7 - 1 =$	$^-9 - ^-9 =$	$4 - 8 =$
5. $^-8 - ^-1 =$	$^-6 - ^-2 =$	$^-12 - ^-7 =$	$^-9 - 10 =$
6. $^-4 - ^-4 =$	$9 - ^-1 =$	$^-4 - ^-6 =$	$^-5 - 5 =$

Unit 7 Algebra: Expressions and Equations

Multiplying and Dividing Integers

When multiplying or dividing two integers, first find the product or quotient of their absolute values. Then use the following rules to determine the sign in the product or quotient.

- The product or quotient of two integers with the same sign is positive.

- The product or quotient of two integers with different signs is negative.

Find: $^-4 \times 6$

> $4 \times 6 = 24$
>
> The signs of $^-4$ and 6 are different, so the product is negative.
>
> $^-4 \times 6 = ^-24$

Find: $^-15 \div {^-3}$

> $15 \div 3 = 5$
>
> The signs of $^-15$ and $^-3$ are the same, so the quotient is positive.
>
> $^-15 \div {^-3} = 5$

PRACTICE

Multiply.

	a	b	c	d
1.	$3 \times {^-3} = {^-9}$	$^-2 \times {^-2} =$	$^-4 \times {^-3} =$	$7 \times {^-6} =$
2.	$^-9 \times {^-3} =$	$6 \times {^-2} =$	$2 \times {^-10} =$	$^-6 \times {^-3} =$
3.	$^-4 \times {^-6} =$	$^-8 \times 3 =$	$5 \times 6 =$	$^-2 \times 5 =$
4.	$^-1 \times 0 =$	$^-5 \times {^-4} =$	$^-7 \times {^-3} =$	$^-4 \times {^-8} =$

Divide.

	a	b	c	d
5.	$18 \div {^-3} = {^-6}$	$^-4 \div 1 =$	$^-9 \div {^-3} =$	$48 \div {^-8} =$
6.	$^-8 \div {^-2} =$	$^-18 \div 9 =$	$^-32 \div {^-4} =$	$^-90 \div 10 =$
7.	$24 \div 4 =$	$42 \div {^-6} =$	$0 \div {^-5} =$	$^-8 \div 8 =$
8.	$^-35 \div {^-5} =$	$^-28 \div {^-7} =$	$^-18 \div {^-2} =$	$^-12 \div 3 =$

Order of Operations

A **numerical expression** has only numbers and at least one operation.

To simplify such an expression, follow the **order of operations** listed at the right.

Order of Operations:

1. Complete operations within parentheses.
2. Multiply and divide from left to right.
3. Add and subtract from left to right.

Find: $48 \div (9 - 3)$

$48 \div (9 - 3) =$	Complete the operation within the parentheses.
$48 \div 6 = 8$	Divide.

Find: $7 + 18 \div 6$

$7 + 18 \div 6 =$	Divide.
$7 + 3 = 10$	Add.

PRACTICE

Simplify.

	a	b	c	d
1.	$3 \times (4 + 6) =$ $3 \times 10 = 30$	$(18 - 4) \div 2 =$	$(11 - 7) \times {}^-5 =$	$56 \div (3 + 4) =$
2.	$14 + 16 \div 4 =$	$20 - 2 \times 9 =$	$15 + 1 \times 6 =$	${}^-17 - 15 \div 5 =$
3.	$5 \times (12 - 5) =$	$36 \div (3 + {}^-6) =$	$(8 + 7) \times 2 =$	$(24 - 12) \div 3 =$
4.	$36 - 4 \times 7 =$	$13 + 42 \div 6 =$	$30 - 20 \div 10 =$	$3 + 9 \times 3 =$
5.	$5 \times 4 \div 2 =$	$20 \div (2 \times 5) =$	$(20 \div 2) \times {}^-5 =$	$(29 - 7) \div 2 =$
6.	${}^-6 + (3 \times 3) =$	$(16 + {}^-4) \div 6 =$	$(9 - 5) \times {}^-2 =$	$(35 \div {}^-7) - 8 =$

Evaluating Expressions

To **evaluate** an expression means to find a single value for it. Use the order of operations to evaluate expressions the same way you simplified numerical expressions on page 152.

If you are given an expression consisting of a numerator and a denominator that each have an operation, evaluate the numerator and the denominator separately. Then divide.

EXAMPLE 1

Evaluate:

$16 + 8 \div 2$

$16 + 4 = 20$

EXAMPLE 2

Evaluate:

$(10 - 8) \cdot 2$

$2 \cdot 2 = 4$

EXAMPLE 3

Evaluate:

$\frac{1}{4}(20 - 4)$

$\frac{1}{4}(16) = 4$

EXAMPLE 4

Evaluate:

$\frac{8 - 2}{2 + 1}$

$\frac{6}{3} = 2$

PRACTICE

Evaluate each expression.

	a	b	c	d
1.	$7 + 10 \div 5 =$ $7 + 2 = 9$	$3(2 + 8) =$	$8 \cdot 2 - 3 =$	$(5 - 1)(4) =$
2.	$2(11 - 3) =$	$4 \cdot 5 + 6 =$	$18 - (6 \div 3) =$	$2 \cdot (15 - 3) =$
3.	$8 + 18 \div 3 =$	$(21 + 4) \div 5 =$	$(10 - 2) \cdot 7 =$	$7 + 9 \div 3 =$
4.	$\frac{1}{3}(6 + 3) =$	$\frac{3}{4}(12) - \frac{1}{2}(2) =$	$\frac{1}{5}(10) + \frac{1}{4}(12) =$	$\frac{1}{2}(8 - 3) =$
5.	$\frac{2}{3 - 1} =$	$\frac{20 - 10}{2 \cdot 5} =$	$\frac{9 - 5}{4 + 4} =$	$\frac{17 + 2(2)}{3} =$
6.	$\frac{15 \div 5}{1 + 2} =$	$\frac{2(9 + 6)}{3 \cdot 1} =$	$\frac{7 + 5}{2(5) - 6} =$	$\frac{12(2) \div 3}{11 - 9} =$

Writing Expressions with Variables

An **algebraic expression** consists of at least one of each of the following: a variable, a number, and an operation. Remember, a variable is a symbol or a letter used to represent a number.

The following are examples of algebraic expressions:

$$9n \qquad a + 4 \qquad d - 18 \qquad \frac{x}{2}$$

Use these examples to help you write algebraic expressions.

Verbal Expression	Operation	Algebraic Expression
the product of 9 and n, 9 times n	multiplication	$9n$, $9(n)$, $9 \cdot n$, or $9 \times n$
4 more than a, a increased by 4	addition	$a + 4$
18 less than d, d decreased by 18	subtraction	$d - 18$
x separated into 2 equal parts	division	$\frac{x}{2}$ or $x \div 2$

PRACTICE

Write an algebraic expression for each verbal expression.

a

1. r more than 10

$10 + r$

2. the product of 7 and s

3. the sum of m and 12

4. a number n subtracted from 25

5. 24 divided by k

6. c decreased by 7

b

9 less than t

a number w divided by 3

h multiplied by $2x$

the difference between p and g

13 increased by b

y separated into 5 equal parts

Unit 7 Algebra: Expressions and Equations

Evaluating Expressions with Variables

A number in an expression is either a **constant** or a **coefficient**. In the expression $4x - 7$, 4 is a coefficient because it is a multiplier of the variable; $^-7$ is a constant because it appears alone.

A **term** in an expression is either a single number or the product of numbers and variables. There are two terms in the expression $3 \div 8xy$. The term 3 is a constant. The term $8xy$ has a coefficient of 8 and two variables.

To evaluate an expression containing one or more variables, substitute a value for each variable. Then simplify the expression.

EXAMPLE 1

Evaluate:
$2t - 8$ if $t = 5$

$2(5) - 8 = 10 - 8$
$\quad\quad\quad = 2$

EXAMPLE 2

Evaluate:
$\frac{1}{3}(q + 3)$ if $q = 6$

$\frac{1}{3}(6 + 3) = \frac{1}{3}(9)$
$\quad\quad\quad = 3$

EXAMPLE 3

Evaluate:
$x(7 + s)$ if $x = 2$ and $s = 3$

$2(7 + 3) = 2(10)$
$\quad\quad\quad = 20$

PRACTICE

Identify each number in the expression as a constant or a coefficient.

	a	b	c	d
1.	$5m + 9$ 5 is a coefficient. 9 is a constant.	$3q - t$	$6s - 2y$	$10x - 7$

Evaluate each expression if $p = 8$, $k = 2$, and $n = 4$.

	a	b	c	d
2.	$pk + n =$	$kp - kn =$	$n(5 + n) =$	$pn - k =$
3.	$\frac{k}{p} =$	$\frac{n}{k} + p =$	$\frac{3n + 3}{5} =$	$\frac{2k + 2p}{n} =$

Evaluate each expression if $s = 15$, $d = 20$, and $u = 5$.

	a	b	c	d
4.	$du - s =$ $20 \times 5 - 15 =$ $100 - 15 = 85$	$u(d - s) =$	$2ds =$	$(d - u)(s + u) =$
5.	$\frac{1}{u}(s + d) =$	$\frac{1}{5}s + u =$	$\frac{u}{d - s} =$	$\frac{d(s - u)}{5} =$

Finding Missing Addends and Missing Factors

When you add two numbers, the numbers that you add are called addends. When you multiply two numbers, the numbers you multiply are called factors. An equation is a statement that two quantities are equal. Variables are often used to stand for unknown, or missing, addends or factors. For example, in the equation $x + 3 = 11$, the variable x stands for the missing addend that you would add to 3 to get 11. In the equation $3a = 27$, the variable a stands for the missing factor you would multiply by 3 to get 27.

Remember, $3a$, $3 \cdot a$, and $3(a)$ all mean 3 times a.

To find a missing addend, subtract the known addend from both sides of the equation. To find a missing factor, divide both sides of the equation by the known factor. Check by substituting the answer into the original equation.

Solve for a missing addend: $x + 3 = 11$

$x + 3 = 11$

$x + 3 - 3 = 11 - 3$ Subtract 3.

$x = 8$

Check: $x + 3 = 11$

        $8 + 3 = 11$

Solve for a missing factor: $3a = 27$

$3a = 27$

$\frac{3a}{3} = \frac{27}{3}$ Divide by 3.

$a = 9$

Check: $3a = 27$

        $3(9) = 27$

GUIDED PRACTICE

Solve. Check.

a	b	c
1. $x + 7 = 10$ $x + 7 - 7 = 10 - 7$ $x = 3$ Check: $x + 7 = 10$ $3 + 7 = 10$	$5x = 20$ $\frac{5x}{5} = \frac{20}{5}$ $x =$	$y + 5 = 15$ $y + 5 - 5 = 15 - 5$ $y =$
2. $10m = 80$ $\frac{10m}{10} = \frac{80}{10}$ $m =$	$n + 12 = 29$ $n + 12 - 12 = 29 - 12$ $n =$	$8x = 96$ $\frac{8x}{8} = \frac{96}{8}$ $x =$
3. $9\frac{1}{3} + x = 30\frac{2}{3}$ $9\frac{1}{3} + x - 9\frac{1}{3} = 30\frac{2}{3} - 9\frac{1}{3}$ $x =$	$7k = 91$ $\frac{7k}{7} = \frac{91}{7}$ $k =$	$40 + x = 93$ $40 + x - 40 = 93 - 40$ $x =$

        Unit 7 Algebra: Expressions and Equations

PRACTICE

Solve. Simplify.

	a	b	c	d
1.	$x + \frac{1}{4} = \frac{3}{4}$	$9n = 315$	$3x = 7$	$1\frac{2}{3} + x = 5$
2.	$k + 15 = 40$	$16x = 90$	$m + 6 = 7\frac{3}{8}$	$12k = 156$
3.	$5x = 37$	$81 + k = 92$	$x + 1\frac{1}{2} = 2\frac{1}{4}$	$11x = 572$
4.	$6k = 70$	$x + 46 = 75$	$3x = 261$	$1\frac{1}{8} + x = 6\frac{1}{4}$
5.	$21n = 105$	$21n = 45$	$63 + x = 79$	$n + 7\frac{1}{2} = 15$
6.	$13 + x = 81$	$5x = 43$	$12x = 144$	$x + 102 = 200$

MIXED PRACTICE

Find each answer.

	a	b	c	d
1.	$\begin{array}{r} 22{,}465 \\ +\,15{,}908 \\ \hline \end{array}$	$\begin{array}{r} 13{,}274 \\ -\quad 296 \\ \hline \end{array}$	$\begin{array}{r} 1{,}296 \\ \times\quad 27 \\ \hline \end{array}$	$26\overline{)2{,}075}$
2.	$\begin{array}{r} 0.437 \\ \times\quad 3 \\ \hline \end{array}$	$0.65\overline{)91}$	20% of 175	$2\frac{1}{5} \div \frac{4}{7}$

Problem-Solving Strategy: Use Logic

Tracey and Kesha live in separate even-numbered apartments. Each of them has a two-digit apartment number. The sum of the two digits of each apartment number is 14. What are the numbers of Tracey's and Kesha's apartments?

Understand the problem.

- **What do you want to know?**
  the numbers of Tracey's and Kesha's apartments

- **What information is given?**
  Clue 1: Each apartment number is even.
  Clue 2: Each number has two digits.
  Clue 3: The sum of the digits in each number is 14.

Plan how to solve it.

- **What strategy can you use?**
  Use logic and the information given to narrow the choices and find the numbers of the apartments. Find all two digit numbers whose digits add up to 14. Do this first, since it narrows the choices quickly. Select the even numbers.

Solve it.

- **How can you use this strategy to solve the problem?**
  Write down all the two-digit numbers whose digits add up to 14. When choosing numbers exclude those with digits 1–4. It is impossible for the digits of a two-digit number, where one digit is 1–4, to add up to 14. Select the even numbers.

- **What is the answer?**

  > The two-digit numbers whose digits add up to 14 are:
  > 59, 68, 77, 86, and 95.
  >
  > The even numbers are 68 and 86.

  Tracey and Kesha live in apartments with numbers 68 and 86.

Look back and check your answer.

- **Is your answer reasonable?**
  You can check the apartment numbers by making sure they satisfy all the requirements. 68 and 86 are both two-digit even numbers. $6 + 8 = 14$ and $8 + 6 = 14$. The answer is reasonable.

Unit 7 Algebra: Expressions and Equations

Use logic to solve each problem.

1. A number greater than 50 has two digits. The sum of those digits is 10, and the difference is 4. What is the number?

Answer _____

2. Jose's dog weighs less than Jose but more than his cat. The sum of the digits of the dog's weight is 9, and the difference is 1. If Jose weighs 52 pounds and the cat weighs $\frac{1}{5}$ the dog's weight, how much does the cat weigh?

Answer _____

3. Tom's age is divisible by 5, and the sum of the digits of his age is 9. Tom's father is 65, and his son is 22. How old is Tom?

Answer _____

4. An even number has 2 digits. The sum of the digits is 11. The difference between the digits is 3. What is the number?

Answer _____

Squares and Exponents

To multiply the number 8 by itself, you write 8×8 or 8^2. The **exponent** 2 tells how many times the **base** 8 is used as a factor. The expression 8^2 is read as 8 **squared** or 8 to the second power.

If a variable x is multiplied by itself, you write x^2.

EXAMPLE 1

$4 \times 4 \times 5 \times 5 \times a = (4)^2(5)^2 a$

EXAMPLE 2

$7 \times a \times a \times b = 7a^2b$

EXAMPLE 3

$5 \times 5 \times a \times a \times b \times b = (5)^2 a^2 b^2$

To evaluate an algebraic expression with one or more exponents, substitute the given value for the variable, then evaluate.

Evaluate each expression if $a = {}^-3$ and $b = 2$.

$6^2 a = 6 \cdot 6 \cdot ({}^-3)$
$= 36 \cdot ({}^-3)$
$= {}^-108$

$7a^2b = 7 \cdot ({}^-3) \cdot ({}^-3) \cdot 2$
$= {}^-21 \cdot ({}^-6)$
$= 126$

${}^-a^2b^2 = ({}^-1) \cdot ({}^-3) \cdot$
$({}^-3) \cdot 2 \cdot 2 = 3 \cdot ({}^-3) \cdot 4$
$= {}^-36$

PRACTICE

Write each expression using exponents.

	a	b	c
1.	$2 \times 2 \times 3 \times 3 \times y =$ $(2)^2(3)^2 y$	$4 \times 4 \times y \times y \times z =$	$10 \times 10 \times 7 \times 7 \times y =$
2.	$5 \times 7 \times 5 \times a =$	$3 \times 3 \times ({}^-1) \times b \times b =$	$6 \times y \times 7 \times 6 \times y =$
3.	$({}^-1) \times ({}^-1) \times a \times a =$	$(3a) \times (5a) =$	$9 \times 9 \times 5 \times 2 \times 5 \times b =$

Evaluate each expression if $x = 4$ and $y = {}^-2$.

	a	b	c
4.	$6x^2y =$ $6 \times 4 \times 4 \times ({}^-2) = {}^-192$	${}^-4 \times 5 \times y^2 =$	${}^-2 \times 3 \times x^2 \times y =$

Cubes and Exponents

When a number is used as a factor three times, we say that the number is **cubed.** You can use an exponent to show that a number is being cubed, or **raised to the third power.**

$$5 \times 5 \times 5 = 5^3 \qquad 10 \times 10 \times 10 = 10^3$$

To evaluate 5^3 multiply $5 \times 5 \times 5$.

$$5^3 = 5 \times 5 \times 5 = 125$$

To evaluate 10^3 multiply $10 \times 10 \times 10$.

$$10^3 = 10 \times 10 \times 10 = 1,000$$

EXAMPLE 1

$$2^3 = 2 \times 2 \times 2 = 8$$

EXAMPLE 2

$$(^-5)^3 = (^-5)(^-5)(^-5) = {}^-125$$

EXAMPLE 3

$$(^-3)^3 = (^-3) \times (^-3) \times (^-3) = -27$$

PRACTICE

Write each expression using an exponent.

	a	b	c	d
1.	$4 \times 4 \times 4 =$ 4^3	$(^-4) \times (^-4) \times (^-4) =$	$3 \times 3 \times 3 =$	$(^-7) \times (^-7) \times (^-7) =$
2.	$1 \times 1 \times 1 =$	$12 \times 12 \times 12 =$	$5 \times 5 \times 5 =$	$(^-20) \times (^-20) \times (^-20) =$

Evaluate each expression.

	a	b	c	d
3.	$6^3 =$ $6 \times 6 \times 6 = 216$	$(^-2)^3 =$	$7^3 =$	$20 \times 20 \times 20 =$
4.	$(^-1) \times (^-1) \times (^-1) =$	$0^3 =$	$9^3 =$	$(^-8)^3 =$

Scientific Notation

Large numbers are sometimes easier to read and understand when they are written in **scientific notation.** A number written in scientific notation has two factors: a number between 1 and 10 and a power of 10.

For example, 40,000 written in scientific notation is 4.0×10^4. 40,000 is the **standard form** of the number.

Write 2,190,000 in scientific notation.	**Write 5.2×10^6 in standard form.**
2,190,000 Move the decimal point to the left until it is behind the 2. *2.190000* Count the number of places the decimal point moved. The decimal moved 6 places to the left. Use 6 as the exponent for the power. *2,190,000 = 2.19 $\times 10^6$*	5.2×10^6 The exponent 6 tells you to move the decimal point 6 places to the right. Fill in zeros to make enough places. *5.2 $\times 10^6$ = 5,200,000* In standard form *5.2 $\times 10^6$ = 5,200,000*

PRACTICE

Write the following numbers in scientific notation.

	a	b	c	d
1.	5,600,000 = *5.6 $\times 10^6$*	6,040,000 =	6,700 =	1,013,000 =
2.	330,000 =	716,000,000 =	2,021,000,000 =	2,070,000 =

Write the following numbers in standard form.

	a	b	c	d
3.	4.1×10^5 = *410,000*	5.99×10^2 =	1.1×10^5 =	2.23×10^4 =
4.	8.9×10^3 =	5.03×10^7 =	3.12×10^9 =	7.5×10^4 =
5.	1.011×10^5 =	6.0×10^8 =	3.14×10^4 =	1.0×10^1 =

Unit 7 Algebra: Expressions and Equations

Square Roots

When you square a number, you multiply the number by itself. To find the **square root** of a number n, ask the following question: What number when multiplied by itself gives the number n as a result?

$9 \times 9 = 81$	$\sqrt{81} = 9$	The square root of 81 is 9 because $9 \times 9 = 81$.
$7 \times 7 = 49$	$\sqrt{49} = 7$	The square root of 49 is 7 because $7 \times 7 = 49$.

The root of a number is called the **radical,** and the number under the radical sign ($\sqrt{}$) is called the **radicand.**

PRACTICE

Square each number. Then find the square root ($\sqrt{}$) of the product.

a	b
1. 8	15
$8 \times 8 = 64 \qquad \sqrt{64} = 8$	
2. 1	6

Find the square root ($\sqrt{}$) of each number.

a	b
3. 25	9
$\sqrt{25} = 5$	
4. 100	4
5. 144	16

Solving Multi-Step Equations

Some equations require two or more operations to solve for the unknown.

Remember:

- Add, subtract, multiply, or divide the same number on both sides of the equal sign.

- You cannot divide by zero.

Solve: $5x - 2 = 38$

$5x - 2 = 38$	Check: $5x - 2 = 38$
$5x - 2 + 2 = 38 + 2$ Add 2.	$5(8) - 2 = 38$
$5x = 40$	$40 - 2 = 38$
$\frac{5x}{5} = \frac{40}{5}$ Divide by 5.	$38 = 38$
$x = 8$	

GUIDED PRACTICE

Solve. Check.

a	b	c
1. $7x + 9 = 51$	$3x - 6 = 30$	$6x + \frac{1}{5} = 65$
$7x + 9 - 9 = 51 - 9$	$3x - 6 + 6 = 30 + 6$	$6x + \frac{1}{5} - \frac{1}{5} = 65 - \frac{1}{5}$
$7x = 42$		
$\frac{7x}{7} = \frac{42}{7}$		
$x = 6$		
Check: $7x + 9 = 51$		
$7(6) + 9 = 51$		
$42 + 9 = 51$		
$51 = 51$		
2. $10x + 9 = 59$	$4x - \frac{1}{2} = 270$	$5x - 10 = 60$
$10x + 9 - 9 = 59 - 9$	$4x - \frac{1}{2} + \frac{1}{2} = 270 + \frac{1}{2}$	$5x - 10 + 10 = 60 + 10$
3. $8x + 32 = 200$	$9x + 11 = 74$	$13x + 13 = 143$
$8x + 32 - 32 = 200 - 32$	$9x + 11 - 11 = 74 - 11$	$13x + 13 - 13 = 143 - 13$

Unit 7 Algebra: Expressions and Equations

PRACTICE

Solve. Check.

	a	b	c
1.	$12x + 7 = 67$	$6x + 1 = 4$	$2x + 16 = 32$
2.	$7x - 5\frac{1}{2} = 12$	$2x + 19 = 29$	$4x + 7 = 10$
3.	$9x + 92 = 128$	$8x - 35 = 37$	$5x - \frac{1}{2} = \frac{1}{2}$
4.	$8x + \frac{1}{3} = \frac{2}{3}$	$2x - \frac{1}{5} = \frac{2}{5}$	$10x - 8 = 32$
5.	$10x - 29 = 11$	$17x + 2 = 49$	$7x - \frac{4}{7} = \frac{3}{7}$
6.	$6x + \frac{1}{4} = \frac{3}{4}$	$11x - 8 = 69$	$13x + 8 = 86$

MIXED PRACTICE

Find each answer.

	a	b	c	d
1.	$\begin{array}{r} 1.735 \\ 967 \\ +\ \ 8.446 \\ \hline \end{array}$	$0.7\overline{)1.54}$	$2\frac{1}{5} \div 3\frac{1}{2} =$	$4x = 120$
2.	$\frac{14}{3} \times \frac{5}{7} =$	$\begin{array}{r} 8,102 \\ -\ \ 906 \\ \hline \end{array}$	$\left\lvert ^-2.35 \right\rvert =$	$15 \div (3 + 2) =$

Collecting Like Terms in Equations

In the equation $2x + 3x = 15$, the two addends, called terms, both contain the unknown x as a factor. They are **like terms**. These two terms, $2x$ and $3x$, can be added to get the single term $5x$ because they are like terms. Check the solution to the equation by substitution.

Collect like terms and solve: $2x + 3x = 15$

$$2x + 3x = 15$$

$5x = 15$ Collect like terms.
$\frac{5x}{5} = \frac{15}{5}$ Divide by 5.
$x = 3$

Check: $2(3) + 3(3) = 15$
$ 6 + 9 = 15$
$ 15 = 15$

Collect like terms and solve: $9x - 3x = 24$

$$9x - 3x = 24$$

$6x = 24$ Collect like terms.
$\frac{6x}{6} = \frac{24}{6}$ Divide by 6.
$x = 4$

Check: $9(4) - 3(4) = 24$
$ 36 - 12 = 24$
$ 24 = 24$

GUIDED PRACTICE

Solve. Check.

	a	b	c
1.	$\frac{1}{2}x + 4x = 45$ $4\frac{1}{2}x = 45$ $\frac{9}{2}x = 45$ $x = 45(\frac{2}{9})$ $x = 10$ Check: $\frac{1}{2}(10) + 4(10) = 45$ $ 5 + 40 = 45$	$6x + 5x = 55$ $11x = 55$	$23x + 27x = 100$ $50x = 100$
2.	$19x - 7x = 84$ $12x = 84$	$16x + 12x = 84$ $28x = 84$	$35x - 2\frac{1}{2}x = 65$ $32\frac{1}{2}x = 65$
3.	$10x + \frac{2}{5}x = 156$ $10\frac{2}{5}x = 156$	$17x + 12x = 87$ $29x = 87$	$12x + 5x = 51$ $17x = 51$

PRACTICE

Collect like terms. Then solve. Check.

a	*b*	*c*
1. $6x - 2x = 4$	$7x - 3x = 20$	$9x + 11x = 80$
2. $15x - 3x = 144$	$20x - 9x = 77$	$5x + 3x = 6$
3. $2x + 14x = 8$	$5x - x = 24$	$7x + 7x = 70$
4. $2x + 5x = 1\frac{1}{2}$	$9x - 4x = 5$	$30x - 10x = 1\frac{1}{3}$
5. $18x - 15x = 39$	$3\frac{1}{2}x - 1\frac{1}{2}x = 18$	$\frac{1}{3}x + \frac{2}{3}x = 10$
6. $7x + x = 72$	$15x - 5x = 20$	$13x - x = 28$

MIXED PRACTICE

Find each answer.

a	*b*	*c*
1. 17% of 50	$\begin{array}{r} 0.63 \\ -0.47 \\ \hline \end{array}$	$\begin{array}{r} 417 \\ \times\ \ 7 \\ \hline \end{array}$
2. $14\overline{)1{,}344}$	1.5% of 44	$\begin{array}{r} 2{,}456 \\ 3{,}489 \\ +1{,}203 \\ \hline \end{array}$

Solving Equations with an Unknown on Both Sides

To solve an equation in which an unknown is on both sides of the equation, use the methods you have learned to move all the unknowns to the same side of the equation. Combine like terms and solve. Check by substitution.

Solve: $7x + 3 = 15 + 5x$

$7x + 3 = 15 + 5x$

$7x + 3 - 3 = 15 + 5x - 3$ Subtract 3 from both sides.

$7x = 12 + 5x$

$7x - 5x = 12 + 5x - 5x$ Subtract 5x from both sides.

$2x = 12$

$\frac{2x}{2} = \frac{12}{2}$ Divide both sides by 2.

$x = 6$

Check: $7(6) + 3 = 15 + 5(6)$

$42 + 3 = 15 + 30$

$45 = 45$

GUIDED PRACTICE

Solve.

a	b	c

1. $9x + 6 = 4x + 36$
$9x + 6 - 6 = 4x + 36 - 6$
$9x = 4x + 30$
$9x - 4x = 4x + 30 - 4x$
$5x = 30$
$\frac{5x}{5} = \frac{30}{5}$
$x = 6$
Check: $9(6) + 6 = 4(6) + 36$
        $54 + 6 = 24 + 36$
        $60 = 60$
	$5x - 9 = 1 + 3x$
	$5x - 9 + 9 = 1 + 3x + 9$
	$5x - 3x = 10 + 3x - 3x$
		$10x = 8 + 2x$
		$10x - 2x = 8 + 2x - 2x$

2. $5x - 3 = 17 - 5x$ $5x - 3 + 3 = 17 - 5x + 3$ $5x + 5x = 20 - 5x + 5x$	$3x + 1 = 41 - 2x$ $3x + 1 - 1 = 41 - 2x - 1$ $3x + 2x = 40 - 2x + 2x$	$11x - 5 = 45 + 6x$ $11x - 5 + 5 = 45 + 6x + 5$ $11x - 6x = 50 + 6x - 6x$
3. $7x + 16 = 32 - x$	$2x = 7 + x$	$20x - 13 = 15x + 62$

PRACTICE

Solve.

a	b	c
1. $25x + 9 = 209 + 5x$	$7x - 10 = 14 - x$	$16x + 5 = 59 + 7x$
2. $3x - 12 = 2x + 5$	$10x + 6 = 7 + 9x$	$23x + 100 = 725 - 2x$
3. $15x + 3 = 13x + 13$	$6x + 8 = 98 + 3x$	$3x + 2 = 50 - 3x$
4. $15x + 7 = 107 + 5x$	$8x - 6 = 42 + 6x$	$6x = 27 + 3x$
5. $20x - 9 = 13x - 7$	$16x - 10 = 89 + 7x$	$25x + 24 = 13x$
6. $17x - 7 = 3x$	$19x + 6 = 31 + 4x$	$^-2x = 100 + 18x$

MIXED PRACTICE

Change each percent to a decimal and then to a fraction. Simplify.

a	b
1. 45%	75%
2. 12%	120%
3. 10%	3%
4. 28%	35%

Using Equations to Solve Problems

Many kinds of problems can be solved by deciding what is unknown, writing an equation, and solving. Check your answer in the original problem.

Jack and Lisa together have $250. Jack has $10 more than 3 times as much as Lisa. How much does each have?

Decide what is unknown.	Solve.	Answer:
Let x = Lisa's money.	x + 3x + 10 = 250	x = $60 Lisa's money
3x + 10 = Jack's money	4x + 10 = 250	3x + 10 = $190 Jack's money
Write an equation.	4x + 10 − 10 = 250 − 10	Check: x + 3x + 10 = 250
Lisa's money + Jack's money = $250	4x = 240	(60) + 3(60) + 10 = 250
x + 3x + 10 = 250	$\frac{4x}{x} = \frac{240}{4}$	60 + 180 + 10 = 250
	x = 60	60 + 190 = 250
		250 = 250

GUIDED PRACTICE

Write an equation for each problem and solve.

1. If 24 is added to a certain number, the result is 52. What is the number?

Let n = the number.

n + 24 = 52

n + 24 − 24 = 52 − 24

n = 28

Answer _____ n = 28 _____

2. Arsenio has $25 more than twice as much money as Malik has. Together they have $145. How much money does each have?

Let x = Malik's money.

2x + 25 = Arsenio's money

x + 2x + 25 = 145

Malik _____

Arsenio _____

3. Pat has three times as much money as does Jerry. Together they have $12.80. How much does each have?

Let x = Jerry's money.

3x = Pat's money

Jerry _____

Pat _____

4. Louisa is thinking of a number. Five times that number equals 240. What is the number?

Let n = the number.

Answer _____

Unit 7 Algebra: Expressions and Equations

PRACTICE

Write an equation for each problem and solve.

1. Elena has five times as much money as Tori does. Together they have $42. How much does each have?

   Elena _____

   Tori _____

2. DeWayne has $15 more than Hakeem. Together they have $55. How much does each have?

   DeWayne _____

   Hakeem _____

3. One package contains 20 envelopes more than a second package does. Together they contain 80 envelopes. How many envelopes does each package contain?

   1st package _____

   2nd package _____

4. One parking lot contains 50 cars less than a second lot. Together the lots contain 200 cars. How many cars are there in each parking lot?

   1st lot _____

   2nd lot _____

5. Ricardo's mother is 3 times as old as Ricardo. The sum of their ages is 72. How old is each?

   Mother _____

   Ricardo _____

6. Natasha's father is 2 years less than three times as old as Natasha. The sum of their ages is 78 years. How old is each?

   Father _____

   Natasha _____

7. Three numbers add up to 180. The second number is twice the first, and the third is three times the first. What is each number? Let n = the first number.

   1st _____

   2nd _____

   3rd _____

8. Three numbers add up to 140. The second number is twice the first, and the third number is twice the second. What are the three numbers?

   1st _____

   2nd _____

   3rd _____

Exponents in Expressions

A numerical expression with exponents can be evaluated using the order of operations or the **rules of exponents.**

When adding or subtracting exponential numbers, use the order of operations. First, evaluate each number with the exponent, then add or subtract.

When multiplying two numbers with the same base, add their exponents. When dividing two numbers with the same base, subtract their exponents.

EXAMPLE 1

$3^2 + 3^4$

$9 + 81$

90

EXAMPLE 2

$4^5 - 4^3$

$1,024 - 64$

960

EXAMPLE 3

$2^2 \times 2^6$

2^{2+6}

2^8

256

EXAMPLE 4

$3^4 \div 3^2$

3^{4-2}

3^2

9

To evaluate a number with an exponent raised to an exponent, multiply the exponents.

EXAMPLE 5 $\quad (5^2)^2 = 5^{2 \times 2} = 5^4 = 625$

GUIDED PRACTICE

Evaluate each expression.

	a	b	c	d
1.	$7^4 - 7^2 =$	$(9^2)^2 =$	$(2^5)^3 =$	$4^4 + 4^5 =$
2.	$3^3 \times 3^4 =$	$2^8 - 2^4 =$	$(7^3)^2 =$	$(4^2)^4 =$
3.	$(8^3)^2 =$	$(2^4)^3 =$	$4^9 \div 4^7 =$	$5^4 - 5^2 =$
4.	$2^8 \div 2^5 =$	$(2^3)^2 \times 2^4 =$	$3^6 - 3^2 =$	$(8^4)^2 \div 8^7 =$
5.	$(3^4)^2 + 3^3 =$	$8^5 - 8^3 =$	$(5^4)^2 \times 5^2 =$	$9^7 \div 9^4 =$

Unit 7 Algebra: Expressions and Equations

PRACTICE

Evaluate each expression.

	a	b	c	d
1.	$6^2 + 6^5 =$	$10^7 \div 10^5 =$	$4^2 \times (4^2)^2 =$	$3^4 - (3^4)^3 =$
2.	$7^9 \div (7^4)^2 =$	$5^3 \times 5^1 =$	$8^4 + 8^2 =$	$9^2 \times 9^2 =$
3.	$2^8 \div (2^3)^2 =$	$7^3 + 7^2 =$	$6^9 \div (6^2)^2 =$	$6^3 \times 6^4 =$
4.	$10^2 \times 10^4 =$	$(8^3)^4 \div 8^8 =$	$5^3 + 5^5 =$	$(4^4)^2 - 4^7 =$
5.	$7^7 \div 7^4 =$	$(9^6)^4 \div (9^3)^5 =$	$10^3 \times 10^6 =$	$(2^3)^2 + (2^2)^4 =$
6.	$6^5 - 6^3 =$	$(10^3)^7 \div (10^4)^5 =$	$8^9 \div 8^6 =$	$2^4 + 2^5 =$

MIXED PRACTICE

Find each answer.

	a	b	c	d
1.	$^-9 \times\ ^-5 =$	$9x + 3x = 36$	$2\frac{2}{5} + 3\frac{1}{3} =$	$\begin{array}{r} 0.23 \\ \times\quad 6 \\ \hline \end{array}$
2.	$\frac{3}{7} \times \frac{4}{9} =$	$0.5\overline{)1.25}$	16% of $\$135 =$	$(9 +\ ^-2) \times\ ^-3 =$

Problem-Solving Strategy: Use a Logic Chart

The last names of Alecia, Darlene, and Tanesha are Watkins, Jackson, and Smith. Darlene's last name is not Smith. Tanesha's last name is Watkins. What are the last names of the three women?

Understand the problem.

- **What do you want to know?**
  the last names of the three women

- **What information is given?**
  Clue 1. Darlene's last name is not Smith.
  Clue 2. Tanesha's last name is Watkins.

Plan how to solve it.

- **What strategy can you use?**
  Use logic and the information given to narrow the choices and find the last name of each woman.

Solve it.

- **How can you use this strategy to solve the problem?**
  Fill in the chart using the clues given.

	Watkins	Jackson	Smith
Alecia	no	no	**YES**
Darlene	no	**YES**	no
Tanesha	**YES**	no	no

- **What is the answer?**
  Alecia's last name is Smith.
  Darlene's last name is Jackson.
  Tanesha's last name is Watkins.

Look back and check your answer.

- **Is your answer reasonable?**
  Make sure your answers agree with the given clues. Tanesha's name is Watkins. Darlene's name is not Smith, so Alecia's name is Smith and Darlene's name is Jackson.

  The answer is reasonable.

Use a logic chart to solve each problem.

1. Charles, Terry, and Tony are wearing blue, red, and green shirts, although not necessarily in that order. Terry is not wearing green. Charles is wearing the red shirt. Who is wearing what color shirt?

   Charles _____

   Terry _____

   Tony _____

2. Martin, Anna, and Julie picked oranges. The amounts picked were 123, 119, and 101. Martin picked more than Anna but less than Julie. How many oranges did each person pick?

   Martin _____

   Anna _____

   Julie _____

3. Raul, Samantha, Pablo, and Mateo counted their baseball cards. They counted 215, 260, 130, and 275, but not necessarily in that order. Pablo has twice as many as Mateo. Samantha has more than Pablo. How many baseball cards does each person have?

   Raul _____

   Samantha _____

   Pablo _____

   Mateo _____

4. Vanessa, Yolanda, Kimberly, and Nicole are in cheerleading, volleyball, softball, and tennis, although not necessarily in that order. Yolanda uses a racket, Nicole uses pompoms, and Kimberly does not use a volleyball. Which activity is each girl in?

   Vanessa _____

   Yolanda _____

   Kimberly _____

   Nicole _____

Problem-Solving Applications

Fill in the numbered circles to show the answers.

1. Evaluate the following expression when $x = 5$ and $y = 10$. $\frac{2(x + 4y)}{5}$

2. The distance from Theron's house to the beach can be written as 8^3 miles. Indicate the distance from Theron's house to the beach in standard form.

3. The mountain-hiking team plans to descend 1,200 feet per day from their current elevation of 7,500 feet. What will their elevation be after 6 days of descent?

4. What is the value of the following expression: $(2^6)^2 \div 2^5$?

5. Juan has a balance of $285 in his checking account. What will his new balance be after he withdraws $40 and pays a utility bill of $72 from his checking account?

6. Evaluate the following expression when $s = 230$. $\frac{1}{2}s + 20$

7. The number of free throws James made during his high school career can be written as 3^5. Indicate the number of free throws James made in standard form.

8. Attendance at the first showing of a movie was 644 people. Attendance at the second showing was 87 fewer people. How many attended the second showing?

Find the absolute value of each number.

	a	b	c	d
1.	$|{}^-30| =$	$|0| =$	$|6| =$	$|{}^-85| =$

Add, subtract, multiply, or divide.

	a	b	c	d
2.	${}^-3 + {}^-2 =$	$9 - {}^-1 =$	${}^-3 \times {}^-1 =$	${}^-64 \div {}^-8 =$

Evaluate each expression.

	a	b	c	d
3.	$(9 \div 3) \times 5 =$	$4(8 - 1) =$	$\frac{18 + 2}{5(4 - 3)} =$	$\frac{24 \div 3}{2(2)} =$

Write each expression using exponents.

	a	b	c
4.	9×9	$z \times z \times z$	17×17

Evaluate each expression if $a = 3$, $b = 4$, and $c = ({}^-2)$.

	a	b	c
5.	$a(2b - c) =$	$\frac{3}{4}b + ac =$	$\frac{6ac}{5b} =$
6.	$4 + 3a^2 =$	$2b^3 - 9 =$	${}^-2bc^2 =$

Change each number from scientific notation to standard form.

	a	b	c	d
7.	9.4×10^6	1.23×10^3	5.7×10^5	8.9×10^4

Solve.

	a	b	c
8.	$\sqrt{9} =$	$2y - 6 = 10$	$5t + 4 + 2t = 18$
9.	$\frac{2}{5} - z = 10\frac{2}{5}$	$3m + 1 = 25 - m$	$\sqrt{144} =$
10.	$3q + 17 = 35$	$12^6 \div 12^4$	$22s = 80 - 18s$

Solve.

11. When 8 is subtracted from twice a certain number, the result is 20. What is that number?

12. The total cost to insure and ship a package was $12.50. If the insurance portion was $1.75, how much was the shipping charge?

Answer _____

Answer _____

Functions and Relations

An **ordered pair** (x, y) is a pair of numbers. For example, $(2, 3)$ is an ordered pair.

A set of ordered pairs is called a **relation.**
The set $\{(^-2, 4), (^-2, 5), (6, 9), (9, 10), (11, 12)\}$ is a relation.

A **function** is a relation in which each x value has only one y value.
The set $\{(2, 3), (4, 5), (6, 5), (9, 10), (11, 12)\}$ is a function.
The set $\{(6, 9), (^-2, 4), (^-2, 5), (8, 12), (11, 13)\}$ is not a function because the x value $^-2$ has more than one y value.

The **domain** is the set of all x values.
The **range** is the set of all y values.
For $\{(1, 2), (3, 4), (5, 6), (7, 8)\}$, the domain is $\{1, 3, 5, 7\}$, and the range is $\{2, 4, 6, 8\}$.

EXAMPLE 1

This is a function.
$\{(^-1, ^-2), (3, 4), (5, 6), (7, ^-2)\}$
domain $\{^-1, 3, 5, 7\}$, range $\{^-2, 4, 6\}$

EXAMPLE 2

This is not a function.
$\{(^-1, ^-2), (4, 5), (4, 6), (7, 8)\}$
domain $\{^-1, 4, 7\}$, range $\{^-2, 5, 6, 8\}$

PRACTICE

Determine whether each of the following relations is a function.

	a	*b*
1.	$\{(0, 3), (^-5, 5), (1, 4), (^-1, ^-1)\}$ _yes_	$\{(2, 1), (^-6, 1), (1, 8), (^-6, ^-7)\}$ ____
2.	$\{(^-4, 3), (^-3, 3), (1, 3)\}$ ____	$\{(3, 3), (^-2, 5), (2, 4), (0, 0)\}$ ____

Find the domain and range for each relation.

	a	*b*
3.	$\{(1, 3), (^-2, 5), (9, 4), (^-10, ^-1)\}$ Domain: Range:	$\{(^-2, 6), (7, 8), (1, ^-3)\}$ Domain: Range:
4.	$\{(4, 9), (4, ^-5), (0, ^-6), (^-1, 0)\}$ Domain: Range:	$\{(2, 9), (5, ^-2), (1, 1)\}$ Domain: Range:

Graphing Ordered Pairs

Ordered pairs can be graphed on a **coordinate plane** like the one shown at the right. The line labeled x is the **horizontal axis,** or x-**axis.** The line labeled y is the **vertical axis,** or y-**axis.** These two lines **intersect** each other at the **origin** (O), and they divide the coordinate plane into four **quadrants.**

The location of a point on a coordinate plane is given by its ordered pair (x, y), sometimes called **coordinates.** The coordinates describe how to get to that point from the origin. The x value tells the left-right position, and the y value tells the up-down position. The origin is at $(0, 0)$.

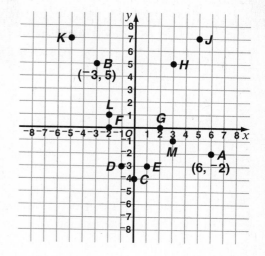

EXAMPLE 1

What are the coordinates of Point A?

To get from the origin to point A, count 6 units right and 2 units down.

Point A has coordinates $(6, {}^-2)$.

EXAMPLE 2

What are the coordinates of Point B?

To get from the origin to point B, count 3 units left and 5 units up.

Point B has coordinates $({}^-3, 5)$.

PRACTICE

Give the coordinates of each point. Refer to the graph above.

a	b	c	d	e
1. C (_0_ , _⁻4_)	D (__, __)	E (__, __)	F (__, __)	G (__, __)
2. H (__, __)	J (__, __)	K (__, __)	L (__, __)	M (__, __)

Plot each point on the graph provided.

a

3. A $(6, 0)$
   B $(6, 4)$
   C $({}^-2, 5)$
   D $(0, 4)$
   E $(0, 0)$

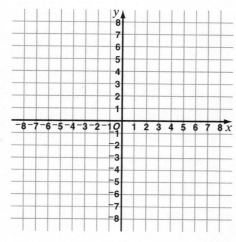

b

F $({}^-6, 3)$
G $({}^-1, {}^-5)$
H $({}^-7, 0)$
J $(4, {}^-1)$
K $(0, {}^-7)$

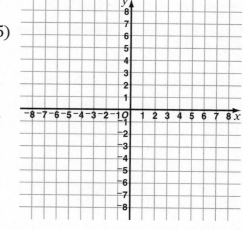

Linear Functions

To graph a function, graph its ordered pairs. If all the points in the graph lie on a line, then that function is a **linear function.** In the top graph, f_1 and f_2 are both linear functions.

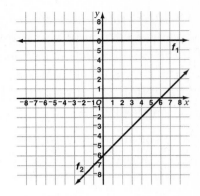

A function can be defined by an equation. Some of the ordered pairs in the linear function defined by $x + y = 3$ are shown in the bottom graph. To determine whether a point lies on the graph of the function, substitute the first coordinate for x and the second coordinate for y. If these substitutions make the equation true, then that point lies on the line. For example, $(4, {}^-1)$ lies on the line, since $4 + ({}^-1) = 3$. $(1, 5)$ does not lie on the line, since $1 + 5 \neq 3$.

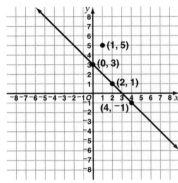

EXAMPLE

Determine which of the given points lies on the graph of the function $x + 2y = 8$.

$(10, {}^-1)$

$x + 2y = 8$
$10 + 2({}^-1) = 8?$
$10 + {}^-2 = 8?$
$8 = 8$

$(10, {}^-1)$ lies on the graph.

$(3, {}^-4)$

$x + 2y = 8$
$3 + 2({}^-4) = 8?$
$3 + {}^-8 = 8?$
${}^-5 \neq 8$

$(3, {}^-4)$ does not lie on the graph.

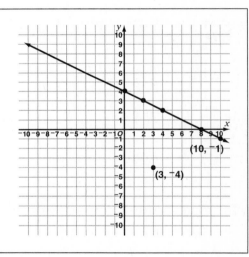

PRACTICE

Determine which of the given points lie on the graph of the given function.

1. $2x + y = {}^-6$	$(3, {}^-12)$ *yes*	$(0, 6)$	$({}^-4, 1)$
2. $-3x + y = 9$	$(3, 0)$	$({}^-2, 3)$	$(4, 3)$
3. $x - 4y = 10$	$(6, {}^-1)$	$(12, 1)$	$(14, 1)$
4. $x + 2y = {}^-5$	$({}^-5, 0)$	$(1, {}^-3)$	$({}^-9, 2)$

Unit 8 Algebra: Functions, Graphs, and Inequalities

Equations with Two Variables

An equation such as $x + y = 4$ has many **solutions**. Each solution is an ordered pair. To find a solution, choose a value to substitute for one of the variables, then solve the equation for the other variable. Study the following examples.

EXAMPLE 1

Solve: $x + y = 4$ when $x = 1$

$$1 + y = 4$$

$$y = 3$$

The equation $x + y = 4$ is true when $x = 1$ and $y = 3$.

(1, 3) is a solution.

EXAMPLE 2

Solve: $x + y = 4$ when $y = {}^-2$

$$x + ({}^-2) = 4$$

$$x = 6$$

The equation $x + y = 4$ is true when $x = 6$ and $y = {}^-2$.

(6, $^-$2) is a solution.

PRACTICE

Solve each equation using the given value of x or y.
Write the ordered pair which makes the equation true.

a	b	c
1. $x + 2y = 7$ when $x = {}^-1$ $^-1 + 2y = 7$ $2y = 8$ $y = 4$ Ordered pair ___(⁻1, 4)___	$x + 2y = 7$ when $x = {}^-3$ Ordered pair _____	$x + 2y = 7$ when $x = 5$ Ordered pair _____
2. $2x + y = 11$ when $x = 3$ $2(3) + y = 11$ $6 + y = 11$ $y = 5$ Ordered pair ___(3, 5)___	$2x + y = 11$ when $x = 0$ Ordered pair _____	$2x + y = 11$ when $x = {}^-1$ Ordered pair _____
3. $x + y = {}^-6$ when $y = {}^-2$ Ordered pair _____	$x + y = {}^-6$ when $y = {}^-1$ Ordered pair _____	$x + y = {}^-6$ when $y = 3$ Ordered pair _____

Graphing Solutions

Remember, an equation with two variables has many solutions.
Each solution is an ordered pair.

EXAMPLE

Graph the solutions to $x + y = 4$ when $x = {}^-2$, 0, and 1.

Substitute each given value for x into the equation, then
solve for y. Write each solution in a table. Finally, plot
each ordered pair solution on the coordinate graph.

Value for x	Substitute into $x + y = 4$.	Solve for y.	Table of solutions

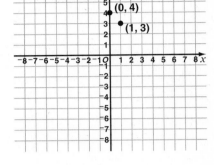

Value for x	Substitute into $x + y = 4$.	Solve for y.	x	y
$^-2$	$^-2 + y = 4$	6	$^-2$	6
0	$0 + y = 4$	4	0	4
1	$1 + y = 4$	3	1	3

These solutions are plotted on the graph.

PRACTICE

Find the values for y using the given values of x. Graph each solution.

1. $2x + y = 5$

x	y
0	
1	
3	

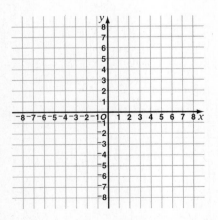

2. $x + y = {}^-4$

x	y
$^-2$	
0	
3	

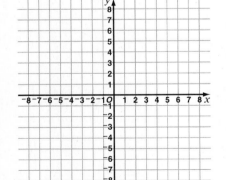

3. $^-3x + y = 2$

x	y
$^-1$	
0	
1	

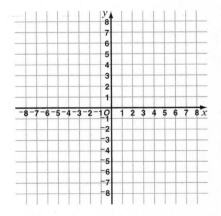

Unit 8 Algebra: Functions, Graphs, and Inequalities

Graphing Linear Equations

For the 2-variable equations that we have studied, the graphs of all the solutions lie on a line. For this reason, equations of this type are called **linear equations.** To graph a linear equation, begin by choosing a value to substitute for either x or y. Then solve for the other variable. Repeat this process to find three or more ordered pair solutions. Finally, graph the solutions and draw the line through those points.

EXAMPLE

Graph the equation $2x - 2y = 4$.

Choose a value.	Solve for the other variable.	Write the solution.
$x = 0$	$2(0) - 2y = 4$ $0 - 2y = 4$ $^-2y = 4$ $y = {}^-2$	$(0, {}^-2)$
$y = 0$	$2x - 2(0) = 4$ $2x - 0 = 4$ $2x = 4$ $x = 2$	$(2, 0)$
$x = 4$	$2(4) - 2y = 4$ $8 - 2y = 4$ $^-2y = {}^-4$ $y = 2$	$(4, 2)$

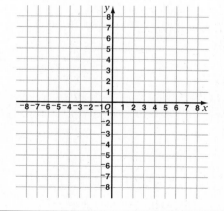

Now plot the points and draw a straight line through them.

PRACTICE

For each equation, find and graph three solutions. Draw a straight line through those points.

1. $3x - y = 2$

(__,__) (__, __) (__, __)

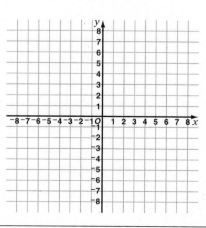

2. $^-x + y = 6$

(__, __) (__, __) (__, __)

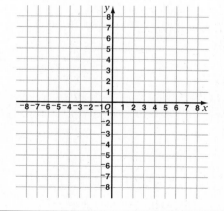

3. $x - 2y = 4$

(__, __) (__, __) (__, __)

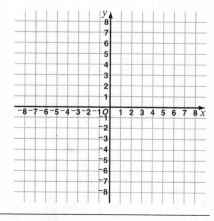

Slope

The **slope** of a line tells how steep the line is. The slope is the **ratio** of the vertical change, or **rise,** to the horizontal change, or **run,** from one point to another point on a line.

$$\text{slope} = \frac{\text{change in } y \text{ (rise)}}{\text{change in } x \text{ (run)}}$$

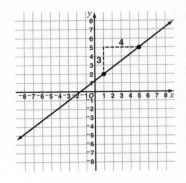

The vertical change, or rise, of the line at right is 3. The horizontal change, or run, of the line is 4. This line has a slope of $\frac{3}{4}$.

The slope of a line can be positive or negative.

EXAMPLE 1

When a line slants upward from left to right, it has a positive slope.

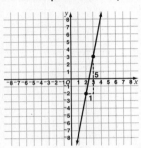

$$\text{slope} = \frac{\text{rise}}{\text{run}} = \frac{5}{1}$$

EXAMPLE 2

When a line slants downward from left to right, it has a negative slope.

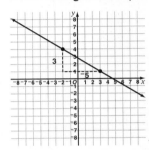

$$\text{slope} = \frac{\text{rise}}{\text{run}} = \frac{3}{-5}$$

PRACTICE

Identify the slope of each line. Write whether the slope is positive or negative.

1.

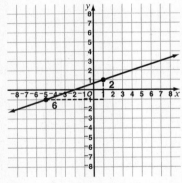

$$\text{slope} = \frac{\text{rise}}{\text{run}} = \frac{2}{6} = \frac{1}{3}$$

The slope is positive.

2.

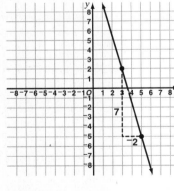

slope =

3.

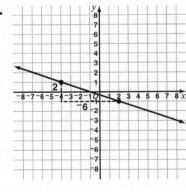

slope =

The Slope Formula

Slope is the ratio of rise to run from one point to another point on a line. If you know two points on a line, you can find its slope by using a formula.

Slope Formula

If (x_1, y_1) and (x_2, y_2) are any two points on a line, then the slope of the line is given by:

$$slope = \frac{rise}{run} = \frac{change\ in\ y}{change\ in\ x} = \frac{(y_2 - y_1)}{(x_2 - x_1)}$$

EXAMPLE

Find the slope of the line.

Write the formula.

$$slope = \frac{(y_2 - y_1)}{(x_2 - x_1)}$$

Substitute the coordinates.
Use (7, 5) and (1, 2).

$$slope = \frac{(5 - 2)}{(7 - 1)}$$

Simplify.

$$slope = \frac{3}{6} = \frac{1}{2}$$

The slope of this line is $\frac{1}{2}$.

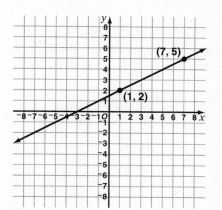

PRACTICE

Find the slope of each line that passes through the given points.

a	b	c
1. $(^-2, 4), (4, 2)$ $\frac{(2 - 4)}{(4 - ^-2)} = \frac{^-2}{6} = \frac{^-1}{3}$	$(3, 5), (4, 7)$	$(6, 2), (8, 0)$
2. $(^-2, ^-2), (1, 4)$	$(^-5, 3), (7, ^-6)$	$(^-3, 2), (1, 4)$
3. $(1, 1), (^-4, 7)$	$(0, ^-2), (9, 3)$	$(1, 1), (4, 10)$

Inequalities

Sometimes the answer to a problem is a set of numbers. Such a set can be represented by using an **inequality.**

For example, the answer to this inequality, $x < 6$, is the set of all numbers less than 6.

Here are the symbols used with inequalities:

$>$ is greater than $<$ is less than
$\geq$ is greater than or equal to $\leq$ is less than or equal to

Greater than or equal to means at least. For example, $x \geq 9$ is read as x is greater than or equal to 9. The answer to this inequality is a set that includes 9 and all numbers greater than 9.

Less than or equal to means at most. For example, $x \leq 3$ is read as x is less than or equal to 3. The answer to this inequality is a set that includes 3 and all numbers less than 3.

EXAMPLE 1

Write $>$, $<$, or $=$.

$^{-}2 \underline{\;<\;} 1$

$5.001 \underline{\;>\;} 1.05$

$11 + 7 \underline{\;=\;} 9 + 9$

EXAMPLE 2

Write $>$, $<$, or $=$.

$\frac{7}{12} \underline{\qquad} \frac{5}{6}$

To compare fractions, convert to a common denominator.

$\frac{5}{6} = \frac{10}{12}$

$\frac{7}{12} < \frac{10}{12}$

$\frac{7}{12} < \frac{5}{6}$

EXAMPLE 3

True or False?

$(\frac{3}{4} - \frac{1}{2}) < (\frac{6}{8} - \frac{2}{4})$?

$(\frac{6}{8} - \frac{4}{8}) < (\frac{6}{8} - \frac{4}{8})$?

$\frac{2}{8} < \frac{2}{8}$? False,

because $\frac{2}{8} = \frac{2}{8}$

PRACTICE

Use $>$, $<$, or $=$ to complete each sentence.

	a	b	c
1.	$^{-}4 \underline{\;>\;} ^{-}8$	$^{-}12 \underline{\qquad} 6$	$3 \underline{\qquad} ^{-}3$
2.	$0.21 \underline{\qquad} 0.12$	$0.050 \underline{\qquad} 0.005$	$7.18 \underline{\qquad} 8.17$
3.	$\frac{1}{2} \underline{\qquad} \frac{5}{6}$	$\frac{3}{5} + \frac{1}{5} \underline{\qquad} \frac{6}{15} + \frac{3}{15}$	$\frac{1}{6} + \frac{2}{3} \underline{\qquad} \frac{17}{18} - \frac{1}{9}$
4.	$(25 - 22) \underline{\qquad} (12 - 9)$	$(8 + 7) \underline{\qquad} (4 + 13)$	$(54 - 6) \underline{\qquad} (36 + 6)$

Tell whether each sentence is true or false.

	a	b	c
5.	$32 > 23$ *true*	$12 < ^{-}18$	$^{-}15 \leq ^{-}5$
6.	$1.34 > 1.4$	$0.06 \geq ^{-}0.17$	$^{-}0.02 < ^{-}0.2$
7.	$\frac{1}{4} < \frac{1}{6}$	$\frac{5}{6} - \frac{1}{2} > \frac{7}{8} - \frac{3}{4}$	$\frac{2}{3} \leq \frac{7}{9}$

Unit 8 Algebra: Functions, Graphs, and Inequalities

Solving Inequalities with Addition and Subtraction

Many inequalities are solved in much the same way equations are. To solve an inequality, you can add or subtract the same amount from both sides without changing its solution.

Solve: $x + 8 < 18$

$x + 8 < 18$

$x + 8 - 8 < 18 - 8$ Subtract 8 from both sides.

$x < 10$

Solve: $15 \geq x - 5$

$15 \geq x - 5$

$15 + 5 \geq x - 5 + 5$ Add 5 to both sides.

$20 \geq x$

PRACTICE

Solve.

	a	b	c
1.	$x - 4 > 12$ $x - 4 + 4 > 12 + 4$ $x > 16$	$x - 9 \leq 6$	$17 > x - 8$
2.	$x + 3 \leq 10$	$16 < x + 13$	$11 \leq x + 5$
3.	$5 < x - 10$	$36 \geq 12 + x$	$x - 9 > 14$
4.	$16 + x > 40$	$x - 6 \geq 19$	$55 \leq x + 20$
5.	$x + 7 < 5$	$x + 6 \geq 2$	$10 > x + 1$
6.	$10 \geq 8 - x$	$14 > 6 - x$	$x + 8 \leq 3$

Solving Inequalities with Multiplication and Division

As with equations, you can multiply or divide both sides of
an inequality by the same number without changing the solution.
However, if you multiply or divide by a negative number, you
must change the direction of the inequality symbol.

Solve: $\frac{x}{2} \leq 4$

$\frac{x}{2} \leq 4$

Multiply both sides
by 2.

$2(\frac{x}{2}) \leq 2(4)$

$x \leq 8$

Check (using any
number ≤ 8):

$\frac{6}{2} \leq 4?$

$3 \leq 4$

Solve: $^-3x < 12$

$^-3x < 12$

Divide both sides
by $^-3$. Reverse the
sign.

$\frac{^-3x}{^-3} > \frac{12}{^-3}$

$x > ^-4$

Check (using any
number $> ^-4$):

$^-3(^-1) < 12?$

$3 < 12$

Solve: $^-2x + 3 < 5x + 10$

$^-2x + 3 < 5x + 10$

First, subtract 3 from both sides.

$^-2x + 3 - 3 < 5x + 10 - 3$

$^-2x < 5x + 7$

Subtract 5x from both sides.

$^-2x - 5x < 5x + 7 - 5x$

$^-7x < 7$

Divide by $^-7$. Reverse the sign.

$\frac{^-7x}{^-7} > \frac{7}{^-7}$

$x > ^-1$

Check (using any number $> ^-1$):

$^-2(0) + 3 < 5(0) + 10?$

$3 < 10$

PRACTICE

Solve.

	a	b	c
1.	$\frac{x}{4} < 5$ $4(\frac{x}{4}) < 4(5)$ $x < 20$	$\frac{x}{2} \geq ^-8$	$6 \leq \frac{x}{^-3}$
2.	$2x > 10$	$^-15 \leq 3x$	$^-6x > ^-24$
3.	$2x + 1 < 7$	$43 > 5x + 8$	$^-4x + 3 \geq 19$
4.	$14 > 3x - 4$	$54 \leq 8x - 2$	$6x - 9 > 21$
5.	$4x - 2 \geq 6x + 8$	$9x + 3 < 12x + 30$	$8x + 6 < 10x - 12$

Unit 8 Algebra: Functions, Graphs, and Inequalities

Solving Problems with Inequalities

Some problems can be solved using inequalities.

EXAMPLE

Michael has 20 cups of flour to complete his baking for the annual family reunion picnic. If he uses 8 cups of flour to make his famous brownies, what is the greatest number of cups of flour that will be left over for making cookies?

$$Let \ x = cups \ of \ flour \ for \ cookies$$

$$8 \ cups \ for \ brownies + x \le 20 \ total \ cups \ of \ flour$$

$$8 + x \le 20$$

$$8 + x - 8 \le 20 - 8$$

$$x \le 12$$

Michael can use no more than 12 cups of flour to make his cookies for the family reunion.

PRACTICE

Solve using inequalities.

1. Holly has 12 feet of ribbon. If she uses 3.5 feet to wrap one gift, what is the maximum length of ribbon Holly can use to wrap the rest of her gifts?

   Answer _____

2. Drew runs less than 30 miles in a week. If he runs 5 miles a day, what is the maximum number of days Drew will run that week?

   Answer _____

3. The Hobbs family has a fixed income of $4,500 per month. Their fixed expenses are $2,200 per month. What is the maximum amount the Hobbs family could save each month?

   Answer _____

4. Sylvia saved $800 to buy furnishings for the living room of her new apartment. She spent $480 on a sofa. If Sylvia buys an antique chair for $80, what is the most she can spend on other items for her living room?

   Answer _____

Problem-Solving Strategy: Use a Line Graph

This graph shows the profits of JBS Industries over a six-month period from July through December. What was the increase in profits from July to August?

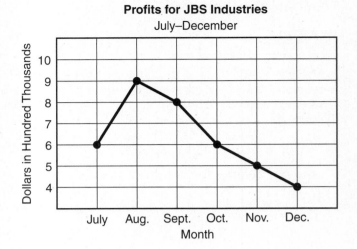

Profits for JBS Industries
July–December

Understand the problem.

- **What do you want to know?**
  the increase in profits from July to August

- **What information is given?**
  a line graph showing the profits of JBS Industries from July to December

Plan how to solve it.

- **What strategy can you use?**
  You can use the line graph to answer questions about the data.

Solve it.

- **How can you use this strategy to solve the problem?**
  Locate July and August on the horizontal axis. From each month, move straight up to the point, then left to get the value on the vertical axis. Write the data for each month. Subtract July's profits from August's profits to find the increase.

  > Data: In July, JBS Industries earned $600,000. In August, JBS Industries earned $900,000.
  >
  > $900,000 − $600,000 = $300,000

- **What is the answer?**
  The profits for JBS Industries increased by $300,000 from July to August.

Look back and check your answer.

- **Is your answer reasonable?**
  You can check your math by counting the number of units the profits increased from July to August. The profits increased by 3 units. Each unit represents $100,000.

  3 × 100,000 = 300,000

  The answer is reasonable.

Unit 8 Algebra: Functions, Graphs, and Inequalities

Use the line graph below to solve.

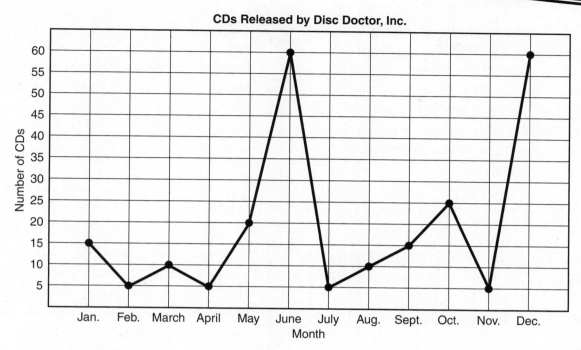

CDs Released by Disc Doctor, Inc.

Number of CDs

Month

1. In which two months were the greatest numbers of CDs released?

Answer _____

2. In which four months were the fewest numbers of CDs released?

Answer _____

3. Between which two months was the greatest increase in the number of CDs released?

Answer _____

4. Between which two months was the greatest decrease in the number of CDs released?

Answer _____

5. During which two months were only fifteen CDs released?

Answer _____

6. How many more CDs were released in October than in March?

Answer _____

7. What was the decrease in number of CDs released from June to July?

Answer _____

8. What was the increase in number of CDs released from November to December?

Answer _____

Problem-Solving Applications

Solve.

1. The temperature on the first day of winter was 12°C. Wanda represented this fact on a coordinate plane with the ordered pair (1, 12). On the ninth day of winter, the temperature was 8°C, which Wanda represented with (9, 8). What is the slope of the line through these two points?

Answer _____

2. There are less than 30 seats on Jill's bus. Shanell's bus has 5 more seats than Jill's bus has. Write an inequality which shows the possible number of seats on Shanell's bus.

Answer _____

3. Tonya's age plus two times Stephen's age is equal to 24. Let Tonya's age be x and let Stephen's age be y. Find Tonya's age if Stephen is 10 years old.

Answer _____

4. The least number of points the Hawks scored during the first football game of the season was 7. The Tigers scored twice as many points as the Hawks did. Write an inequality to show the possible points scored by the Tigers.

Answer _____

5. Leslie has a dozen eggs for baking. If she uses 3 eggs per day, what is the maximum number of days she can bake before buying more eggs?

Answer _____

6. Jacob planted a tree and kept track of its growth on a coordinate plane. The growth rate during April was given by the slope of the line from (2, 6) to (3, 10). The rate for May was given by the slope from (3, 10) to (4, 13). Which month had the higher rate of growth?

Answer _____

7. The bonuses for employees of the Fresh-Baked Pie Company are given by the equation $^-x + 4y = 8$. Which of the following points would not lie on the graph of this equation?
(4, 3), (8, 4), (10, 5)

Answer _____

8. The Jackson family income is $800 per week. If their regular expenses are $510 per week, what is the maximum amount they could save each week?

Answer _____

Unit 8 Algebra: Functions, Graphs, and Inequalities

Determine whether each of the following relations is a function. Find the domain and range for each.

a

1. $\{(2, 2), (1, 4), (3, 6), (^-1, 2)\}$

Function? _____

Domain _____

Range _____

b

2. $\{(^-4, 6), (5, ^-3), (1, 1), (^-4, 7)\}$

Function? _____

Domain _____

Range _____

For each equation, find and graph three solutions. Draw a straight line through those points.

a

3. $2x - y = 6$

x	y

b

$x + 2y = 7$

x	y

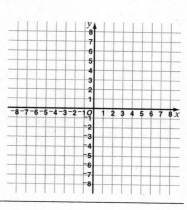

Find the slope of each line that passes through the given points.

a

4. $(1, 7), (2, 4)$

b

$(2, 5), (4, 9)$

c

$(^-3, 3), (4, ^-4)$

Solve.

a

5. $x + 13 > 45$

b

$49 \geq x - 17$

c

$^-3x \leq 15$

6. $6 + 5x < 8 + 4x$

$2x - 21 > 11 - 6x$

$2 + 3x \geq 12 - 2x$

Points and Lines

A **point** is an exact location in space.

A **line** is an endless straight path.

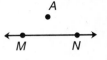

point *A*

line *MN* or line *NM*

A **line segment** is a straight path between two points.

line segment *ST* or line segment *TS*

$\overline{ST}$ or $\overline{TS}$

A **ray** is an endless straight path starting at one point.

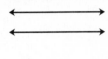

ray *GH*

$\overrightarrow{GH}$

Lines can have different relationships. Two lines can be intersecting lines, perpendicular lines, or parallel lines.

Lines that cross at one point are **intersecting lines.**	Lines that intersect to form four 90° angles are **perpendicular lines.**	Lines that never intersect and are always the same distance apart are **parallel lines.**
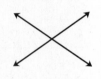	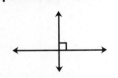	

PRACTICE

Name each figure. Write *point, line, line segment,* or *ray.*

         a   *b*   *c*   *d*

1.    *D*

         _____ray_____   _____   _____   _____

Describe each pair of lines. Write *intersecting, perpendicular,* or *parallel.*

         a   *b*   *c*   *d*

2.

     _____   _____   _____   _____

Types of Angles

An **angle** is formed by two rays or line segments with a common endpoint called a **vertex.** The symbol for angle is ∠.

Angles are measured in **degrees** (°).

They also are classified by their size.

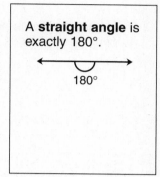

angle *QRS* or angle *SRQ*
or angle *R*

∠*QRS* or ∠*SRQ* or ∠*R*

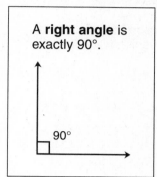

A **right angle** is exactly 90°.

90°

An **acute angle** is less than 90°.

An **obtuse angle** is greater than 90°.

A **straight angle** is exactly 180°.

180°

PRACTICE

Name each angle using symbols.

a	b	c	d

1.

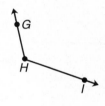

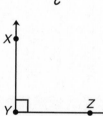

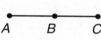

_____ ∠GHI _____ _____ _____ _____

Classify each angle. Write *right, acute, obtuse,* or *straight*.

a	b	c	d

2.

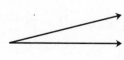

_____ _____ _____ _____

Types of Triangles

A **triangle** is a closed figure with three sides and three angles.

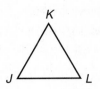

triangle *JKL*
Δ *JKL*

Triangles can be classified by their **congruent** (equal) sides.

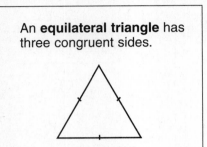

An **equilateral triangle** has three congruent sides.

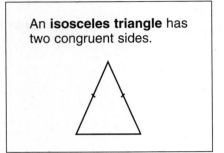

An **isosceles triangle** has two congruent sides.

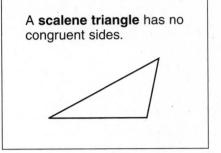

A **scalene triangle** has no congruent sides.

Triangles can also be classified by their angles.

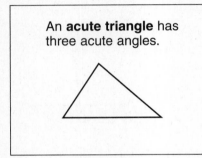

An **acute triangle** has three acute angles.

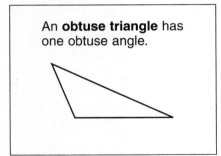

An **obtuse triangle** has one obtuse angle.

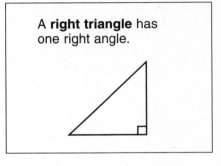

A **right triangle** has one right angle.

PRACTICE

Classify each triangle by its sides. Write *equilateral, isosceles,* or *scalene*.

    a   *b*   *c*   *d*

1.

    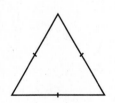      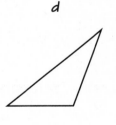

_____isosceles_____   _____   _____   _____

Classify each triangle by its angles. Write *acute, obtuse,* or *right*.

    a   *b*   *c*   *d*

2.

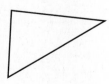   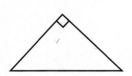   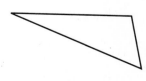   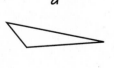

_____   _____   _____   _____

                     Unit 9 Geometry

Polygons

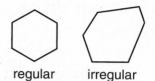

A **polygon** is a closed **plane** figure having three or more sides. A polygon having all sides congruent and all angles congruent is called a **regular polygon**. An **irregular polygon** has sides of different lengths and angles of different measures.

regular   irregular

Polygons are classified by the number of sides and angles.

Triangle	Quadrilateral	Pentagon	Hexagon	Octagon
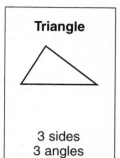	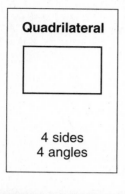	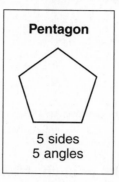	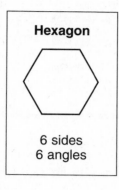	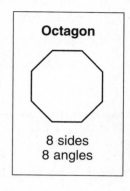
3 sides 3 angles	4 sides 4 angles	5 sides 5 angles	6 sides 6 angles	8 sides 8 angles

PRACTICE

Write whether each polygon is *regular* or *irregular*.

       a   *b*   *c*   *d*

1.   

    regular

2.   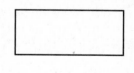

Classify each polygon. Write *triangle*, *quadrilateral*, *pentagon*, *hexagon*, or *octagon*.

       a   *b*   *c*   *d*

3.   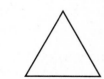

    triangle

4.      

Perimeter of a Triangle

To find the **perimeter** of a triangle, add the lengths of the sides.

EXAMPLE

Find the perimeter of this triangle.

P = side 1 + side 2 + side 3

P = *58* + *75* + *48*

P = *181*

The perimeter is 181 inches.

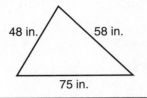

48 in.   58 in.

75 in.

PRACTICE

Draw a picture and write in the lengths of each side. Solve.

1. Find the perimeter of an equilateral triangle in which each side measures 9.6 centimeters.

Answer _____

2. Roger needs trim for a triangular-shaped bandanna for his western costume. The bandanna measures 15 inches on 2 sides and 20 inches on the third side. How much trim does he need?

Answer _____

3. How many meters of wire will be required to enclose a triangular-shaped park in which the sides measure 50, 45, and 69 meters?

Answer _____

4. Find the perimeter of an equilateral triangle in which each side measures 0.068 kilometers.

Answer _____

5. What is the perimeter of an isosceles triangle that has two sides 8 yards long and a third side 6 yards long?

Answer _____

6. The sides of a triangular garden measure 130, 120, and 60 feet. What is the perimeter of the garden?

Answer _____

Perimeter of a Rectangle

To find the perimeter of a rectangle, you can use a **formula.**
Notice that the opposite sides of a rectangle are equal.

The formula $P = 2l + 2w$ means the perimeter of a rectangle
equals 2 times the length plus 2 times the width.

EXAMPLE

Find the perimeter of this rectangle.

Write the formula.	$P = 2l + 2w$
Substitute the data.	$P = (2 \times 60) + (2 \times 40)$
Solve the problem.	$P = 120 + 80$
	$P = 200$

$l = 60$ m

$w = 40$ m

The perimeter of the rectangle is 200 meters.

PRACTICE

Use the formula for perimeter of a rectangle. Solve.

1. Ned wants to fence his garden. It is
   10 feet wide and 12 feet long. How much
   fencing does he need?

   Answer _____

2. Montaña Park is 0.25 kilometer wide
   and 0.75 kilometer long. What is the
   perimeter of the park?

   Answer _____

3. A pillow measures 54 centimeters by
   62 centimeters. How much trim is needed
   to go around the pillow?

   Answer _____

4. A desk measures 159 centimeters by
   120 centimeters. What is the perimeter
   of the desk?

   Answer _____

5. A farm measures 1.4 kilometers by
   1.2 kilometers. What is the perimeter of
   the farm?

   Answer _____

6. Lin's bedroom window is a rectangle
   which is twice as long as it is wide. The
   window is 36 inches wide. What is the
   perimeter of the window?

   Answer _____

Problem-Solving Strategy: Make a Table

The city wants fencing around the playground, the basketball court, and the tennis court in the new park. The playground is 100 feet by 100 feet, the basketball court is 94 feet by 50 feet, and the tennis court is 78 feet by 36 feet. If the fencing costs $3.00 a foot, how much will the city pay for fencing in the new park?

Understand the problem.

- **What do you want to know?**
  how much the fencing will cost in the new park

- **What information is given?**
  Playground: 100 feet by 100 feet
  Basketball court: 94 feet by 50 feet
  Tennis court: 78 feet by 36 feet
  Cost of fencing: $3.00 per foot

Plan how to solve it.

- **What strategy can you use?**
  You can make a table to organize the information.

Solve it.

- **How can you use this strategy to solve the problem?**
  Make a table that includes calculations for the perimeter and cost of fencing for each section. Complete the table, then add the section costs to find the total cost of the fencing in the new park.

Section	Perimeter	Cost of Fencing
Playground	$P = 2(100) + 2(100) = 400$	$400 \times \$3 = \$1{,}200$
Basketball Court	$P = 2(94) + 2(50) = \quad 288$	$288 \times \$3 = \quad \$864$
Tennis Court	$P = 2(78) + 2(36) = \quad 228$	$228 \times \$3 = \quad \$684$
Total Cost of the Fencing		$\$2{,}748$

- **What is the answer?**
  The total cost of the fencing for the new park is $2,748.

Look back and check your answer.

- **Is your answer reasonable?**
  You can check your answer by rounding the original information to the nearest 100 or 50 and then calculating the cost.

  Playground: $2(100) + 2(100) = 400$ $400 \times 3 = \$1{,}200$

  Basketball Court: $2(100) + 2(50) = 300$ $300 \times 3 = \quad \$900$

  Tennis Court: $2(100) + 2(50) = 300$ $300 \times 3 = \quad \underline{\$900}$

                                                        $\$3{,}000$

  $3,000 is close to $2,748. The answer is reasonable.

Make a table to solve each problem.

1. Antoinette is putting wallpaper borders around each bedroom in her house. The master bedroom is 25 feet by 15 feet. Her son's and daughter's rooms are 15 feet by 10 feet each. If the wallpaper border costs $1.50 a foot, how much will Antoinette spend on borders?

Answer _____

2. Brian just finished three paintings. He makes his own frames for each painting. The first painting is 42 in. by 42 in.; the second is 60 in. by 36 in.; and the third is 84 in. by 24 in. How many inches of wood does Brian need to frame all three paintings?

Answer _____

3. Rosa has a border around her vegetable garden and both flower beds. The vegetable garden is 6 meters by 3 meters. Both flower beds are 3 meters by 1 meter. How many meters of border did Rosa use?

Answer _____

4. Caitlin is putting weatherstripping around each of her windows. She has two windows 30 in. by 90 in. and two windows 40 in. by 85 in. How much weatherstripping does Caitlin need?

Answer _____

Formula for Area of a Triangle

The **height** of a triangle is a perpendicular line segment from any vertex to the opposite side. The opposite side is called the **base**.

To find the **area** (number of square units) of a triangle, you can use a formula. The formula $A = \frac{1}{2}bh$ means the area of a triangle equals one-half the base times the height. The answer will be in square units.

EXAMPLE

Find the area of this triangle.

Write the formula.

$A = \frac{1}{2}bh$

Substitute the data.

$A = \frac{1}{2} \times 12 \times 15$

Solve the problem.

$A = \frac{12 \times 15}{2} = \frac{180}{2} = 90$

The area of the triangle is 90 square centimeters.

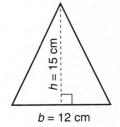

PRACTICE

Use the formula for area of a triangle. Solve.

1. What is the area of a triangle that has a base of 16 meters and a height of 20 meters?

   Answer _____

2. How much sod will be needed to cover a triangular-shaped park whose base measures 105 feet and height measures 87 feet?

   Answer _____

3. A triangular-shaped park has one side, the base, measuring 120 meters, and one side, the height, measuring 80 meters. What is the area of the park?

   Answer _____

4. A new highway cut off part of the town and formed a triangle. The base of the triangle measures 30 kilometers, and one side, the height, measures 25 kilometers. What is the area of this part of the town?

   Answer _____

5. The top of the front wall of a barn forms a triangle. The triangle is 3.5 meters tall and 10 meters wide. What is the area of this part of the wall?

   Answer _____

6. A group of students are making school banners shaped like triangles. The base of each triangle is 11 inches. The height of each triangle is 25 inches. How much fabric is needed to make each banner?

   Answer _____

Formula for Area of a Rectangle

To find the area of a rectangle, you can use a formula.

The formula $A = lw$ means the area of a rectangle equals the length times the width.

EXAMPLE

Find the area of this rectangle.

Write the formula. $A = lw$

Substitute the data. $A = 12 \times 8$

Solve the problem. $A = 96$

The area of the rectangle is 96 square meters.

Remember, write your answer in square units.

$w = 8$ m

$l = 12$ m

PRACTICE

Use the formula for area of a rectangle. Solve.

1. How many square meters is the floor area of a room that measures 8 meters by 6.9 meters?

   Answer _____

2. What is the area of a window that measures 16 inches by 24 inches?

   Answer _____

3. A pillow measures 62 centimeters by 40 centimeters. How much fabric will be needed to cover one side of the pillow?

   Answer _____

4. How much sod is needed to cover a yard that measures 20 meters by 15 meters?

   Answer _____

5. What is the area of a concrete sidewalk that measures 100 meters by 1.5 meters?

   Answer _____

6. How much tile is needed to cover a floor that measures 54 feet by 42 feet?

   Answer _____

7. How many square inches of glass are needed to cover a picture that measures 8 inches by 10 inches?

   Answer _____

8. How much carpeting is needed to cover a floor that measures 3 meters by 4.4 meters?

   Answer _____

Surface Area of a Rectangular Prism

The **surface area** of a rectangular **prism** is the sum of the areas of each **face.** Because the surface area measures two **dimensions,** it is measured in square units.

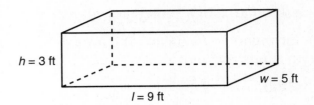

EXAMPLE

Find the surface area of this figure.

Find the sum of the areas of each face.

$A = 9 \times 3 = 27$ sq. ft

$B = 9 \times 5 = 45$ sq. ft

$C = 9 \times 3 = 27$ sq. ft

$D = 9 \times 5 = 45$ sq. ft

$E = 5 \times 3 = 15$ sq. ft

$F = 5 \times 3 = 15$ sq. ft

The sum of the areas of each face is:

$27 + 45 + 27 + 45 + 15 + 15 = 174$ sq. ft

The surface area of the rectangular prism is 174 square feet.

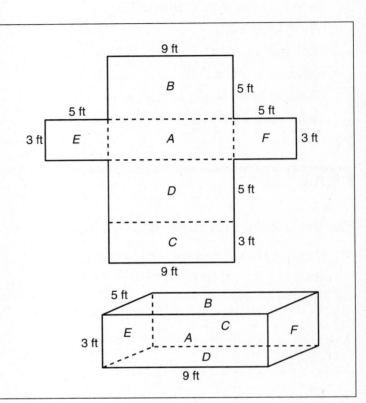

Find the surface area of each figure.

1.

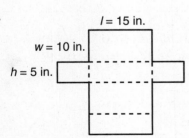

$A = 15(10) + 15(5) + 15(10)$
$\quad + 15(5) + 10(5) + 10(5)$

$= 150 + 75 + 150$
$\quad + 75 + 50 + 50$

$= 550$ square inches

2.

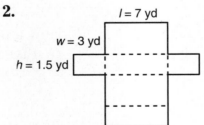

3.

$w = 3.5$ m
$h = 2$ m
$l = 6.5$ m

Find the surface area of each figure.

1.

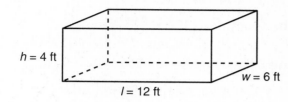

Answer _____

2.

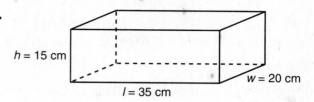

Answer _____

3.

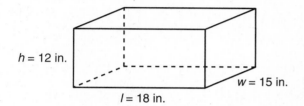

Answer _____

4.

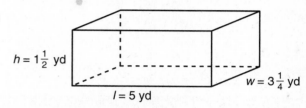

Answer _____

Solve.

5. Doreen bought a storage box that is 5 feet long, 3 feet wide, and 1 foot high. What is the surface area of the storage box?

Answer _____

6. A necklace came in a box that is 5 cm by 8 cm by 15 cm. What is the surface area of the box?

Answer _____

---

7. Antonio is building a toy chest for his son. The toy chest is 30 inches high, 40 inches wide, and 50 inches long. What is the surface area of the toy chest?

Answer _____

8. Stacey is sending her mother a package that is 3 feet long, 1 foot wide, and $1\frac{1}{2}$ feet tall. What is the surface area of the package?

Answer _____

Area of Parallelograms and Trapezoids

A **parallelogram** is a quadrilateral with 2 sets of parallel sides.

The formula $A = b \times h$ means the area of a parallelogram is the product of the base and the height.

Find the area of the parallelogram.

The area of the parallelogram is 66 square feet.

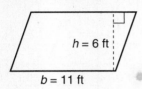

$h = 6$ ft
$b = 11$ ft

A **trapezoid** is a quadrilateral with exactly 1 pair of parallel sides.

The formula $A = \frac{(b_1 + b_2)h}{2}$ means the area of a trapezoid equals the sum of the bases times the height divided by 2.

Find the area of the trapezoid.

The area of the trapezoid is 36 square inches.

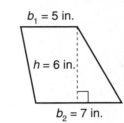

$b_1 = 5$ in.
$h = 6$ in.
$b_2 = 7$ in.

$A = \frac{(5 + 7)6}{2}$

$A = 36$

GUIDED PRACTICE

Find the area of each parallelogram or trapezoid.

      a   **b**   **c**

1.

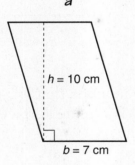

$h = 10$ cm
$b = 7$ cm

$b_1 = 2.3$ m
$h = 1.8$ m
$b_2 = 5.2$ m

$h = 6$ yd
$b = 9\frac{2}{3}$ yd

$A = b \times h$
$A = 7 \times 10$
$A = 70$ sq. cm

2.

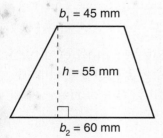

$b_1 = 45$ mm
$h = 55$ mm
$b_2 = 60$ mm

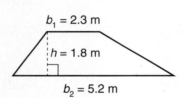

$h = 7.8$ ft
$b = 9.2$ ft

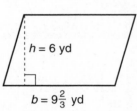

$b_1 = 3$ in.
$h = 5$ in.
$b_2 = 7$ in.

Find the area of each parallelogram or trapezoid.

1.

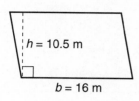

$b_1 = 3.4$ yd

$h = 4.9$ yd

$b_2 = 5.6$ yd

$h = 17$ in.

$b = 27$ in.

2.

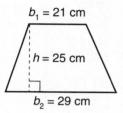

$b_1 = 21$ cm

$h = 25$ cm

$b_2 = 29$ cm

$h = 30$ mm

$b = 65$ mm

$b_1 = 18$ ft

$h = 16$ ft

$b_2 = 20$ ft

Solve.

3. What is the area of a trapezoid that is 8 inches high with bases that are 10 inches and 15 inches long?

4. What is the area of a parallelogram with a height of $3\frac{1}{4}$ feet and a base of $6\frac{1}{2}$ feet?

Answer _____

Answer _____

5. Dion drew a trapezoid with a height of 12 centimeters and bases of 25 centimeters and 17 centimeters. What is the area of Dion's trapezoid?

6. What is the area of a parallelogram that has a base of 16 yards long and is 8 yards high?

Answer _____

Answer _____

Formula for Volume of a Rectangular Prism

To find the **volume** (number of **cubic** units) of a rectangular prism, you can use a formula.

The formula $V = lwh$ means the volume of a rectangular prism equals the length times the width times the height. The answer will be in cubic units.

EXAMPLE

Find the volume of this rectangular prism.

Write the formula.	$V = lwh$
Substitute the data.	$V = 10 \times 15 \times 4$
Solve the problem.	$V = 600$

The volume is 600 cubic meters.

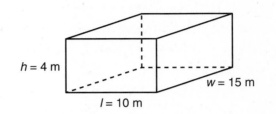

$h = 4$ m $w = 15$ m $l = 10$ m

PRACTICE

Use the formula for volume of a rectangular prism. Solve.

1. How many cubic meters of concrete are needed for a driveway that measures 2 meters wide, 27 meters long, and 0.1 meters thick?

   Answer _____

2. A classroom measures 14 meters by 7 meters by 3.5 meters. How many cubic meters of air are in the room?

   Answer _____

3. How much dirt was removed to form a hole that measures 80 feet long, 54 feet wide, and 4 feet deep?

   Answer _____

4. What is the volume of a basement that measures 7 yards by 9 yards by 3 yards?

   Answer _____

5. Tom built a toolbox that is 55 centimeters by 35 centimeters by 31 centimeters. What is the volume of Tom's toolbox?

   Answer _____

6. What is the volume of water in a tank that measures 10 feet by 12 feet by 8 feet?

   Answer _____

7. How much soil is needed to fill a box that is 12 inches by 19 inches by 18 inches?

   Answer _____

8. What is the volume of a bin that measures 5 meters by 2 meters by 3.5 meters?

   Answer _____

Formula for Circumference of a Circle

Circumference is the distance around a circle. To find the circumference, you can use a formula.

The formula $C = \pi d$ means the circumference equals **pi** times the **diameter.** This formula uses the symbol π for pi. We use 3.14 for the value of π. The diameter is a straight line across the circle and through the center.

You can also use the formula $C = 2\pi r$ which means the circumference equals two times pi times the **radius.** The radius is a straight line from the center of the circle to the circumference. It is one half of the diameter, so $2r = d$.

EXAMPLE

Find the circumference of this circle.

Write the formula.	$C = \pi d$
Substitute the data.	$C = 3.14 \times 12$
Solve the problem.	$C = 37.68$

The circumference of the circle is 37.68 millimeters.

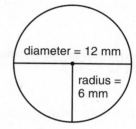

diameter = 12 mm

radius = 6 mm

PRACTICE

Use the formula for circumference of a circle. Solve.

1. What is the circumference of a circle that has a diameter of 7 inches?

   Answer _____

2. The wheel of a bicycle has a radius of 35 centimeters. What is the circumference of the wheel?

   Answer _____

3. What is the circumference of a circle with a radius of 175 millimeters?

   Answer _____

4. What is the circumference of a circle with a diameter of 3.5 yards?

   Answer _____

5. At the Alamo, a circular flower garden encloses the star of Texas. The garden has a radius of 3.15 meters. How much border is needed to enclose the garden? Round your answer to hundredths.

   Answer _____

6. The diameter of the inside of the ring of a basketball hoop is 45.71 centimeters. What is the circumference of the ring? Round your answer to the nearest hundredth.

   Answer _____

Formula for Area of a Circle

To find the area of a circle, you can use a formula.

The formula $A = \pi r^2$ means the area of a circle is equal to pi times the radius squared, or the radius times the radius.

EXAMPLE

Find the area of this circle.

Write the formula.

$$A = \pi r^2$$

Substitute the data.

$$A = 3.14\ (7 \times 7)$$

Solve the problem.

$$A = 3.14 \times 49 = 153.86$$

The area of the circle is 153.86 square centimeters.

Remember, write your answer in square units.

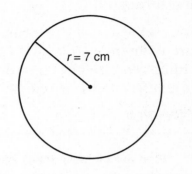

$r = 7$ cm

PRACTICE

Use the formula for area of a circle. Solve.

1. Find the area of a circle that has a radius of 3.5 feet.

   Answer _____

2. What is the area of a circle that has a diameter of 28 inches? (Hint: The radius is one half the diameter.)

   Answer _____

3. A bandstand in the shape of a circle is to be 7 meters across. How many square meters of flooring will be required? Round your answer to the nearest hundredth.

   Answer _____

4. A circular canvas net used by firefighters has a radius of 2.1 meters. What is the area of the net?

   Answer _____

5. A gallon of paint covers 56 square meters. How many gallons of paint will be needed to cover a circular ceiling that is 22 meters in diameter?

   Answer _____

6. The circular top of an auto piston has a radius of 4.2 centimeters. What is the area of the top of the piston? Round your answer to the nearest hundredth.

   Answer _____

Formula for Volume of a Cylinder

To find the volume of a cylinder, you can use a formula.

The formula $V = \pi r^2 h$ means the volume of a cylinder equals pi times the radius squared times the height.

Remember, diameter = $2r$.

EXAMPLE

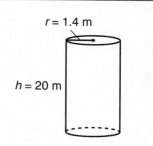

Find the volume of this cylinder.

Write the formula. $V = \pi r^2 h$

Substitute the data. $V = 3.14 \, (1.4 \times 1.4) \times 20$

Solve the problem. $V = 123.088$

The volume of the cylinder is 123.088 cubic meters.

Remember, write your answer in cubic units.

$r = 1.4$ m

$h = 20$ m

PRACTICE

Use the formula for volume of a cylinder. Solve.

1. A cylindrical water tank has a diameter of 2.8 yards and is 6.5 yards high. What is the volume of the tank? Round your answer to the nearest hundredth.

   Answer _____

2. The inside radius of a pipe is 0.35 meters. One section of the pipe is 6 meters long. How much water will this piece of pipe hold?

   Answer _____

3. A small pipe has a radius of 1 inch and is 3.5 inches long. How much liquid can the pipe hold?

   Answer _____

4. A storage tank has a radius of 5.25 meters and a height of 12 meters. How much liquid can the storage tank hold? Round your answer to the nearest hundredth.

   Answer _____

5. The tank of a gasoline truck has a radius of 1.75 meters and is 7 meters long. What is the volume of the tank? Round your answer to the nearest hundredth.

   Answer _____

6. A cylinder-shaped container is 9 centimeters in diameter and 15 centimeters in height. How much liquid will this container hold? Round your answer to the nearest hundredth.

   Answer _____

Problem-Solving Strategy: Use a Formula

The volume (V) of a rectangular prism is 288 cubic inches. The length (l) is 9 inches, and the width (w) is 4 inches. What is the height (h) of the prism?

Understand the problem.

- **What do you want to know?**
  the height of the rectangular prism

- **What information is given?**
  volume = 288 cubic inches
  length = 9 inches
  width = 4 inches

Plan how to solve it.

- **What strategy can you use?**
  Use the formula for the volume of a rectangular prism.

Solve it.

- **How can you use this strategy to solve the problem?**
  Replace V, l, and w in the formula with the numbers given. Then solve for h.

$$V = lwh$$
$$288 = 9 \times 4 \times h$$
$$288 = 36 \times h$$
$$288 \div 36 = 36 \times h \div 36$$
$$288 \div 36 = h$$
$$8 = h$$

- **What is the answer?**
  The height of the prism is 8 inches.

Look back and check your answer.

- **Is your answer reasonable?**
  You can check the height by multiplying it by the given length and width of the prism in order to get the volume.

$$V = lwh = 9 \times 4 \times 8$$
$$= 288$$

The volume matches the given data. The answer is reasonable.

Solve using a formula.

1. The area of a trapezoid is 45 square centimeters. The bases of the trapezoid are 10 centimeters and 8 centimeters. What is the height of the trapezoid?

   Answer _____

2. The height of a cylinder is 3 feet. The volume of the cylinder is 2.355 cubic feet. What is the diameter of the cylinder?

   Answer _____

3. The volume of a rectangular prism is 84 cubic inches. The height of the prism is 3 inches. The length is 7 inches. What is the width of the prism?

   Answer _____

4. The area of a triangle is 12 square inches. The height of the triangle is 4 inches. What is the base of the triangle?

   Answer _____

5. One triangular face of a pyramid has a base of 20 meters and a height of 30 meters. What is the area of the triangular face?

   Answer _____

6. A triangular stained-glass window has a base of 36 inches and a height of 48 inches. What is the area of the window?

   Answer _____

7. A rectangular wastebasket has a length of 20 inches, a width of 10 inches, and a height of 24 inches. What is the volume of the wastebasket?

   Answer _____

8. A rectangular mailbox has a length of 18 inches, a width of 20 inches, and a height of 5 inches. What is the volume of the box?

   Answer _____

Problem-Solving Applications

Solve.

1. What is the length of a side of an equilateral triangle whose perimeter is 375 feet?

   Answer _____

2. What is the radius of a circle whose area is 113.04 meters? (Hint: Use 3.14 for π.)

   Answer _____

3. The volume of a rectangular shed is 700 cubic yards. If the shed's length is 7 yards and the width is 10 yards, what is the height?

   Answer _____

4. The area of a triangle is 88 square feet. The height is 8 feet. What is the base of the triangle?

   Answer _____

5. The volume of a cylinder that is 25 inches high is 2,826 cubic inches. What is the diameter of the cylinder?

   Answer _____

6. What is the radius of a circle with a circumference of 78.5 centimeters?

   Answer _____

7. A professional football field measures $53\frac{1}{3}$ yards wide. Its area is 6,400 square yards. What is the length of a professional football field?

   Answer _____

8. The volume of a rectangular prism is 160 cubic inches. The length and width of the rectangular prism are 5 inches and 2 inches. What is the height of this rectangular prism?

   Answer _____

Classify each angle. Write *right*, *acute*, *obtuse*, or *straight*.

      a   b   c   d

1.

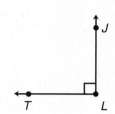
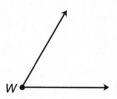
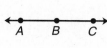
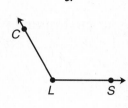

_____   _____   _____   _____

Classify each polygon. Write *regular* or *irregular*.

      a   b   c   d

2.

_____   _____   _____   _____

Classify each triangle. Write *right*, *obtuse*, *equilateral*, or *scalene*.

      a   b   c   d

3.

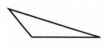

_____   _____   _____   _____

Solve.

4. The diameter of a cylinder is 32 centimeters, and the height is 60 centimeters. What is the volume of the cylinder?

Answer _____

5. What is the surface area of a rectangular prism that is 3 yards long, 4 yards wide, and 5 yards high?

Answer _____

6. Find the area of a parallelogram with a base of 10 feet and a height of 7.5 feet.

Answer _____

7. What is the perimeter of an isosceles triangle that has two sides 16 inches long and one side 8 inches long?

Answer _____

UNIT 10 Measurement, Ratios, and Proportions

Customary Measurement

Some **customary** units of length are inch, foot, yard, and mile. Study the relationship of one unit of length to another.

1 foot (ft) = 12 inches (in.)
1 yard (yd) = 3 ft
= 36 in.
1 mile (mi) = 1,760 yd
= 5,280 ft

Some customary units of weight are ounce, pound, and ton. Study the relationship of one unit of weight to another.

1 pound (lb) = 16 ounces (oz)
1 ton (T) = 2,000 pounds

Some customary units of **capacity** are cup, pint, quart, and gallon. Study the relationship of one unit of capacity to another.

1 pint (pt) = 2 cups (c)
1 quart (qt) = 2 pt
= 4 c
1 gallon (gal) = 4 qt
= 8 pt
= 16 c

PRACTICE

Change each measurement to the larger unit.

a	b	c
1. 39 in. = _**3**_ ft _**3**_ in.	52 in. = ____ ft ____ in.	2,500 lb = ____ T ____ lb
2. 35 oz = ____ lb ____ oz	60 oz = ____ lb ____ oz	5,550 yd = ____ mi ____ yd
3. 17 pt = ____ qt ____ pt	7 c = ____ pt ____ c	21 qt = ____ gal ____ qt

Change each measurement to the smaller unit.

a	b	c
4. 6 yd = _**216**_ in.	4 ft = ____ in.	2 mi = ____ ft
5. 8 lb = ____ oz	12 lb = ____ oz	3 T = ____ lb
6. 7 qt 1 c = ____ c	16 pt = ____ c	5 gal = ____ pt

Metric Length

The meter (m) is the basic **metric** unit of length. A meter can be measured with a meter stick. A baseball bat is about 1 meter long.

A centimeter (cm) is one hundredth of a meter (*centi*- means 0.01). The centimeter is used to measure small lengths. Your small finger is about 1 centimeter across.

A millimeter (mm) is one thousandth of a meter (*milli*- means 0.001). The millimeter is used to measure very small lengths. The head of a pin is about 1 millimeter across.

A kilometer (km) is one thousand meters (*kilo*- means 1,000). The kilometer is used to measure long distances. The distance between two cities can be measured in kilometers.

To change between two units, write a number sentence using the units you have, the units you want to find, and the relationship between the units. Make sure the units you have cancel so that the remaining unit is the one you want to find.

1 km = 1,000 m	
1 m = 100 cm	
1 cm = 10 mm	

1 m = 0.001 km	
1 cm = 0.01 m	
1 mm = 0.1 cm	

Find: 9.4 m = _____ cm

units you have	relationship between units	units you want to find
↓	↓	↓
9.4 m	× $\frac{100 \text{ cm}}{1 \text{ m}}$ =	940 cm

Find: 15 m = _____ km

units you have	relationship between units	units you want to find
↓	↓	↓
15 m	× $\frac{0.001 \text{ km}}{1 \text{ m}}$ =	0.015 km

PRACTICE

Circle the best measurement.

	a	b	c
1.	height of a tree 15 m 15 km	width of a rubber band 4 mm 4 m	length of a race 3 m 3 km
2.	length of a canoe 5 cm 5 m	height of a step 20 mm 20 cm	width of a bus 200 m 200 cm

Change each measurement to the smaller unit.

	a	b	c
3.	7 m = _____ cm	15 cm = _____ mm	1,200 km = _____ m
4.	225 m = _____ cm = _____ mm	136 km = _____ m	84 m = _____ cm

Change each measurement to the larger unit.

	a	b	c
5.	120 cm = _____ m	4,346 m = _____ km	890 mm = _____ cm
6.	930 mm = _____ cm = _____ m	750 m = _____ km	11 cm = _____ m

Metric Mass

Every person and object are made of **matter**. **Mass** is a measure of the amount of matter in a person or object.

The **gram** (g) is the basic unit of mass. The gram is used to measure the mass of very light objects. A paper clip's mass is about 2 grams.

The **kilogram** (kg) is one thousand grams. It is used to measure the mass of heavier objects. The mass of a computer would be given in kilograms. Remember, *kilo-* means 1,000.

$$1 \text{ kg} = 1,000 \text{ g} \qquad 1 \text{ g} = 0.001 \text{ kg}$$

To change between two units, write a number sentence using the units you have, the units you want to find, and the relationship between the units. Make sure the units you have cancel so that the remaining unit is the one you want to find.

Find: 3.54 kg = _____ g

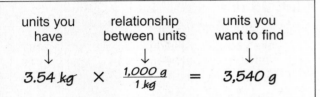

Find: 13.6 g = _____ kg

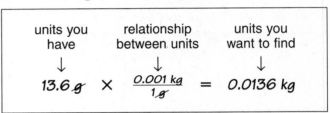

PRACTICE

Circle the best measurement.

	a	*b*	*c*
1.	mass of a postage stamp 1 g 1 kg	mass of an infant child 4 g 4 kg	mass of a couch 100 g 100 kg
2.	mass of an orange 500 g 500 kg	mass of a bowling ball 5 g 5 kg	mass of an insect 20 g 20 kg

Change each measurement to the smaller unit.

a   *b*   *c*

3. 10 kg = _____ g   4.8 kg = _____ g   0.76 kg = _____ g

4. 0.004 kg = _____ g   1.092 kg = _____ g   305 kg = _____ g

Change each measurement to the larger unit.

a   *b*   *c*

5. 2.8 g = _____ kg   7 g = _____ kg   3,094 g = _____ kg

6. 925 g = _____ kg   52.43 g = _____ kg   61 g = _____ kg

Unit 10 Measurement, Ratios, and Proportions

Metric Capacity

The **liter** (L) is the basic metric unit of capacity. A liter of liquid will fill a box that has 10-centimeter edges. A large bottle of milk holds about 4 liters.

A **milliliter** (mL) is one thousandth of a liter. It is used to measure very small amounts of liquid. A milliliter of liquid will fill a box that is 1 centimeter on each edge. A container of yogurt holds about 200 milliliters. Remember, *milli-* means 0.001.

1 L = 1,000 mL	1 mL = 0.001 L

To change between two units, write a number sentence using the units you have, the units you want to find, and the relationship between the units. Make sure the units you have cancel so that the remaining unit is the one you want to find.

Find: 75 L = _____ mL

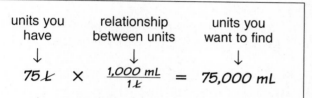

Find: 1,250 mL = _____ L

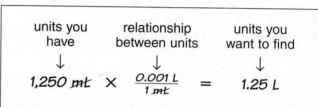

PRACTICE

Circle the best measurement.

	a	b	c
1.	capacity of a gas tank	capacity of a container of cottage cheese	capacity of a bathtub
	60 mL 60 L	750 mL 750 L	350 mL 350 L
2.	capacity of a tea cup	capacity of an eye dropper	capacity of a coffeepot
	300 mL 300 L	50 mL 50 L	3 mL 3 L

Change each measurement to the smaller unit.

	a	b	c
3.	0.7 L = _____ mL	8 L = _____ mL	1.6 L = _____ mL
4.	421 L = _____ mL	3.09 L = _____ mL	0.424 L = _____ mL

Change each measurement to the larger unit.

	a	b	c
5.	8,883 mL = _____ L	390.7 mL = _____ L	14 mL = _____ L
6.	12.5 mL = _____ L	208 mL = _____ L	79 mL = _____ L

Ratios

A **ratio** is a fraction used to compare two quantities. For example, if a baseball player gets 3 hits for every 6 times at bat, the ratio of hits to times at bat is $\frac{3}{6}$ or $\frac{1}{2}$. The ratio of times at bat to hits is $\frac{6}{3}$ or $\frac{2}{1}$.

PRACTICE

Write a fraction for each ratio. Simplify.

a

1. the ratio of inches in a foot to inches in a yard

    Ratio: $\frac{12}{36}$ or $\frac{1}{3}$

2. the ratio of cups in a pint to cups in a quart

    Ratio: _____

3. the ratio of cents in a quarter to cents in a dollar

    Ratio: _____

4. the ratio of cents in a half dollar to cents in a dime

    Ratio: _____

5. the ratio of 17 "yes" votes to 20 "no" votes

    Ratio: _____

6. the ratio of the number of days in December to the number of days in January

    Ratio: _____

7. the ratio of minutes in an hour to minutes in a half hour

    Ratio: _____

b

the ratio of hours in a day to hours in a week

Ratio: _____

the ratio of 3 apples on a table to 6 apples in a bowl

Ratio: _____

the ratio of 8 men to 10 women

Ratio: _____

the ratio of 10 women to 8 men

Ratio: _____

the ratio of 5 wall outlets to 3 wall switches

Ratio: _____

the ratio of 8 hours asleep to 16 hours awake

Ratio: _____

the ratio of 8 computers to 8 desks

Ratio: _____

Unit 10 Measurement, Ratios, and Proportions

Ratios in Measurement

Here you will form ratios using what you know about finding areas of squares and rectangles and volumes of rectangular prisms.

$$A = lw$$
$$V = lwh$$

EXAMPLE

The ratio of the sides of two squares is $\frac{1}{2}$. What is the ratio of the areas?

$$\frac{\text{Area A}}{\text{Area B}} = \frac{lw}{lw} = \frac{1 \times 1}{2 \times 2} = \frac{1}{4}$$

square A $\Big]$1   square B $\Big]$2

The ratio of the two areas is $\frac{1}{4}$.

The area of square B is 4 times greater than the area of square A.

Or, the area of square A is $\frac{1}{4}$ the area of square B.

PRACTICE

Solve.

1. The ratio of the sides of two squares is $\frac{1}{3}$. What is the ratio of the areas?

    Answer _____

2. The ratio of the sides of two squares is $\frac{1}{4}$. What is the ratio of the areas?

    Answer _____

3. The ratio of the edges of two cubes is $\frac{1}{5}$. What is the ratio of the volumes?

    Answer _____

4. The ratio of the edges of two cubes is $\frac{3}{4}$. What is the ratio of the volumes?

    Answer _____

5. The ratio of the edges of two cubes is $\frac{2}{3}$. What is the ratio of the volumes?

    Answer _____

6. The ratio of the sides of two squares is $\frac{10}{1}$. What is the ratio of the areas?

    Answer _____

Proportions

A **proportion** is an equation stating that two ratios are equal. For example, if you mix 2 gallons of red paint with 3 gallons of white, the ratio of red to white is $\frac{2}{3}$. If you mix 4 gallons of red paint with 6 gallons of white, the ratio of red to white is $\frac{4}{6}$. The shades of pink for the two mixtures are the same, because $\frac{2}{3} = \frac{4}{6}$ is a true proportion.

A quick way to check that two ratios are equal is to **cross-multiply.** Write the ratios side by side and draw double-pointed arrows that cross. Multiply the pairs of numbers and see if you get the same result both times. It does not matter which pair of numbers is multiplied first. Look at this example.

EXAMPLE

Is $\frac{2}{3} = \frac{4}{6}$ a true proportion? $\frac{2}{3} \diagdown\!\!\!\!\diagup \frac{4}{6}$ Cross-multiply.

$$(2)(6) = 12 \text{ and } (3)(4) = 12$$

Since you get the same result (12), then $\frac{2}{3} = \frac{4}{6}$ is a true proportion. If you get different results when you cross-multiply, the ratios are not equal.

PRACTICE

Use cross-multiplying to tell whether the proportion is true or false. Write *true* or *false*.

a	b	c

1. $\frac{8}{12} = \frac{6}{9}$ _____true_____ $\frac{4}{5} = \frac{9}{10}$ _____ $\frac{16}{24} = \frac{2}{3}$ _____

$\frac{8}{12} \diagdown\!\!\!\!\diagup \frac{6}{9}$ $72 = 72$

2. $\frac{8}{10} = \frac{11}{15}$ _____ $\frac{6}{10} = \frac{12}{20}$ _____ $\frac{7}{8} = \frac{21}{24}$ _____

3. $\frac{18}{20} = \frac{9}{10}$ _____ $\frac{8}{16} = \frac{10}{20}$ _____ $\frac{8}{27} = \frac{2}{6}$ _____

Solving Proportions with an Unknown

To solve a proportion that contains an unknown, cross-multiply and solve the resulting equation. Check your answer in the original proportion.

Solve: $\frac{4}{6} = \frac{x}{18}$

$$\frac{4}{6} = \frac{x}{18}$$

$(4)(18) = 6x$ Cross-multiply.

$72 = 6x$

$\frac{72}{6} = \frac{6x}{6}$ Divide.

$12 = x$

Check: $\frac{4}{6} = \frac{x}{18}$

$\frac{4}{6} = \frac{12}{18}$

$4(18) = 6(12)$

$72 = 72$

PRACTICE

Solve.

        a   *b*   *c*

1. $\frac{5}{10} = \frac{10}{x}$ $\frac{50}{60} = \frac{5}{x}$ $\frac{25}{3} = \frac{100}{x}$

     $5x = (10)(10)$

     $5x = 100$

     $\frac{5x}{5} = \frac{100}{5}$

     $x = 20$

2. $\frac{7}{9} = \frac{21}{x}$ $\frac{4}{15} = \frac{8}{x}$ $\frac{5}{8} = \frac{x}{16}$

3. $\frac{5}{x} = \frac{15}{9}$ $\frac{20}{x} = \frac{5}{4}$ $\frac{x}{12} = \frac{25}{3}$

4. $\frac{12}{4} = \frac{x}{7}$ $\frac{x}{4} = \frac{5}{10}$ $\frac{x}{11} = \frac{10}{55}$

Using Proportions to Solve Problems

There are many problems that you can solve by setting up and solving proportions.

EXAMPLE

If Paul can walk 15 miles in 6 hours, how far can he walk, at the same rate, in 8 hours?

Let x = number of miles he can walk in 8 hours.

$\frac{15}{6} = \frac{x}{8}$

$6x = 120$

$x = 20$ He can walk 20 miles in 8 hours.

Check: $\frac{15}{6} = \frac{x}{8}$

$\frac{15}{6} = \frac{20}{8}$

$8(15) = 6(20)$

$120 = 120$

PRACTICE

Solve.

1. Martina bought 6 feet of wire for $21.66. How much would 10 feet of the same wire have cost?

Let x = the cost of 10 feet of wire.

$\frac{21.66}{6} = \frac{x}{10}$

$6x = 216.60$

$x = \$36.10$

Answer _____$36.10_____

2. Kristen bought a 14-ounce bottle of catsup for 91¢. At the same rate, how much would a 20-ounce bottle cost?

Answer _____

3. Carlos used $3.20 worth of gasoline to drive 68 miles. How many dollars worth of gas will he use to drive 85 miles?

Answer _____

4. The tax on a piece of property valued at $20,000 was $264. At the same rate, what would be the tax on a piece of property valued at $22,000?

Answer _____

5. A train is traveling at the rate of 75 miles per hour. At this speed, how far will it travel in 40 minutes? (Hint: Change 1 hour to minutes.)

Answer _____

6. Clint bought 3 yards of fabric for $15.75. How much would 5 yards of the same fabric have cost?

Answer _____

Unit 10 Measurement, Ratios, and Proportions

Direct Variation

In the formula $D = rt$, distance equals the rate times the time. If a car travels at a constant rate of r miles per hour for 3 hours, the distance D that it travels can be found by using the equation $D = r \times 3$. If the car doubles its time, it will double its distance. If the car triples its time, it will triple its distance. The distance traveled **varies directly** as the time varies. This is an example of **direct variation**.

PRACTICE

Complete the tables.

1. $D = rt$

r	50	50	50	50	50
t	1	2	3	4	5
D	50				

Distance varies directly as the time varies.

2. $A = lw$

w	10	10	10	10	10	10	10
l	2	4	6	8	10	12	14
A	20						

Area varies directly as the length varies.

3. $A = \frac{1}{2}bh$

b	6	6	6	6	6	6	6
h	2	4	6	8	10	12	14
A	6						

Area varies directly as the height varies.

Similar Triangles

Two triangles are **similar** if the **corresponding** angles are the same size and if the ratios of the lengths of the corresponding sides are equal. Since the ratios are equal, they form a proportion.

Find the length of side YZ.

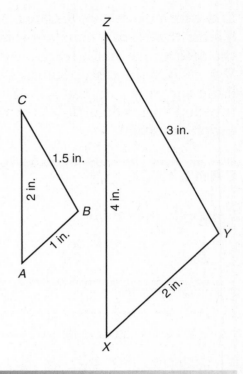

$$\frac{side\ AB}{side\ XY} = \frac{side\ BC}{side\ YZ}$$

$$\frac{AB}{XY} = \frac{BC}{YZ}$$

$$\frac{1}{2} = \frac{1.5}{x}$$

$$1(x) = 2(1.5)$$

$$x = 3$$

The length of YZ is 3 in.

Check: $1(3) = 2(1.5)$

$$3 = 3$$

PRACTICE

Complete these proportions for the similar triangles above.

      a   b   c   d

1. $\dfrac{AB}{BC} = \dfrac{XY}{\boxed{YZ}}$ $\dfrac{BC}{YZ} = \dfrac{AC}{\boxed{}}$ $\dfrac{XY}{AB} = \dfrac{\boxed{}}{BC}$ $\dfrac{AB}{AC} = \dfrac{XY}{\boxed{}}$

$\dfrac{1}{1.5} = \dfrac{2}{\boxed{3}}$ $\dfrac{1.5}{3} = \dfrac{2}{\boxed{}}$ $\dfrac{2}{1} = \dfrac{\boxed{}}{1.5}$ $\dfrac{1}{2} = \dfrac{2}{\boxed{}}$

2. $\dfrac{AC}{XZ} = \dfrac{\boxed{AB}}{XY}$ $\dfrac{BC}{\boxed{}} = \dfrac{YZ}{XY}$ $\dfrac{YZ}{BC} = \dfrac{\boxed{}}{AC}$ $\dfrac{XY}{AB} = \dfrac{\boxed{}}{AC}$

$\dfrac{\boxed{2}}{\boxed{4}} = \dfrac{\boxed{1}}{\boxed{2}}$ $\dfrac{\boxed{}}{\boxed{}} = \dfrac{\boxed{}}{\boxed{}}$ $\dfrac{\boxed{}}{\boxed{}} = \dfrac{\boxed{}}{\boxed{}}$ $\dfrac{\boxed{}}{\boxed{}} = \dfrac{\boxed{}}{\boxed{}}$

3. $\dfrac{XY}{XZ} = \dfrac{\boxed{}}{\boxed{}}$ $\dfrac{YZ}{XZ} = \dfrac{\boxed{}}{\boxed{}}$ $\dfrac{AC}{BC} = \dfrac{\boxed{}}{\boxed{}}$ $\dfrac{AC}{AB} = \dfrac{\boxed{}}{\boxed{}}$

$\dfrac{\boxed{}}{\boxed{}} = \dfrac{\boxed{}}{\boxed{}}$ $\dfrac{\boxed{}}{\boxed{}} = \dfrac{\boxed{}}{\boxed{}}$ $\dfrac{\boxed{}}{\boxed{}} = \dfrac{\boxed{}}{\boxed{}}$ $\dfrac{\boxed{}}{\boxed{}} = \dfrac{\boxed{}}{\boxed{}}$

Using Similar Triangles

Proportions can help you solve for the lengths of sides in similar triangles.

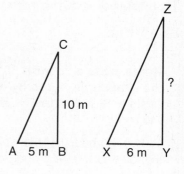

EXAMPLE

Triangles ABC and XYZ are similar. What is the length of YZ?

You can solve this using two methods.

$$\frac{AB}{XY} = \frac{BC}{YZ}$$

$$\frac{5}{6} = \frac{10}{YZ}$$ or

$$5YZ = 60$$

$$YZ = 12$$

$$\frac{AB}{BC} = \frac{XY}{YZ}$$

$$\frac{5}{10} = \frac{6}{YZ}$$

$$5YZ = 60$$

$$YZ = 12$$

PRACTICE

Set up and solve a proportion to solve each problem.

1. Triangles ABC and XYZ are similar. What is the length of XY?

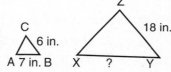

$$\frac{7}{XY} = \frac{6}{18}$$

$$6XY = 126$$

$$XY = 21$$

Answer _____ *XY = 21 in.* _____

2. Triangles ABC and XYZ are similar. What is the length of YZ?

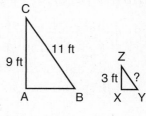

Answer _____

3. Triangles ABC and XYZ are similar. What is the length of BC?

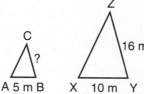

Answer _____

4. Triangles ABC and XYZ are similar. What is the length of BC?

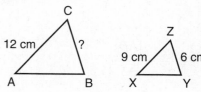

Answer _____

5. Triangles ABC and XYZ are similar. What is the length of XY?

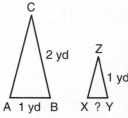

Answer _____

6. Triangles ABC and XYZ are similar. What is the length of YZ?

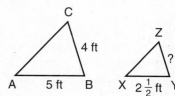

Answer _____

Using Proportion in Similar Figures

You can use proportions to solve problems about similar figures.

EXAMPLE

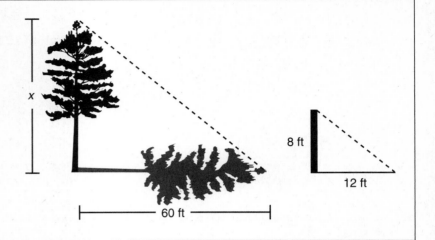

A tree casts a shadow 60 feet long. At the same time, a nearby 8-foot post casts a 12-foot shadow. How tall is the tree?

To find the height of the tree, use similar triangles to form a proportion. Then solve.

$$\frac{x}{60} = \frac{8}{12}$$

$$12x = 8(60)$$

$$x = \frac{8(60)}{12}$$

$$x = 40 \quad \text{The tree is 40 feet tall.}$$

PRACTICE

Draw a picture. Use a proportion. Solve.

1. A flagpole casts a 75-foot shadow at the same time a nearby tree 20 feet tall casts a shadow of 30 feet. How tall is the flagpole?

   Answer _____

2. A skyscraper casts a shadow 111 feet long at the same time a nearby 50-foot telephone pole casts a shadow of 10 feet long. How high is the skyscraper?

   Answer _____

3. A telephone pole casts a shadow 30 feet long while a nearby fence post 4 feet high casts a shadow 3 feet long. How high is the pole?

   Answer _____

4. A grain silo casts a shadow of 40 feet while a nearby fence post casts a shadow of 2 feet. The fence post is 5 feet high. How tall is the grain silo?

   Answer _____

Unit 10 Measurement, Ratios, and Proportions

The Pythagorean Theorem

The side opposite the right angle in a right triangle is called the **hypotenuse.** Every right triangle has the property that the square of the hypotenuse is equal to the sum of the squares of the **legs.** This is called the **Pythagorean Theorem.**

The Pythagorean Theorem is written $c^2 = a^2 + b^2$. It can be used to find the length of one side of a right triangle if you know the lengths of the other two sides.

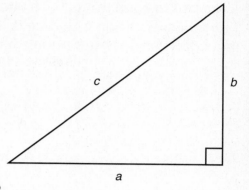

EXAMPLE 1

Solve for the hypotenuse.

$c^2 = a^2 + b^2$

$c^2 = (8)^2 + (6)^2$

$c^2 = 64 + 36$

$c^2 = 100$

$c = \sqrt{100}$

$c = 10$

The hypotenuse of the triangle is 10.

EXAMPLE 2

Solve for the missing leg.

$c^2 = a^2 + b^2$

$(15)^2 = (9)^2 + (b)^2$

$225 = 81 + b^2$

$225 - 81 = b^2$

$144 = b^2$

$144 = b$

$12 = b$

The missing leg of the triangle is 12.

PRACTICE

Find the missing length in each right triangle, using $c^2 = a^2 + b^2$.

a	b	c
1. $a = 5, b = 12, c = ?$	$a = 7, c = 25, b = ?$	$a = 3, b = 4, c = ?$
2. $b = 40, c = 41, a = ?$	$a = 1.2, b = 1.6, c = ?$	$a = 15, c = 17, b = ?$

Problem-Solving Strategy: Select a Strategy

A marathon runner has been running for $1\frac{1}{2}$ hours at 11.6 miles per hour. The race is 26.2 miles long. How much farther does the runner have to run?

Problem-Solving Strategies

Choose an Operation
Make a Drawing
Complete a Pattern
Use Logic
Use Estimation
Use a Formula
Use Guess and Check
Work Backwards

Understand the problem.

- **What do you want to know?**
  how many miles the runner has to run to finish

- **What information is given?**
  The runner has been running $1\frac{1}{2}$ hours at 11.6 miles per hour; the race is 26.2 miles long.

Plan how to solve it.

- **What strategy can you use?**
  You can choose operations to calculate how much farther the runner has to run.

Solve it.

- **How can you use this strategy to solve the problem?**
  Since this is a two-step problem, select the strategy *Choose an Operation* for each step. Multiply the time by the speed to find the distance the runner has already run. Then subtract this from the total distance of the race.

  $$\begin{array}{r} \textbf{11.6 miles per hour} \\ \times\ \textbf{1.5 hours} \\ \hline \textbf{17.4 miles traveled} \end{array}$$

  $$\begin{array}{r} \textbf{26.2 miles total} \\ -\textbf{17.4 miles traveled} \\ \hline \textbf{8.8 miles to go} \end{array}$$

- **What is the answer?**
  The runner has to run another 8.8 miles to complete the race.

Look back and check your answer.

- **Is your answer reasonable?**
  You can check both steps by using addition and division.

  $$\begin{array}{r} \textbf{8.8 miles to go} \\ +\textbf{17.4 miles traveled} \\ \hline \textbf{26.2 miles total} \end{array}$$

  $$\textbf{1.5 hours}\overline{)\textbf{17.4 miles traveled}}^{\textbf{11.6 miles per hour}}$$

  The answer is reasonable.

Select a strategy to solve.

1. Eduardo deposited $1,500 in a savings account. The interest rate was 3.75% annually. How much interest will he earn in 5 years, if the interest remained the same each year?

Answer _____

2. A rectangular picture has a width of 48 centimeters. The area of the picture is 3,456 square centimeters. How long is the picture?

Answer _____

3. Two years ago the average attendance at a Spartans basketball game was 1,811 people. Last year the average attendance was 1,960. This year the average attendance was 2,109. If this trend continues, what will the average attendance be next year?

Answer _____

4. The sum of the ages of Diane and her younger brother is 18. The product of their ages is 45. How old is each person?

Diane _____

Diane's brother _____

5. Raheem, Katarina, and Harold live in Richmond, Brookdale, and Montague, but not necessarily in that order. Katarina did not choose a home in Richmond. Neither Katarina nor Raheem lives in Brookdale. Which person lives in which town?

Richmond _____

Brookdale _____

Montague _____

6. Theodora wants to install wallpaper on a wall in her den. The wall is 18 feet long and 8 feet high. Wallpaper costs $0.45 per square foot. How much will the wallpaper cost?

Answer _____

Change each measurement to the unit given.

	a		b		c

1. 60 g = _____ kg   6 gal = _____ pt   16 mL = _____ L

2. 200 cm = _____ m   10 L = _____ mL   66 in. = _____ ft _____ in.

3. 1.5 T = _____ lb   42.41 kg = _____ g   5.2 km = _____ m

Write a fraction for each ratio.

          a   b

4. the ratio of seconds in one minute to   the ratio of 7 pencils to 13 erasers
   minutes in two hours

   Ratio: _____   Ratio: _____

Use cross-multiplication to tell whether the proportion is true or false. Write *true* or *false*.

          a   b   c

5. $\frac{2}{6} = \frac{5}{15}$ _____ $\frac{4}{7} = \frac{12}{14}$ _____ $\frac{3}{12} = \frac{10}{40}$ _____

Solve.

          a   b   c

6. $\frac{4}{10} = \frac{x}{50}$ $\frac{18}{30} = \frac{6}{x}$ $\frac{7}{3} = \frac{x}{15}$

Solve.

7. Jack swam 4 laps in 15 minutes. At the same rate, how long will it take him to swim 12 laps?

8. The length of the hypotenuse of a right triangle measures 2.5 inches. If one leg measures 1.5 inches, what is the length of the other leg?

   Answer _____   Answer _____

---

9. The ratio of the edges of two cubes is $\frac{1}{3}$. What is the ratio of the volumes?

10. A tree cast a 24-foot shadow at the same time a fence post 5 feet high cast a 4-foot shadow. How tall is the tree?

   Answer _____   Answer _____

Write the value of the underlined digit.

	a	*b*	*c*	*d*
1.	7<u>8</u>,309 _____	3<u>0</u>8 _____	7.<u>2</u>15 _____	1.00<u>6</u> _____

Find each answer.

	a	*b*	*c*	*d*
2.	8,0 9 8 +1,4 5 6	2 3,0 6 7 + 8,6 9 2	6 5 9 −1 9 3	3,8 7 0 −1,7 7 9

3.	3 6 ×2 4	8 2 5 ×1 7 3	18)‾4 6 9	9)‾8 2 8

Line up the digits. Then find each answer.

	a	*b*	*c*
4.	294 − 41 = _____	785 + 928 = _____	11,382 − 807 = _____
5.	27 × 316 = _____	168 ÷ 3 = _____	2,543 ÷ 62 = _____

Simplify.

	a	*b*	*c*	*d*	*e*
6.	$\frac{6}{15}$ = _____	$\frac{12}{8}$ = _____	$\frac{12}{36}$ = _____	$\frac{42}{9}$ = _____	$\frac{6}{50}$ = _____

Add or subtract. Simplify.

	a	*b*	*c*	*d*
7.	$\frac{3}{8}$ $+\frac{5}{8}$	$9\frac{3}{10}$ $+4\frac{4}{5}$	$9\frac{5}{8}$ $-6\frac{1}{3}$	$\frac{1}{3}$ $-\frac{1}{10}$

Solve.

8. The storekeeper sold $9\frac{1}{4}$ yards of fabric from a piece of fabric 53 yards long. How much was left in the original piece?

9. Oranges sell for 46¢ per pound. How much will Ted have to pay for $1\frac{1}{2}$ pounds?

Answer _____

Answer _____

Final Review

Multiply or divide. Use cancellation when possible. Simplify.

	a	*b*	*c*
10.	$\frac{5}{6} \times 12 =$	$1\frac{3}{5} \times 10 =$	$1\frac{2}{3} \times 2\frac{1}{4} =$
11.	$\frac{3}{5} \div \frac{2}{5} =$	$3\frac{3}{10} \div \frac{2}{5} =$	$2\frac{1}{4} \div 1\frac{1}{2} =$

Write each decimal as a fraction or mixed number.

	a	*b*	*c*	*d*
12.	$0.3 =$ _____	$1.17 =$ _____	$0.009 =$ _____	$0.01 =$ _____

Write each fraction as a decimal.

	a	*b*	*c*	*d*
13.	$\frac{8}{10} =$ _____	$\frac{23}{100} =$ _____	$\frac{5}{100} =$ _____	$\frac{8}{1,000} =$ _____

Find each answer. Write zeros as needed.

	a	*b*	*c*	*d*
14.	7.3 8 +0.1 9	4 8.0 2 +2 1.0 8 6	8.9 5 −1.6 8	1 5.3 − 7.2 9
15.	9.0 6 × 1 3	7.6 9 ×0.1 3	$92\overline{)2\ 2.7\ 7}$	$1.5\overline{)1\ 0.0\ 5}$

Write each percent as a decimal and as a fraction. Simplify.

	a	*b*
16.	$35\% =$ _____ = _____	$8\% =$ _____ = _____

Find each number.

	a	*b*
17.	25% of 80	What percent of 40 is 8?
18.	10% of what number is 9?	72% of 50

Find the simple interest.

	a	*b*
19.	\$350 at $4\frac{1}{2}\%$ for 1 year	\$600 at 7.1% for 2 years

Final Review

Evaluate each expression if $x = 2$, $y = {}^-3$, and $z = 5$.

             a   *b*   *c*   *d*

20. $12 \div 2y = $ _____ $4x - y = $ _____ $^-3z^2 = $ _____ $\dfrac{x^2 + 16}{z} = $ _____

Find the slope of each line that passes through the given points.

             a   *b*   *c*

21. $(2,3)$, $(4,5)$ $(^-9,1)$, $(2,^-8)$ $(6,0)$, $(7,^-6)$

Classify each angle. Write *right, acute, obtuse,* or *straight.*

             a   *b*   *c*   *d*

22.

_____ _____ _____ _____

Classify each polygon. Write *regular* or *irregular.*

             a   *b*   *c*   *d*

23.

_____ _____ _____ _____

Classify each triangle by its sides. Write *equilateral, isosceles,* or *scalene.*

             a   *b*   *c*   *d*

24.

      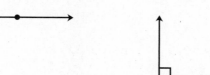   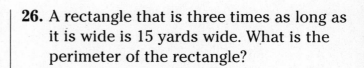   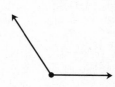

_____ _____ _____ _____

Solve.

25. A triangle has a base of 9 meters and a height of 12 meters. What is the area?

26. A rectangle that is three times as long as it is wide is 15 yards wide. What is the perimeter of the rectangle?

Answer _____   Answer _____

Final Review

Solve each equation using the given value of *x* or *y*. Write the ordered pair which makes the equation true.

a	*b*	*c*

27. $3x + 2y = 9$ when $x = {}^-3$ $4x - y = 3$ when $y = 1$ $^-2x + 3y = 7$ when $x = 4$

Change each measurement to the unit given.

a	*b*	*c*

28. 10 qt = _____ gal _____ qt   8 pt = _____ c   6,500 m = _____ cm

29. 16 in. = _____ ft _____ in.   1.5 T = _____ lb   6 mL = _____ L

30. 4 kg = _____ g   230 mm = _____ cm   9 L = _____ mL

Solve.

a	*b*	*c*	*d*

31. $x - 15 = 7$ $6x + 9 = 29 + 2x$ $7x = {}^-42$ $6x + 1 = 61$

32. $3x + 5x = 72$ $10x - 4x = 36$ $x + 5 = 19$ $\frac{12}{5} = \frac{x}{15}$

33. $\frac{5}{x} = \frac{40}{64}$ $\frac{x}{8} = \frac{12}{16}$ $5x - 1 = 24$ $6 = 2x - 20$

Write a fraction for each ratio.

a	*b*

34. the ratio of days in a week to months in a year

Ratio: _____

the ratio of 3 teachers to 24 students

Ratio: _____

Solve.

a	*b*	*c*	*d*

35. $3 + 10x \geq 33$ $17 < 2 + x$ $10x > 5x + 15$ $^-2x - 50 \leq 30$

Solve.

36. A right triangle with a hypotenuse 17 centimeters long has a side 15 centimeters long. What is the length of the third side?

Answer _____

37. A museum has five floors. On each floor there are 3 bathrooms. What is the ratio of floors to bathrooms in this museum?

Answer _____

about how many an approximate number (p. 14)

absolute value the distance a number is from 0 on a number line (p. 148)

acute angle an angle whose measure is less than 90° (p. 195)

acute triangle a triangle with all three angles less than 90° (p. 196)

addends numbers being added (p. 11)

algebra the study of variables and operations with variables (p. 146)

algebraic expression a combination including one or more variables and possibly one or more numbers and operations (p. 154)

angle a figure formed by two rays or line segments with a common endpoint (p. 195)

area number of square units (p. 202)

base a number used as a repeated factor (p. 160)

base (of a triangle) any segment to which the height of the triangle is drawn (p. 202)

cancellation the process of dividing a common factor from a numerator and a denominator in order to simplify a fractional expression before multiplying (p. 75)

capacity the volume of a container in terms of liquid measure (p. 216)

circumference the distance around a circle (p. 209)

coefficient a number multiplied by a variable in an expression (p. 155)

common factor a number that is a factor of two or more numbers (p. 75)

congruent figures that are the same shape and size (p. 196)

constant a number or symbol whose value does not change (p. 155)

coordinate plane a reference system used to locate points (p. 179)

coordinates a pair of numbers (x,y) locating a point on a coordinate plane (p. 179)

corresponding matching (p. 226)

cross-multiply to multiply each numerator in a proportion by the denominator on the other side of the equation in order to see if the fractions or ratios are equal (p. 222)

cubed raised to the third power (p. 161)

cubic made up of three dimensions (p. 208)

current value the amount an item is worth at the present time (p. 140)

customary units (of measurement) basic units of length, capacity, and weight as used in the United States (p. 216)

decimal a number with a decimal point (p. 96)

decimal point a dot in a decimal that separates the whole number and decimal parts (p. 96)

degrees units for measuring angles (p. 195)

denominator the bottom number of a fraction (p. 52)

diameter a line segment crossing through the center point of a circle, with both ends on the circle (p. 209)

digit one of the ten numerals 0, 1, 2, 3, 4, 5, 6, 7, 8, and 9 (p. 12)

dimensions measureable amounts, such as length, width, and height, of a figure (p. 204)

direct variation the manner in which one value of a variable changes as another variable's value changes (p. 225)

dividend an amount being divided (p. 44)

divisor a number that divides another number (p. 38)

domain the set of all x values (p. 178)

equal to having the same value (pp. 13, 97)

equilateral triangle a triangle with three sides of equal length (p. 196)

equivalent fraction a fraction that has the same value as another fraction (p. 54)

estimate to find an answer that is close to the exact answer (p. 18)

evaluate to find the simplest value for an expression (p. 153)

exponent a number that indicates how many times a given base is used as a factor (p. 160)

face a flat surface on a solid figure (p. 204)

factors numbers which when multiplied by other numbers form a product (p. 33)

formula an equation for a mathematical rule (p. 199)

fraction a number in the form of $\frac{a}{b}$ (p. 52)

function a set of ordered pairs in which each x-value has only one y-value (p. 178)

gram (g) the basic unit of mass (p. 218)

greater than (>) a comparison of two numbers, where the greater number is left of the > symbol (pp. 13, 97)

height (of a triangle) a perpendicular line segment from any vertex to the opposite side (p. 202)

hexagon a polygon with six sides and six angles (p. 197)

higher terms an equivalent fraction that is not in its simplest form (p. 54)

horizontal axis the left-right axis on a coordinate plane (p. 179)

hypotenuse the side opposite the right angle in a right triangle (p. 229)

improper fraction a fraction with a numerator that is greater than or equal to the denominator (p. 53)

inequality a mathematical sentence that compares amounts that are not equal (p. 186)

integers whole numbers and their opposites (p. 147)

interest an amount of money that is paid for borrowed money (p. 138)

intersect to cross at one point (p. 179)

intersecting lines two lines that cross at one point (p. 194)

invert to switch the numerator and the denominator (p. 84)

irrational numbers numbers that cannot be written as $\frac{a}{b}$, where a and b are integers and $b \neq 0$. Non-terminating, non-repeating decimals are irrational numbers. (p. 147)

irregular polygon a polygon where not all the sides or angles are of equal measure (p. 197)

isosceles triangle a triangle with two sides of equal length (p. 196)

kilogram (kg) one thousand grams (p. 218)

least common denominator (LCD) the least number (other than 0) that is a multiple of two or more denominators (p. 54)

legs the two sides that form the right angle of a right triangle (p. 229)

less than (<) a comparison of two numbers where the lesser number is left of the < symbol (pp. 13, 97)

like terms two or more terms with the same variable or variables (p. 166)

line an endless straight path (p. 194)

linear equations two-variable equations whose solutions lie on lines (p. 183)

linear function a function whose graph is a straight line (p. 180)

line segment a straight path between two points (p. 194)

liter (L) metric unit of capacity (p. 219)

lowest terms a fraction in which the only common factor of the numerator and denominator is 1; also called **simplest terms** (p. 55)

mass a measure of the amount of matter in an object (p. 218)

matter what objects are made of (p. 218)

metric the system of measurement that uses base 10 and meters, liters, grams, etc. (p. 217)

milliliter (mL) one thousandth of a liter (p. 219)

mixed number a number that includes a whole number and a fraction (p. 53)

multiplier a number by which a given number is multiplied (p. 118)

natural numbers counting numbers (p. 147)

numerator the top number of a fraction (p. 52)

numerical expression a combination of numbers and at least one operation (p. 152)

obtuse angle an angle whose measure is greater than 90° (p. 195)

obtuse triangle a triangle with one angle greater than 90° (p. 196)

octagon a polygon with eight sides and eight angles (p. 197)

opposites same numbers with opposite signs (positive and negative) (p. 147)

ordered pair a pair of numbers in the form (x,y) (p. 178)

order of operations the order in which operations in an expression or equation should be performed (p. 152)

origin the point (0,0) on a coordinate plane (p. 179)

parallel lines lines that never intersect and are always the same distance apart (p. 194)

parallelogram a quadrilateral with 2 sets of parallel sides (p. 206)

part a percent of a number (p. 134)

pentagon a polygon with five sides and five angles (p. 197)

percent out of one hundred, per hundred (p. 126)

percent of decrease the percent to which a number becomes lesser (p. 141)

percent of increase the percent to which a number becomes greater (p. 140)

perimeter the distance around the outside of a figure (p. 198)

periods groups of three digits in large numbers that are separated by commas (p. 12)

perpendicular lines lines that intersect to form four 90° angles (p. 194)

pi (π) the ratio of the circumference of a circle to the diameter, about $\frac{22}{7}$, or 3.14. (p. 209)

place-value chart a table of the positional value that each digit in a number represents (p. 12)

plane a flat surface that extends without end (p. 197)

point an exact location in space (p. 194)

polygon a closed plane figure that has three or more sides (p. 197)

power of ten the number obtained when 10 is raised to an exponent (p. 118)

principal an amount loaned or borrowed (p. 138)

prism a three-dimensional figure with two parallel and congruent bottom faces and with lateral faces that are parallelograms (p. 204)

product the answer to a multiplication problem (p. 33)

proportion an equation stating that two ratios are equal (p. 222)

Pythagorean Theorem the rule that the square of a right triangle's hypotenuse equals the sum of the squares of the legs ($c^2 = a^2 + b^2$) (p. 229)

quadrants four parts formed by the x- and y-axes on a coordinate plane (p. 179)

quadrilateral a polygon with four sides and four angles (p. 197)

quotient the answer to a division problem (p. 37)

radical the root of a number (p. 163)

radicand the number under the radical sign (p. 163)

radius a straight line from the center point of a circle to a point on the circle (p. 209)

range the set of all y values (p. 178)

rate the percent in a percent problem (p. 134)

ratio a fraction used to compare two quantities (pp. 184, 220)

rational numbers numbers that can be written as fractions of the form $\frac{a}{b}$, where a and b are integers and $b \neq 0$ (p. 147)

ray an endless straight path starting at a point (p. 194)

real numbers all rational and irrational numbers (p. 147)

reciprocal the number that when multiplied by another number results in 1 (p. 84)

regroup to exchange amounts of equal value to rename a number. For example, 56 is 5 tens and 6 ones, or 4 tens and 16 ones. (p. 16)

regular polygon a polygon having all sides of equal length and all angles of equal measure (p. 197)

relation a set of ordered pairs (p. 178)

remainder a number left after one number is divided by another (p. 38)

right angle an angle of 90° (p. 195)

right triangle a triangle with one angle equal to 90° (p. 196)

rise vertical change on a coordinate plane (p. 184)

rounded numbers numbers close to the actual values, usually in multiples of ten (p. 14)

rules of exponents the standard rules of using exponents in computations (p. 172)

run horizontal change on a coordinate plane (p. 184)

scalene triangle a triangle with no sides the same length (p. 196)

scientific notation a method of writing numbers using powers of 10 (p. 162)

set a group (p. 147)

similar having corresponding angles of equal measures and corresponding sides of proportional lengths (p. 226)

simple interest interest paid only on the amount of money borrowed (p. 138)

simplest terms the form $\frac{a}{b}$ in which the only common factor of the numerator and denominator is 1 (p. 55)

simplify to reduce a fraction or expression to its simplest form (p. 55)

slope the ratio of vertical change (rise) to horizontal change (run) (p. 184)

solutions values that make an equation or inequality true (p. 181)

squared raised to the second power (p. 160)

square root a number that when multiplied by itself results in a given number (p. 163)

standard form the customary method of writing whole numbers (p. 162)

straight angle an angle of 180° (p. 195)

sum the answer to an addition problem (p. 11)

surface area the total area of all faces of a prism or other object (p. 204)

term a number, variable, or combination of a number and variable(s) between the operation signs of an expression (p. 155)

trapezoid a quadrilateral with exactly one pair of parallel sides (p. 206)

trial quotient a possible answer to a division problem (p. 38)

triangle a polygon with three sides and three angles (p. 196)

variable a letter or symbol that represents a number (p. 146)

vertex a common endpoint of two rays or line segments that form an angle (p. 195)

vertical axis the up-down axis on a coordinate plane (p. 179)

volume number of cubic units that will fit inside a three-dimensional area (p. 208)

whole a number at 100 percent (p. 134)

whole numbers natural numbers (counting numbers) and the number 0 (pp. 12, 147)

x-axis the horizontal axis on a coordinate plane (p. 179)

y-axis the vertical axis on a coordinate plane (p. 179)

Page 5

	a	b	c
1.	>	>	<

	a		b
2.	135 398 516		0.486 40.9 48.6

3. a. 8 hundreds   b. 6 thousands
    c. 4 hundredths   d. 3 tenths

	a	b	c	d
4.	400	800	800	25,400
5.	1,098	6,611	167,810	15 R3
6.	9,127	49,737	8,808	79 R5

	a	b	c	d	e
7.	$\frac{2}{3}$	$5\frac{3}{5}$	$\frac{1}{7}$	$4\frac{8}{9}$	6
8.	$\frac{3}{4}$	$9\frac{13}{30}$	$1\frac{5}{7}$	$1\frac{1}{2}$	

Page 6

	a	b	c		a	b	c
9.	20	$4\frac{4}{7}$	$\frac{2}{3}$	10.	$1\frac{2}{3}$	$8\frac{1}{4}$	$\frac{7}{10}$

	a	b	c	d
11.	$\frac{3}{10}$	$4\frac{13}{20}$	$3\frac{3}{50}$	$\frac{1}{8}$
12.	6.7	2.55	0.16	0.005
13.	4.54	76.67	0.06006	40.1

	a	b		a	b
14.	0.08; $\frac{2}{25}$	0.52; $\frac{13}{25}$	15.	40	25%
16.	85	91.2			

17. $301.50   18. $8.75

Page 7

	a	b
19.	$13.13	$36.80

	a	b	c	d
20.	3	2	4	601
21.	⁻2	⁻11	⁻78	19
22.	11	5	50	50

23. $50x$ $z - 17$

	a	b	c	d
24.	⁻11	32	⁻24	7
25.	$x = 29$	$x = 24$	$x = 5$	$x = 9$
26.	$x = 12$	$x = 6$	$x = 13$	$x = 5$
27.	36	⁻8	7	81
28.	3,000	12,000	607,000	890

29. (2, 3) and (⁻4, ⁻3)

Page 8

	a	b	c
30.	(2, ⁻4)	(⁻1, ⁻3$\frac{1}{3}$)	(3, 4)

31. a.   b.

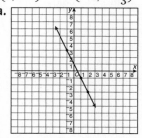

	a	b	c	d
32.	⁻1	$\frac{7}{2}$	$\frac{9}{7}$	
33.	$x > ⁻17$	$x \leq 32$	$x \geq ⁻15$	$x < ⁻8$
34.	scalene	right	equilateral	obtuse
35.	regular	irregular	irregular	regular

Page 9

	a	b	c
36.	3 gal 3 qt	0.04 km	2 lb
37.	3 ft 4 in.	56,000 g	0.334 L
38.	$\frac{1}{4}$	$\frac{7}{12}$	
39.	$x = 35$	$x = 30$	$x = 2$

40. XY is 12 feet.   41. MO is 30 feet.

	a	b	c
42.	$b = 4$	$c = 10$	$a = 5$

43. 21 feet   44. 108 square inches

Page 10

	a	b	c	d	e	f	g	h	i	j
1.	2	3	1	5	6	8	7	4	10	9
2.	7	3	4	11	9	10	2	8	6	5
3.	6	3	7	4	8	5	12	9	11	10
4.	9	13	11	5	6	10	8	4	7	12
5.	8	10	6	14	9	7	12	11	5	13
6.	12	10	6	11	15	8	14	7	13	9
7.	10	8	12	15	11	14	7	16	9	13
8.	8	11	17	10	15	9	14	12	16	13
9.	10	15	13	11	17	9	14	18	12	16

Page 11

	a	b	c	d	e	f	g	h	i
1.	12	13	11	10	15	17	12	15	16
2.	19	15	13	14	13	15	13	19	18
3.	20	18	19	20	20	23	20	22	23
4.	21	22	21	19	21	23	22	21	23
5.	24	19	20	22	22	23	17	22	20

Page 12

	a	b
1.	tens	ten thousands
2.	hundred thousands	millions
3.	5 ten thousands	9 ones
4.	3 millions	4 thousands

5. 645,310   6. 87,416
7. 10,089   8. eighty thousand, four hundred sixty-two
9. five hundred six   10. twelve thousand, nine hundred thirty-four

Page 13

	a	b	c		a	b	c
1.	<	>	<	2.	<	<	>
3.	=	>	<	4.	>	>	>
5.	<	>	=	6.	>	>	>
7.	<	<	>	8.	12	26	34
9.	425	523	643	10.	247	338	617
11.	133	245	873	12.	71	107	170
13.	335	683	836	14.	134	538	647
15.	384	700	916	16.	3,871	4,266	7,109

Page 14

	a	b	c	d
1.	60	80	50	40
2.	30	60	80	50
3.	30	90	20	100
4.	500	700	900	400
5.	800	500	300	200
6.	100	500	700	400
7.	2,500	5,500	6,200	3,700
8.	8,800	6,800	3,300	8,600
9.	18,300	44,200	36,700	11,800

Page 15

	a	b	c	d	e
1.	897	794	579	779	399
2.	777	970	937	999	797
3.	7,879	6,799	7,689	8,888	9,699
4.	7,618	5,899	9,899	9,969	7,378
5.	4,796	9,194	8,899	8,829	7,987
6.	37,787	57,735	68,886	58,788	99,999

Page 16

	a	b	c	d	e
1.	881	581	763	783	591
2.	764	571	882	954	863
3.	673	782	591	764	753
4.	827	508	518	927	756
5.	727	929	439	908	937
6.	871	637	827	884	454

Page 17

	a	b	c	d	e
1.	930	821	737	1,220	1,049
2.	602	1,016	658	202	1,372
3.	3,673	7,822	7,804	5,902	23,176
4.	796	381	5,534	10,590	23,024
5.	1,025	6,636	10,340		
6.	6,060	10,905	6,375		

Page 18

	a	b	c	d
1.	800	800	600	600
2.	1,100	800	700	900
3.	1,000	1,200	1,000	1,000
4.	1,600	1,400	900	700
5.	2,000	2,700	3,200	4,400

Page 19

	a	b	c	d	e
1.	924	862	1,333	862	1,528
2.	1,211	1,303	1,352	1,303	657
3.	887	1,505	1,042	899	1,742
4.	8,613	9,188	10,988	7,406	5,800
5.	12,453	4,821	7,569	6,191	12,001
6.	8,583	15,306	8,639	6,025	4,001
7.	1,049	689	6,584		
8.	4,853	7,003	7,180		
9.	9,876	9,029	10,201		

Page 20

	a	b	c	d	e	f	g	h	i	j
1.	5	4	4	1	9	4	3	2	5	3
2.	9	4	7	2	9	7	0	5	2	1
3.	7	2	7	3	2	6	3	2	4	8
4.	3	0	9	8	7	1	4	1	4	6
5.	7	8	9	7	8	9	6	8	9	7
6.	6	4	8	6	9	5	2	3	2	1

	a	b	c	d	e	f	g	h	i	j
7.	9	7	6	3	4	1	6	4	3	8
8.	6	0	5	0	0	3	0	9	5	5
9.	5	2	0	1	3	5	1	8	2	8

Page 21

	a	b	c	d	e
1.	13	43	10	61	22
2.	62	64	81	83	51
3.	24	48	65	55	61
4.	27	17	10	50	51
5.	112	534	233	411	126
6.	222	132	403	335	304

Page 22

	a	b	c	d	e
1.	233	110	513	450	448
2.	365	10	317	531	116
3.	5,223	6,432	1,520	3,151	1,636
4.	2,071	1,153	3,153	1,230	2,110
5.	161	2,203	1,260	1,200	1,140
6.	2,313	1,115	2,439	4,535	10

Page 23

	a	b	c	d	e
1.	38	44	27	74	32
2.	52	26	17	46	48
3.	47	38	47	59	39
4.	29	19	48	26	77
5.	42	37	32	71	35
6.	48	42	49	32	81

Page 24

	a	b	c	d	e
1.	277	363	661	81	154
2.	792	197	80	495	486
3.	558	181	280	699	132
4.	266	23	150	481	272
5.	190	215	781	205	345
6.	555	91	761	475	141

Page 25

	a	b	c	d	e
1.	359	188	189	266	265
2.	99	267	327	647	86
3.	83	398	578	186	79
4.	473	245	383	273	237
5.	599	199	472		

Page 26

	a	b	c	d
1.	300	300	200	100
2.	500	200	200	300
3.	100	600	0	100
4.	400	700	1,700	1,700
5.	2,000	1,700	4,000	2,300

Page 27

	a	b	c	d	e
1.	117	85	777	963	1,042
2.	45	55	334	335	264
3.	9,898	13,838	6,493	15,713	6,691
4.	6,223	3,217	3,737	6,232	3,573
5.	939	2,183	2,185	1,663	9,999
6.	12,241	33,427	22,166	34,850	77,458
7.	68,799	160,331	31,252	98,899	114,000
8.	21,070	742,500			

Page 29

1. Earl is 17, and Denise is 25.
2. 58 and 65
3. Jupiter has 16 moons, and Saturn has 18 moons.
4. Five 3-point and eleven 2-point.
5. Five minutes   6.   130 dB

Page 30

1. thirty-five thousand, eight hundred fourteen
2. two hundred eighty-one million, four hundred twenty-one thousand, nine hundred
3. 1,056   4.   100,800
5. fifty-six thousand, nine hundred forty-six
6. four thousand, four hundred
7. 1903   8.   5,526 miles
9. 29,035 feet   10.   8 red balls

Page 31

	a	b	c	d	e
1.	400	8,800	500	4,600	
2.	77	57	78	84	489
3.	747	918	752	1,104	10,223
4.	23	45	36	57	56
5.	523	306	294	558	3,461

6. 29,510 days   7.   18 years old and 20 years old

Page 32

	a	b	c	d	e	f	g	h	i	j
1.	5	24	0	2	9	28	12	0	30	0
2.	27	32	35	2	45	7	0	25	14	8
3.	49	10	42	24	12	24	18	18	12	32
4.	3	0	18	24	56	6	36	7	16	18
5.	14	72	36	21	48	72	30	64	63	28
6.	12	20	56	42	81	10	6	27	8	3
7.	54	63	54	21	4	9	36	8	15	40
8.	48	0	15	0	0	9	0	6	45	35
9.	40	16	5	1	6	20	4	8	4	16

Page 33

	a	b	c	d	e
1.	48	96	147	208	48
2.	144	299	882	671	528
3.	176	861	121	726	736

Page 34

	a	b	c	d	e
1.	236	84	351	782	
2.	162	100	378	108	136
3.	456	756	672	975	580
4.	768	216	559	651	1,003

Page 35

	a	b	c	d	e
1.	1,786	8,544	7,592	16,606	
2.	2,166	980	12,644	11,662	4,296
3.	5,504	7,315	7,056	7,350	23,644
4.	28,880	7,644	25,550	33,792	347,655

Page 36

	a	b	c	d	e
1.	693	824	448	996	848
2.	6,152	4,950	7,136	4,347	3,752
3.	6,792	6,075	4,675	4,788	2,592
4.	1,260	1,120	1,470	1,850	250
5.	1,325	2,162	5,220	2,166	448
6.	5,928	5,544	35,144	19,470	9,614
7.	16,716	34,632	1,704		

Page 37

	a	b		a	b
1.	3	6	2.	2	5

	a	b	c	d	e	f	g	h	i	j
3.	5	4	0	1	9	4	3	0	5	1
4.	9	4	7	2	9	1	0	5	2	1
5.	7	2	7	3	2	6	3	2	4	8
6.	3	0	9	8	7	1	4	6	4	6
7.	7	8	9	7	8	9	6	8	9	7
8.	6	4	8	6	9	5	2	3	2	0
9.	9	7	6	3	4	1	6	4	3	8
10.	6	0	5	0	7	3	1	0	5	5
11.	5	2	0	1	3	5	1	8	2	8

Page 38

	a	b	c	d
1.	15 R1	28 R2	12 R6	13 R3
2.	38 R3	60	103	26 R1

Page 39

	a	b	c	d	e
1.	23	21 R3	10 R4	10 R2	9 R5
2.	142	121	114 R2	144 R2	34 R2
3.	29 R3	20	31 R5	185 R3	178
4.	16 R4	100 R7	123 R4	62 R6	163
5.	64	6 R3	70 R3		

Mixed Practice

	a	b	c	d
1.	708	4,417	52,939	19,079
2.	3,000	963	14,432	49,932

Page 40

	a	b	c	d
1.	42 R1	22 R2	22 R1	19
2.	61 R1	51 R2	71 R3	258 R1
3.	209	61 R3	31 R3	315 R1

Page 41

	a	b	c	d
1.	22 R3	21 R7	20 R10	204
2.	9 R5	22 R20	4 R24	8 R55
3.	52 R1	113 R39	31 R31	70 R1

Page 42

	a	b	c	d
1.	3 R27	4 R42	5 R10	5 R5
2.	7 R9	7 R48	6 R37	6 R26
3.	3 R79	7 R28	5 R6	6 R4
4.	7 R6	7 R8	9	6 R48
5.	5 R90	6 R9	5 R11	6 R6

Page 43

	a	b	c	d
1.	314	1,294 R16	971	1,075 R45
2.	845 R37	516	1,733 R25	183 R33

Page 44

	a	b	c	d
1.	233 R107	40 R207	14 R13	9 R132
2.	73 R44	82 R872	860	501 R210

Page 45

	a	b	c	d
1.	288	957	15,552	203,200

	a	b	c	d
2.	888	4,368	44,620	618,372
3.	358,812	2,980,055	136,752	2,270,436
4.	13 R15	939 R1	640 R3	5,219
5.	4	213 R25	73 R10	314 R10
6.	847	483 R8	608 R20	126

Page 46

	a	b	c	d
1.	3,200	300	1,800	2,400
2.	2,400	4,800	2,000	2,700
3.	8,000	24,000	12,000	12,000
4.	350,000	180,000	240,000	280,000
5.	2,800	9,000	140,000	
6.	720,000	12,000	1,200	

Page 47

	a	b	c		a	b	c
1.	90	80	50	2.	600	800	400
3.	20	20	30	4.	70	20	15
5.	10	18	16				

Page 49

1. addition; 2,089 miles
2. multiplication; 405 hours
3. subtraction; 87,427 miles
4. subtraction; 1,578 strikeouts
5. multiplication; 280 miles
6. multiplication; 720 days
7. addition; the year 2062
8. division; 7 pints

Page 50

1. 19 gallons 2. 432 people 3. $1,000
4. 216 feet 5. 3 miles a day; 84 miles in 4 weeks
6. $520 7. 28 teams 8. about 12,000 gallons

Page 51

	a	b	c	d
1.	400	2,000	100	40
2.	2,550	9,228	1,426	2,668
3.	13,480	57,204	126,763	170,856
4.	173	446 R4	4,218	3 R13
5.	232 R31	117 R8	2,314 R11	315 R46

6. 2,268 miles 7. 425 miles per hour

Page 52

1. a. $\frac{2}{6}$ or two sixths b. $\frac{5}{10}$ or five tenths
   c. $\frac{3}{8}$ or three eighths

	a	b	c		a	b	c
2.	$\frac{3}{5}$	$\frac{2}{3}$	$\frac{5}{8}$	3.	$\frac{1}{6}$	$\frac{9}{9}$	$\frac{4}{7}$
4.	$\frac{7}{10}$	$\frac{1}{8}$	$\frac{1}{2}$				

5. a. Two sevenths b. Six sixths c. Three tenths
6. a. Eight ninths b. Four fifths c. Seven eighths
7. a. One fifth b. Three sevenths c. One third

Page 53

	a	b	c	d
1.	4	3	2	1
2.	$1\frac{1}{12}$	$1\frac{1}{2}$	$1\frac{1}{3}$	$1\frac{1}{4}$
3.	$1\frac{3}{8}$	6	$1\frac{3}{4}$	3
4.	16	$2\frac{1}{5}$	2	$4\frac{1}{6}$

	a	b	c	d
5.	$\frac{9}{2}$	$\frac{29}{5}$	$\frac{20}{3}$	$\frac{29}{4}$
6.	$\frac{27}{10}$	$\frac{74}{9}$	$\frac{88}{5}$	$\frac{77}{8}$

Page 54

	a	b	c	d
1.	$\frac{6}{9}$	$\frac{15}{30}$	$\frac{9}{12}$	$\frac{6}{15}$
2.	$\frac{7}{14}$	$\frac{15}{18}$	$\frac{8}{10}$	$\frac{6}{16}$
3.	$\frac{9}{12}$	$\frac{5}{15}$	$\frac{8}{20}$	$\frac{20}{24}$
	$\frac{12}{12}$	$\frac{12}{15}$	$\frac{5}{20}$	$\frac{21}{24}$
4.	$\frac{14}{21}$	$\frac{18}{20}$	$\frac{5}{10}$	$\frac{2}{6}$
	$\frac{15}{21}$	$\frac{15}{20}$	$\frac{6}{10}$	$\frac{3}{6}$

Page 55

	a	b	c	d		a	b	c	d
1.	$\frac{3}{4}$	$\frac{1}{2}$	$\frac{1}{3}$	$\frac{3}{4}$	2.	$\frac{5}{6}$	$\frac{2}{5}$	$\frac{1}{4}$	$\frac{2}{3}$
3.	$\frac{1}{3}$	$\frac{7}{8}$	$\frac{1}{2}$	$\frac{2}{5}$	4.	$\frac{1}{2}$	$\frac{2}{3}$	$\frac{1}{3}$	$\frac{5}{3}$
5.	$\frac{2}{3}$	$\frac{1}{3}$	$\frac{1}{5}$	$\frac{3}{7}$	6.	$\frac{4}{7}$	$\frac{1}{6}$	$\frac{3}{5}$	$\frac{1}{3}$

Page 56

	a	b	c	d	e
1.	$\frac{1}{2}$	$\frac{3}{5}$	$\frac{1}{3}$	1	$\frac{4}{5}$
2.	$1\frac{1}{5}$	$\frac{7}{8}$	$1\frac{1}{3}$	1	$\frac{10}{11}$
3.	$\frac{1}{2}$	$\frac{1}{5}$	$\frac{1}{5}$	$\frac{1}{2}$	$\frac{4}{5}$

Page 57

	a	b	c	d
1.	$1\frac{1}{3}$	$\frac{7}{8}$	$\frac{7}{8}$	$1\frac{1}{8}$
2.	$1\frac{4}{9}$	$\frac{8}{9}$	$\frac{1}{2}$	$\frac{6}{7}$
3.	$1\frac{2}{15}$	1	$\frac{11}{14}$	$\frac{3}{4}$
4.	$1\frac{1}{10}$	$1\frac{7}{16}$	$\frac{2}{3}$	

Page 58

	a	b	c	d
1.	$1\frac{5}{18}$	$1\frac{7}{15}$	$\frac{19}{30}$	$\frac{13}{14}$
2.	$1\frac{5}{12}$	$1\frac{13}{30}$	$\frac{19}{28}$	$\frac{3}{4}$
3.	$1\frac{8}{45}$	$1\frac{24}{55}$	$1\frac{13}{24}$	$\frac{29}{56}$
4.	$1\frac{5}{24}$	$1\frac{7}{12}$	$\frac{20}{21}$	

Page 59

	a	b	c	d
1.	$5\frac{1}{2}$	$2\frac{1}{2}$	$3\frac{5}{14}$	$9\frac{2}{3}$
2.	$15\frac{7}{9}$	$5\frac{3}{8}$	$5\frac{7}{8}$	$9\frac{3}{5}$
3.	$8\frac{39}{56}$	$6\frac{7}{12}$	$9\frac{9}{10}$	$19\frac{19}{20}$
4.	$7\frac{3}{5}$	$4\frac{11}{12}$	$10\frac{13}{24}$	$15\frac{9}{10}$

Page 61

1. $61\frac{1}{2}$ 2. 2,060 km
3. Add $1\frac{1}{3}$; 14 4. Multiply by 3; 405, 1,215
5. Add $\frac{5}{8}$; $3\frac{1}{2}$ 6. Divide by 4; 80
7. Add $1,780; $43,600 8. Add $\frac{1}{4}$ inch; $4\frac{1}{2}$ inches

Page 62

	a	b	c
1.	$4\frac{5}{12}$	$10\frac{7}{12}$	$3\frac{39}{88}$
2.	$10\frac{17}{56}$	$11\frac{1}{3}$	$11\frac{5}{9}$
3.	$6\frac{1}{6}$	$9\frac{1}{18}$	$8\frac{5}{12}$
4.	$5\frac{1}{2}$	$14\frac{4}{5}$	$9\frac{5}{12}$

Page 63

1. $\frac{2}{3}$ of the residents   2. $\frac{1}{5}$ mile farther
3. 62 feet of rope   4. $23\frac{9}{16}$ pounds total
5. $44\frac{1}{3}$ yards left   6. $2\frac{1}{4}$ ounces total
7. $127\frac{19}{20}$ inches total   8. $64\frac{7}{10}$ cm total

Page 64

	a	b	c	d
1.	$\frac{1}{5}$	$\frac{1}{6}$	$\frac{5}{16}$	$\frac{1}{20}$
2.	$\frac{19}{70}$	$\frac{1}{12}$	$\frac{1}{10}$	$\frac{5}{12}$
3.	$\frac{11}{35}$	$\frac{23}{40}$	$\frac{1}{12}$	$\frac{5}{8}$
4.	$\frac{7}{24}$	$\frac{1}{2}$	$\frac{2}{15}$	$\frac{1}{10}$

Page 65

	a	b	c	d
1.	$\frac{1}{24}$	$\frac{19}{36}$	$\frac{11}{24}$	$\frac{12}{55}$
2.	$\frac{3}{10}$	$\frac{37}{72}$	$\frac{1}{2}$	$\frac{3}{5}$
3.	$\frac{7}{12}$	$\frac{5}{18}$	$\frac{3}{5}$	$\frac{3}{8}$
4.	$\frac{13}{24}$	$\frac{5}{8}$	$\frac{3}{10}$	

Mixed Practice

	a	b	c	d
1.	11,036	31,391	$13\frac{5}{12}$	$10\frac{7}{10}$
2.	741	7,314	1,110	79 R21

Page 66

	a	b	c	d
1.	$11\frac{2}{2}$	$2\frac{9}{9}$	$20\frac{10}{10}$	$41\frac{24}{24}$
2.	$6\frac{5}{5}$	$13\frac{7}{7}$	$15\frac{11}{11}$	$34\frac{6}{6}$
3.	$7\frac{3}{5}$	$4\frac{1}{4}$	$2\frac{1}{6}$	$1\frac{2}{3}$
4.	$7\frac{6}{11}$	$1\frac{1}{3}$	$7\frac{5}{7}$	$5\frac{1}{6}$
5.	$7\frac{2}{3}$	$1\frac{2}{5}$	$4\frac{1}{2}$	$2\frac{3}{4}$

Page 67

	a	b	c	d
1.	$5\frac{1}{6}$	$1\frac{5}{7}$	$6\frac{5}{6}$	$12\frac{2}{7}$
2.	$3\frac{5}{9}$	$3\frac{3}{4}$	$17\frac{8}{9}$	$2\frac{7}{16}$
3.	$5\frac{1}{6}$	$11\frac{2}{3}$	$1\frac{5}{8}$	$2\frac{3}{5}$
4.	$\frac{3}{10}$	$2\frac{4}{5}$	$7\frac{2}{5}$	$4\frac{3}{8}$
5.	$9\frac{1}{4}$	$5\frac{4}{5}$	$6\frac{5}{12}$	
6.	$2\frac{4}{9}$	$1\frac{1}{2}$	$8\frac{7}{10}$	

Mixed Practice

	a	b	c	d
1.	104 R20	2,185,556	256	1,682,862

Page 68

	a	b	c		a	b	c
1.	$8\frac{5}{4}$	$2\frac{7}{5}$	$11\frac{9}{8}$	2.	$4\frac{4}{3}$	$5\frac{10}{7}$	$6\frac{11}{6}$
3.	$3\frac{1}{2}$	$2\frac{2}{3}$	$2\frac{3}{5}$	4.	$5\frac{4}{9}$	$1\frac{5}{8}$	$5\frac{3}{4}$
5.	$3\frac{7}{36}$	$2\frac{5}{12}$	$4\frac{7}{24}$				

Page 69

	a	b	c		a	b	c
1.	$1\frac{2}{5}$	$1\frac{2}{3}$	$6\frac{9}{10}$	2.	$2\frac{1}{2}$	$2\frac{5}{12}$	$5\frac{23}{28}$
3.	$3\frac{27}{40}$	$1\frac{2}{3}$	$14\frac{3}{8}$	4.	$12\frac{7}{8}$	$5\frac{7}{8}$	$7\frac{1}{18}$
5.	$1\frac{1}{4}$	$2\frac{1}{6}$	$5\frac{23}{40}$				

Mixed Practice

	a	b	c	d
1.	1,100	22,000	21,100	6,000

Page 71

1. $18\frac{1}{4}$ feet   2. Ted, David, Shawna, Ellen, Carlos
3. Sam will have picked more.
4. 8,364 feet below the cloud
5. $\frac{3}{4}$ mile   6. $1\frac{3}{4}$ inches

Page 72

1. $\frac{3}{10}$ did not use a computer.   2. $2\frac{1}{2}$ inches
3. Bentley stock is $\frac{3}{8}$ dollar less.   4. $4\frac{3}{4}$ pounds
5. $199\frac{5}{6}$ carat difference
6. $3\frac{3}{4}$ miles from town
7. $3\frac{1}{5}$ inches of rain   8. $6\frac{1}{4}$ inches

Page 73

	a	b	c	d
1.	$\frac{13}{3}$	$\frac{17}{3}$	$\frac{32}{5}$	$\frac{69}{8}$
2.	$5\frac{2}{3}$	$4\frac{3}{4}$	$6\frac{1}{5}$	$5\frac{2}{9}$
3.	3	$2\frac{2}{9}$	3	$5\frac{1}{5}$
4.	$\frac{6}{9}$	$\frac{12}{16}$	$\frac{28}{35}$	$\frac{14}{20}$
5.	1	1	$1\frac{2}{5}$	$1\frac{2}{3}$
6.	$1\frac{17}{30}$	$9\frac{7}{20}$	$\frac{2}{5}$	$9\frac{3}{5}$
7.	$1\frac{3}{8}$	$5\frac{14}{15}$	$\frac{3}{4}$	$6\frac{13}{20}$
8.	$1\frac{1}{12}$ yards		9.	$8\frac{13}{20}$ miles

Page 74

	a	b		a	b
1.	$\frac{8}{15}$	$\frac{8}{35}$	2.	$\frac{1}{6}$	$\frac{2}{15}$
3.	$\frac{21}{32}$	$\frac{16}{45}$	4.	$\frac{2}{5}$	$\frac{3}{16}$
5.	$\frac{1}{3}$	$\frac{2}{15}$	6.	$\frac{2}{7}$	$\frac{1}{3}$
7.	$\frac{1}{6}$	$\frac{1}{4}$			

Page 75

	a	b		a	b
1.	$\frac{2}{35}$	$\frac{3}{56}$	2.	$\frac{3}{5}$	$\frac{4}{7}$
3.	$\frac{7}{22}$	$\frac{1}{10}$	4.	$\frac{1}{7}$	$\frac{6}{13}$
5.	$\frac{1}{6}$	$\frac{2}{3}$	6.	$\frac{1}{6}$	$\frac{1}{4}$
7.	$\frac{1}{9}$	$\frac{1}{3}$	8.	$\frac{1}{6}$	$\frac{1}{4}$

Page 76

	a	b	c	d
1.	$\frac{1}{1}$	$\frac{27}{1}$	$\frac{19}{1}$	$\frac{52}{1}$
2.	$\frac{7}{1}$	$\frac{36}{1}$	$\frac{125}{1}$	$\frac{11}{1}$

	a	b			a	b
3.	15	8		4.	10	$2\frac{2}{3}$
5.	50	15		6.	9	$13\frac{1}{2}$
7.	5	9		8.	$6\frac{3}{4}$	4

Page 77

	a	b			a	b
1.	$4\frac{4}{5}$	7		2.	15	$3\frac{1}{2}$
3.	30	6		4.	$2\frac{2}{3}$	15
5.	11	3		6.	25	25
7.	$\frac{4}{7}$	12		8.	15	9

Mixed Practice

	a	b	c	d
1.	5,656	466	16,209	5,866
2.	12,673	41	31,863	8,894

Page 78

	a	b			a	b
1.	6	$14\frac{1}{4}$		2.	21	9
3.	$7\frac{13}{15}$	$100\frac{1}{10}$		4.	242	$43\frac{1}{2}$
5.	10	$25\frac{3}{7}$		6.	$4\frac{9}{10}$	$16\frac{1}{10}$
7.	$19\frac{1}{4}$	$10\frac{1}{3}$		8.	$27\frac{1}{2}$	$5\frac{1}{2}$

Page 79

	a	b			a	b
1.	$1\frac{3}{4}$	2		2.	$3\frac{1}{2}$	1
3.	$\frac{4}{5}$	$1\frac{3}{4}$		4.	3	$1\frac{1}{2}$
5.	$1\frac{5}{16}$	$\frac{1}{2}$		6.	$3\frac{5}{6}$	2
7.	$\frac{5}{6}$	$1\frac{3}{16}$		8.	2	$2\frac{3}{16}$

Page 80

	a	b			a	b
1.	$5\frac{13}{24}$	$3\frac{1}{3}$		2.	$10\frac{4}{5}$	$4\frac{19}{20}$
3.	$1\frac{7}{8}$	10		4.	10	$14\frac{7}{16}$
5.	9	$8\frac{2}{3}$		6.	$12\frac{2}{15}$	$6\frac{3}{4}$
7.	$2\frac{1}{5}$	$10\frac{5}{8}$		8.	$3\frac{1}{5}$	$10\frac{11}{15}$

Page 81

1. 12 gallons 2. $14\frac{1}{4}$ cups 3. $\frac{5}{16}$ mile
4. $1\frac{1}{2}$ miles 5. $3\frac{1}{3}$ yards 6. $\frac{3}{16}$ mile
7. $102.00 8. $232\frac{4}{5}$ inches

Page 83

1. 30 feet 2. $24\frac{1}{2}$ cups 3. 250 gallons
4. 32 cars 5. 74 feet 6. $\frac{3}{8}$ mile
7. 10 minutes 8. 10 inches

Page 84

	a	b	c	d	e
1.	$\frac{9}{2}$	$\frac{4}{3}$	$\frac{6}{5}$	$\frac{10}{7}$	$\frac{8}{1}$
2.	$\frac{9}{8}$	$\frac{7}{1}$	$\frac{5}{2}$		$\frac{11}{5}$

	a	b			a	b
3.	$\frac{1}{2}$	$1\frac{1}{9}$		4.	$1\frac{1}{4}$	$\frac{2}{3}$
5.	$\frac{2}{3}$	$1\frac{13}{32}$		6.	$5\frac{1}{3}$	$1\frac{1}{2}$
7.	$1\frac{7}{9}$	$1\frac{5}{11}$		8.	$1\frac{1}{5}$	$1\frac{1}{2}$

Page 85

	a	b			a	b
1.	$\frac{3}{8}$	$\frac{5}{9}$		2.	$1\frac{1}{2}$	$2\frac{1}{3}$
3.	$2\frac{1}{10}$	$6\frac{2}{3}$		4.	1	$\frac{5}{8}$
5.	$\frac{8}{27}$	2		6.	$\frac{24}{35}$	$\frac{2}{3}$
7.	$1\frac{1}{3}$	$\frac{2}{3}$		8.	2	$1\frac{2}{3}$

Mixed Practice

	a	b	c	d
1.	126,513	22	966	10,915
2.	61,824	531	61,104	118

Page 86

	a	b	c	d	e
1.	$\frac{1}{3}$	$\frac{1}{9}$	$\frac{1}{7}$	$\frac{1}{2}$	$\frac{1}{16}$
2.	$\frac{1}{10}$	$\frac{1}{125}$	$\frac{1}{36}$	$\frac{1}{21}$	$\frac{1}{48}$

	a	b			a	b
3.	$\frac{1}{4}$	$\frac{2}{7}$		4.	$\frac{5}{42}$	$\frac{2}{15}$
5.	$\frac{1}{10}$	$\frac{12}{125}$		6.	$\frac{1}{9}$	$\frac{2}{25}$
7.	$\frac{1}{12}$	$\frac{2}{9}$		8.	$\frac{11}{84}$	$\frac{3}{32}$

Page 87

	a	b			a	b
1.	$\frac{1}{16}$	$\frac{5}{54}$		2.	$\frac{1}{25}$	$\frac{13}{64}$
3.	$\frac{2}{7}$	$\frac{1}{16}$		4.	$\frac{1}{16}$	$\frac{11}{36}$
5.	$\frac{1}{28}$	$\frac{1}{20}$		6.	$\frac{1}{45}$	$\frac{3}{16}$

Mixed Practice

	a	b	c	d
1.	1,742	593	83,551	20,194
2.	2,303	1,928	22,646	40,185
3.	24	56	32	11

Page 88

	a	b			a	b
1.	2	8		2.	8	16
3.	20	48		4.	18	$4\frac{1}{2}$
5.	60	48		6.	36	$9\frac{1}{3}$
7.	6	$3\frac{1}{3}$		8.	12	$1\frac{1}{5}$

Page 89

	a	b			a	b
1.	$\frac{1}{2}$	$\frac{1}{3}$		2.	$1\frac{1}{2}$	$\frac{3}{4}$
3.	$1\frac{4}{7}$	$1\frac{3}{8}$		4.	$\frac{2}{3}$	$\frac{3}{7}$
5.	$3\frac{1}{3}$	$\frac{2}{3}$		6.	$\frac{5}{16}$	$\frac{2}{3}$
7.	$\frac{2}{9}$	$2\frac{1}{5}$		8.	$\frac{3}{4}$	$\frac{3}{8}$

Page 90

	a	b			a	b
1.	14	2		2.	$2\frac{1}{9}$	$7\frac{1}{2}$
3.	11	$7\frac{3}{4}$		4.	2	$1\frac{1}{2}$

Page 90 (cont.)

	a	b		a	b
5.	$2\frac{3}{4}$	$2\frac{7}{9}$	6.	$2\frac{7}{10}$	11
7.	$15\frac{3}{4}$	4	8.	6	9

Page 91

	a	b		a	b
1.	$\frac{1}{2}$	$1\frac{29}{46}$	2.	$3\frac{2}{3}$	$1\frac{29}{41}$
3.	$3\frac{3}{10}$	$\frac{2}{3}$	4.	$3\frac{1}{33}$	$6\frac{1}{2}$
5.	2	$5\frac{2}{3}$	6.	$3\frac{3}{5}$	$5\frac{1}{3}$
7.	$1\frac{7}{8}$	$\frac{3}{8}$	8.	$2\frac{26}{27}$	$2\frac{2}{3}$

Page 93

In each of the following, any extra information should be crossed out in the text.

1. $145.00
2. $72.00
3. $\frac{1}{2}$ foot, or 6 inches
4. 5 feet
5. $12.00
6. $1\frac{1}{6}$, or $1.16
7. 2,250 yards
8. 6,982 square miles

Page 94

1. 40 cups
2. 26 T-shirts
3. 48 shingles
4. 4 days
5. $10\frac{2}{3}$ tons
6. 4 pieces
7. 8 batches
8. 7 sets

Page 95

	a	b		a	b
1.	$\frac{2}{15}$	$\frac{1}{8}$	2.	$\frac{7}{12}$	$\frac{1}{3}$
3.	4	2	4.	$\frac{40}{43}$	2
5.	$6\frac{2}{3}$	$3\frac{3}{4}$	6.	$2\frac{5}{8}$	$3\frac{7}{9}$
7.	$21\frac{3}{7}$	$\frac{4}{5}$	8.	$5\frac{47}{50}$	$1\frac{1}{6}$
9.	$13\frac{1}{2}$	15	10.	13	1
11.	8 spacers		12.	4 hours	

Page 96

	a	b		a	b
1.	0.3	0.25	2.	0.015	1.5
3.	10.04	5.055	4.	0.175	

5. five thousandths
6. thirty-nine and three hundred seventy-four thousandths
7. one dollar and twenty-three cents
8. fourteen dollars and eight cents
9. six hundredths

	a	b	c
10.	$9.00	$0.90	$0.09
11.	$0.66	$0.11	$42.00
12.	$110.74	**13.** $2,005.03	**14.** $1.19

Page 97

	a	b	c		a	b	c
1.	<	<	=	2.	<	>	=
3.	=	=	<	4.	>	>	>
5.	<	>	<	6.	=	<	<

	a		b
7.	$0.675 < 60.80 < 67.5$		$7.026 < 7.230 < 7.260$
8.	$1.025 < 1.1 < 1.20$		$0.034 < 0.304 < 0.34$

Page 98

	a	b	c	d
1.	$\frac{2}{5}$	$\frac{3}{5}$	$\frac{2}{25}$	$\frac{1}{500}$
2.	$\frac{21}{100}$	$\frac{83}{1,000}$	$\frac{901}{1,000}$	$\frac{9}{500}$
3.	$4\frac{1}{2}$	$1\frac{31}{50}$	$10\frac{1}{10}$	$1\frac{11}{40}$
4.	$9\frac{7}{100}$	$38\frac{6}{25}$	$5\frac{23}{50}$	$13\frac{4}{5}$
5.	0.1	0.2	0.5	0.7
6.	0.06	0.8	0.052	0.416
7.	5.6	3.1	7.6	0.65
8.	1.03	5.09	1.643	2.051

Page 99

	a	b	c
1.	0.125	0.4	0.15
2.	0.8	0.34	0.44
3.	0.035	0.32	0.375
4.	6.5	2.15	7.4
5.	6.25	1.38	1.56
6.	1.45	2.84	
7.	6.12	13.02	
8.	19.5	4.875	

Page 100

	a	b	c	d
1.	$5.41	$0.59	$16.86	$42.24
2.	0.306	29.228	315.3	54.25
3.	$11.43	37.525	1.603	16.737
4.	72.204	23.294	535.00	99.068

Page 101

	a	b	c	d
1.	9.52	10.345	22.536	20.401
2.	38.662	82.233	88.183	44.739
3.	$23.63	45.475	1.815	22.771
4.	5.755	2.849	8.87	7.901
5.	13.1	$24.89		
6.	58.2	54.073		

Mixed Practice

	a	b	c	d
1.	3,510	8,820	22	225

Page 102

	a	b	c	d
1.	3.136	1.16	5.599	$23.77
2.	3.915	4.75	2.04	1.897
3.	4.242	17.20	0.808	$4.14
4.	3.834	1.112	22.36	10.63

Page 103

	a	b	c	d
1.	5.122	2.158	2.014	0.16
2.	$6.96	$24.50	$79.78	$9,032.30
3.	1.625	1.226	1.089	7.45
4.	3.834	79.78	4.505	1.112
5.	4.015	2.04	22.26	
6.	7.45	4.75	1.089	

Mixed Practice

	a	b		a	b
1.	0.006	0.12	2.	0.020	0.04
3.	0.9	0.040	4.	3.3	6.008

	a	b	c	d
5.	=	<	>	=
6.	<	>	=	<

Page 105

1. $49.49
2. 30 invitations
3. $12.09
4. 225 miles
5. 7:15 A.M.
6. $13.00

Page 106

1. 7.53 million square miles
2. $43.85
3. 9.06 inches
4. 13.25 pounds
5. 580.9 kilometers
6. 1,485.6 kilometers
7. 635.3 kilometers
8. 698.7 kilometers

Page 107

	a	b	c	d
1.	$13	$34	$221	29
2.	80	$1	4	$0
3.	$4	55	125	22
4.	10.2	8.2	9.9	
5.	20.0	4.1	325.6	
6.	29.9	20.5	200.0	

Page 108

	a	b	c	d
1.	0.9	0.08	3.55	12.37
2.	10.24	0.19	0.83	1.00
3.	3.761	5.653	10.31	442.96
4.	0.6	9.2	0.19	0.07
5.	0.281	11.9	3.704	6.54
6.	0.2322	0.9283	47.40	6.258
7.	4.218	16.1357	248.692	

Page 109

	a	b	c	d
1.	4.846	11.31	18.337	27.97
2.	16.9594	16.57	45.92	390.44
3.	12.174	39.254		
4.	8.25	56.85		
5.	0.234	21.77	3.828	2.76
6.	11.257	5.7645	4.5008	53.997
7.	11.486	3.125	6.42	
8.	26.9933	0.0266	15.47	

Page 110

	a	b	c
1.	5.1	2.16	1.414
2.	0.4	0.840	0.95
3.	0.012	0.06	0.054
4.	134.40	5.940	2,134.40
5.	468.66	2,622.87	116.256

Page 111

	a	b	c	d
1.	1.724	0.252	9.78	11.7
2.	40.8	114.08	16.9	33.8
3.	98.4	21.7	350.0	49.5
4.	76.75	3.936	13.806	487.83
5.	91.2	28.148	855.65	

Mixed Practice

	a	b	c	d
1.	199	202	122 R60	69 R54
2.	102 R10	77 R5	160 R40	114 R6

Page 112

	a	b	c
1.	0.64	0.477	0.38
2.	0.072	0.027	0.0008
3.	0.01288	0.408	0.1557
4.	1.425	4.858	46.2
5.	182.508	16.324	14.6016

Page 113

	a	b	c	d
1.	0.18	0.018	4.9	0.252
2.	0.0032	0.0024	1.096	0.01096
3.	0.0021	0.0165	32.86	14.382
4.	0.0086	0.07622	53.4432	

Mixed Practice

	a	b	c	d
1.	26.355	3.696	20.909	5.197
2.	1.094	0.459	9.09	48.6
3.	$105.02	$471.05	$90.69	$199.01
4.	$9\frac{1}{8}$	$16\frac{1}{2}$	$70\frac{3}{4}$	$6\frac{13}{21}$

Page 114

	a	b	c	d
1.	8.2	$0.69	2.76	0.112
2.	0.04	$1.50	0.203	$3.14
3.	4.16	$4.12	0.018	0.007
4.	1.5	$0.67	1.4	

Page 115

	a	b	c	d
1.	4.8	5.29	0.003	$13.70
2.	29.9	6.2	$81.00	4.5
3.	2.06	0.7	$46.00	

Page 116

	a	b	c	d
1.	160	30	5	$340
2.	150	500	$650	400
3.	$35	26	600	$140
4.	$15	108	820	

Page 117

	a	b	c	d
1.	0.5	$0.30	0.4	$0.75
2.	0.02	0.05	$0.80	0.95
3.	0.25	0.125	0.025	0.6
4.	0.5	0.75	0.004	0.25

Page 118

	a	b	c
1.	75	460	0.7
2.	70	460	7.5
3.	0.05	0.008	0.0125
4.	0.125	0.000125	0.1492
5.	6,200	64.215	6.4215
6.	3,150	4.8	0.00048
7.	0.0375	0.375	3.75
8.	37.5	375	7
9.	71,935	16,147	14,920
10.	2.6178	0.0026178	2,617.8

Page 119

	a	b	c		a	b	c
1.	64	64	120	2.	130	8	78
3.	4	2	11	4.	3	6	25
5.	414	3	128				

	a	b	c	d
1.	2.4	1.032	30.186	4.7173
2.	36	0.06	0.098	0.008
3.	56.52	0.18	0.06	0.348
4.	2.3	826	26,078	12,483
5.	1.28	18.5	5.9	25.3
6.	2.664	1.12	8.96	934.16

Page 121

	a	b	c	d
1.	123.93	6.888	315.375	4.176
2.	0.084	0.2072	0.0005	0.729
3.	30.52875	0.00441	2.3562	0.003776
4.	0.092	0.017	0.03	0.04
5.	2.54	90.6	93.8	1,250
6.	0.625	20	200	430

Page 123

1. about 2,000 quarters
2. about $4.00
3. about 1 meter
4. about 9 bracelets
5. about $10 per hour, about $15,600 per year
6. about 90 miles
7. about $1,200
8. about $8.00

Page 124

1. $606.30
2. 0.92 meters
3. about $10.00
4. Sam paid $1.24 more per CD.
5. 640.9 kilometers
6. 3.0 meters tall
7. 1,100 pounds
8. $0.17 per brick

Page 125

	a	b	c	d
1.	0.1	0.03	0.2	0.75
2.	0.125	0.625	1.25	2.6
3.	$1\frac{1}{10}$	$1\frac{1}{2}$	$\frac{3}{4}$	$5\frac{1}{2}$
4.	18.82	6.309	1.608	40.317
5.	3.38	0.3168	259.64	0.9996
6.	0.05	36.96	8.4	0.166
7.	0.06	0.12	1,200	6.0
8.	22.5	225	2,250	
9.	3.52	0.186	14,920	

Page 126

	a	b		a	b
1.	$\frac{41}{50}$	$\frac{7}{100}$	2.	$\frac{1}{100}$	$1\frac{21}{50}$
3.	$\frac{19}{20}$	$\frac{11}{20}$	4.	$1\frac{9}{100}$	$\frac{73}{100}$
5.	$\frac{49}{50}$	$\frac{3}{25}$	6.	$\frac{1}{25}$	$\frac{11}{25}$
7.	$1\frac{3}{4}$	$\frac{83}{100}$	8.	$\frac{13}{50}$	$1\frac{37}{100}$

Page 127

	a	b	c
1.	30%	8%	45%
2.	91%	56%	149%
3.	73%	67.2%	2%
4.	325%	9%	70%
5.	133.3%	54%	62%
6.	37.5%	40%	70%
7.	21%	31.25%	25%
8.	60%	35%	41.67%

Page 128

1. $\frac{6}{10} = 0.6 = 60\%$
2. $\frac{1}{4} = 0.25 = 25\%$
3. $\frac{1}{5} = 0.2 = 20\%$
4. $\frac{17}{20} = 0.85 = 85\%$
5. $\frac{1}{2} = 0.5 = 50\%$
6. $\frac{3}{4} = 0.75 = 75\%$
7. 37%
8. 0.075
9. 0.1
10. 32%
11. $\frac{3}{20}$
12. 0.625

Page 129

	a	b	c
1.	2.05	5	1.75
2.	9.999	3.2	1.013
3.	4.5	6.09	11
4.	8.07	7.255	1.98

5. 2.1 6. 1.52 7. 3.33 8. 1.35

Page 130

	a	b	c
1.	0.005	0.0033	0.0025
2.	0.004	0.0041	0.0005
3.	0.0025	0.005	0.004
4.	0.008	0.00625	0.00875
5.	0.009		
6.	0.0064		
7.	0.0055		
8.	$0.0045 > 0.00375$		

Page 131

1. 20%
2. 75%
3. 0.0725
4. $\frac{9}{25}$
5. 9.75%
6. 15%
7. 0.085
8. 80%

Page 133

1. 25%
2. $\frac{3}{20}$
3. 0.3
4. $\frac{1}{10}$, 0.1, 10%
5. $\frac{1}{5}$, 0.2, 20%
6. 0.5
7. $\frac{2}{5}$
8. 30%

Page 134

	a	b		a	b
1.	45	180	2.	96	60
3.	30	180	4.	250	54.45

5. $237.60 6. $65.70

Page 135

	a	b		a	b
1.	4	$\frac{2}{3}$	2.	34	$1\frac{1}{3}$
3.	33	3	4.	$1\frac{1}{5}$	$4\frac{2}{3}$

5. $22.00 6. 400 students

Page 136

	a	b		a	b
1.	500%	60%	2.	15%	30%
3.	45%	15%	4.	67%	125%
5.	40%		6.	45%	
7.	11%		8.	55%	

Page 137

	a	b		a	b
1.	68	125	2.	80	200
3.	55	200	4.	730	160
5.	$40.00		6.	$3,000.00	
7.	13,000 miles		8.	40 questions	

Page 138

	a	b		a	b
1.	$13.75	$14.63	2.	$144.00	$100.00
3.	$8.25	$36.00	4.	$700.00	$17.00

Page 139

	a	b
1.	$112.45	$3.94
2.	$13.36	$577.80
3.	$79.95	$1,072.00
4.	$58.59	$32.81
5.	$317.52	$33.13
6.	$1,207.50	$2,846.25

Mixed Practice

	a	b	c	d
1.	144.24	$255.60	$25.01	0.63
2.	81,536	55	51,788	295

Page 140

1. 63.6 pounds 2. $7.80 3. $108,972
4. 19,812 students 5. $23,540 6. $24.75

Page 141

1. 475 students 2. $24.00 3. $12,800
4. 69 points 5. 548,800 people 6. $119.38

Page 143

1. $2,520 2. $1,275 3. $7,000
4. $3,600 5. $4,400 6. $8,500

Page 144

1. $99 2. $450 3. 75
4. $860 5. 25% increase 6. $320
7. 20% 8. $320

Page 145

	a	b
1.	$26\% = 0.26 = \frac{13}{50}$	$0.2\% = 0.002 = \frac{1}{500}$
2.	$115\% = 1.15 = 1\frac{3}{20}$	$5\% = 0.05 = \frac{1}{20}$
3.	$\frac{7}{20} = 0.35 = 35\%$	
4.	$\frac{81}{100} = 0.81 = 81\%$	
5.	40.5	1.8
6.	15%	200%
7.	30	50

8. $200.00 9. 35%
10. $23.10 11. $1,020.00

Page 146

1. a. $a \times b = b \times a$ b. $x - x = 0$
   c. $n + n = 2n$ d. $0 \times m = 0$
2. Answers may vary.
   a. $0 + 3 = 3$ b. $8 \div 2 = 4$
      $0 + 5 = 5$ $10 \div 2 = 5$
      $0 + 8 = 8$ $12 \div 2 = 6$

Page 147

1. a. natural, whole, integers, rational
   b. integers, rational number
   c. rational number
2. a. rational number
   b. rational number c. rational number

Page 148

	a	b	c	d
1.	6	9	8	13
2.	18	3	10	15
3.	7	0	17	22
4.	12	19	11	26
5.	30, ⁻30	14, ⁻14	32, ⁻32	29, ⁻29
6.	21, ⁻21	23, ⁻23	42, ⁻42	99, ⁻99

Page 149

	a	b	c			a	b	c
1.	<	<	>		2.	>	=	<
3.	>	<	>		4.	<	<	>
5.	=	>	=		6.	>	>	<
7.	>	=	>		8.	<	<	>

	a	b
9.	⁻6 < 0 < 7	⁻9 < ⁻5 < 7
10.	⁻1 < 1 < 11	⁻21 < 12 < 27
11.	⁻2 < 3 < 8	⁻13 < ⁻3 < 0
12.	⁻11 < 4 < 5	⁻20 < ⁻16 < 19

Page 150

	a	b	c	d
1.	2	⁻10	2	⁻4
2.	⁻12	7	⁻7	⁻18
3.	⁻3	⁻8	9	13
4.	8	⁻8	0	⁻4
5.	⁻7	⁻4	⁻5	⁻19
6.	0	10	2	⁻10

Page 151

	a	b	c	d
1.	⁻9	4	12	⁻42
2.	27	⁻12	⁻20	18
3.	24	⁻24	30	⁻10
4.	0	20	21	32
5.	⁻6	⁻4	3	⁻6
6.	4	⁻2	8	⁻9
7.	6	⁻7	0	⁻1
8.	7	4	9	⁻4

Page 152

	a	b	c	d
1.	30	7	⁻20	8
2.	18	2	21	⁻20
3.	35	⁻12	30	4
4.	8	20	28	30
5.	10	2	⁻50	11
6.	3	2	⁻8	⁻13

Page 153

	a	b	c	d
1.	9	30	13	16
2.	16	26	16	24
3.	14	5	56	10
4.	3	8	5	$\frac{5}{2}$
5.	1	1	$\frac{1}{2}$	7
6.	1	10	$\frac{1}{3}$	4

Page 154

	a	b		a	b
1.	$10 + r$	$t - 9$	2.	$7s$	$w \div 3$
3.	$m + 12$	$2hx$	4.	$25 - n$	$p - g$
5.	$24 \div k$	$13 + b$	6.	$c - 7$	$y \div 5$

Page 155

1.
 a. 5 is a coefficient, 9 is a constant
 b. 3 is a coefficient, $^-1$ is a coefficient
 c. 6 is a coefficient, $^-2$ is a coefficient
 d. 10 is a coefficient, $^-7$ is a constant

	a	b	c	d
2.	20	8	36	30
3.	$\frac{1}{4}$	10	3	5
4.	85	25	600	300
5.	7	8	1	40

Page 156

	a	b	c
1.	$x = 3$	$x = 4$	$y = 10$
2.	$m = 8$	$n = 17$	$x = 12$
3.	$x = 21\frac{1}{3}$	$k = 13$	$x = 53$

Page 157

	a	b	c	d
1.	$x = \frac{1}{2}$	$n = 35$	$x = 2\frac{1}{3}$	$x = 3\frac{1}{3}$
2.	$k = 25$	$x = 5\frac{5}{8}$	$m = 1\frac{3}{8}$	$k = 13$
3.	$x = 7\frac{2}{5}$	$k = 11$	$x = \frac{3}{4}$	$x = 52$
4.	$k = 11\frac{2}{3}$	$x = 29$	$x = 87$	$x = 5\frac{1}{8}$
5.	$n = 5$	$n = 2\frac{1}{7}$	$x = 16$	$n = 7\frac{1}{2}$
6.	$x = 68$	$x = 8\frac{3}{5}$	$x = 12$	$x = 98$

Mixed Practice

	a	b	c	d
1.	38,373	12,978	34,992	79 R21
2.	1.311	140	35	$3\frac{17}{20}$

Page 159

1. The number is 73. 2. The cat weighs 9 pounds.
3. Tom is 45 years old. 4. The number is 74.

Page 160

	a	b	c
1.	$(2)^2(3)^2y$	$(4)^2(y)^2z$	$(10)^2(7)^2y$
2.	$7(5)^2a$	$(^-1)(3)^2(b)^2$	$7(6)^2(y)^2$
3.	$(^-1)^2(a)^2$	$15(a)^2$	$2(9)^2(5)^2b$
4.	$^-192$	$^-80$	192

Page 161

	a	b	c	d
1.	4^3	$(^-4)^3$	3^3	$(^-7)^3$
2.	$(1)^3$	$(12)^3$	5^3	$(^-20)^3$
3.	216	$^-8$	343	8,000
4.	$^-1$	0	729	$^-512$

Page 162

1.
 a. 5.6×10^6
 b. 6.04×10^6
 c. 6.7×10^3
 d. 1.013×10^6

2.
 a. 3.3×10^5
 b. 7.16×10^8
 c. 2.021×10^9
 d. 2.07×10^6

3.
 a. 410,000
 b. 599
 c. 110,000
 d. 22,300

4.
 a. 8,900
 b. 50,300,000
 c. 3,120,000,000
 d. 75,000

5.
 a. 101,100
 c. 31,400

 b. 600,000,000
 d. 10

Page 163

1.
 a. $8 \times 8 = 64; \sqrt{64} = 8$
 b. $15 \times 15 = 225; \sqrt{225} = 15$

2.
 a. $1 \times 1 = 1; \sqrt{1} = 1$
 b. $6 \times 6 = 36; \sqrt{36} = 6$

3. a. $\sqrt{25} = 5$ b. $\sqrt{9} = 3$
4. a. $\sqrt{100} = 10$ b. $\sqrt{4} = 2$
5. a. $\sqrt{144} = 12$ b. $\sqrt{16} = 4$

Page 164

	a	b	c
1.	$x = 6$	$x = 12$	$x = 10\frac{4}{5}$
2.	$x = 5$	$x = 67\frac{5}{8}$	$x = 14$
3.	$x = 21$	$x = 7$	$x = 10$

Page 165

	a	b	c
1.	$x = 5$	$x = \frac{1}{2}$	$x = 8$
2.	$x = 2\frac{1}{2}$	$x = 5$	$x = \frac{3}{4}$
3.	$x = 4$	$x = 9$	$x = \frac{1}{5}$
4.	$x = \frac{1}{24}$	$x = \frac{3}{10}$	$x = 4$
5.	$x = 4$	$x = 2\frac{13}{17}$	$x = \frac{1}{7}$
6.	$x = \frac{1}{12}$	$x = 7$	$x = 6$

Mixed Practice

	a	b	c	d
1.	977.181	2.2	$\frac{22}{35}$	$x = 30$
2.	$3\frac{1}{3}$	7,196	2.35	3

Page 166

	a	b	c
1.	$x = 10$	$x = 5$	$x = 2$
2.	$x = 7$	$x = 3$	$x = 2$
3.	$x = 15$	$x = 3$	$x = 3$

Page 167

	a	b	c
1.	$x = 1$	$x = 5$	$x = 4$
2.	$x = 12$	$x = 7$	$x = \frac{3}{4}$
3.	$x = \frac{1}{2}$	$x = 6$	$x = 5$
4.	$x = \frac{3}{14}$	$x = 1$	$x = \frac{1}{15}$
5.	$x = 13$	$x = 9$	$x = 10$
6.	$x = 9$	$x = 2$	$x = 2\frac{1}{3}$

Mixed Practice

	a	b	c
1.	8.5	0.16	2,919
2.	96	0.66	7,148

Page 168

	a	b	c
1.	$x = 6$	$x = 5$	$x = 1$
2.	$x = 2$	$x = 8$	$x = 10$
3.	$x = 2$	$x = 7$	$x = 15$

Page 169

	a	b	c
1.	$x = 10$	$x = 3$	$x = 6$
2.	$x = 17$	$x = 1$	$x = 25$
3.	$x = 5$	$x = 30$	$x = 8$
4.	$x = 10$	$x = 24$	$x = 9$
5.	$x = \frac{2}{7}$	$x = 11$	$x = {}^-2$
6.	$x = \frac{1}{2}$	$x = 1\frac{2}{3}$	$x = {}^-5$

Mixed Practice

	a	b		a	b
1.	$0.45; \frac{9}{20}$	$0.75; \frac{3}{4}$	2.	$0.12; \frac{3}{25}$	$1.2; 1\frac{1}{5}$
3.	$0.10; \frac{1}{10}$	$0.03; \frac{3}{100}$	4.	$0.28; \frac{7}{25}$	$0.35; \frac{7}{20}$

Page 170

1. $n = 28$
2. Arsenio has $105, and Malik has $40.
3. Jerry has $3.20, and Pat has $9.60.
4. $n = 48$

Page 171

1. Elena has $35, and Tori has $7.
2. DeWayne has $35, and Hakeem has $20.
3. 1st package has 50. 2nd package has 30.
4. 1st lot has 75 cars. 2nd lot has 125 cars.
5. Mother is 54, and Ricardo is 18.
6. Father is 58, and Natasha is 20.
7. The three numbers are 30, 60, and 90.
8. The three numbers are 20, 40, and 80.

Page 172

	a	b	c	d
1.	2,352	6,561	32,768	1,280
2.	2,187	240	117,649	65,536
3.	262,144	4,096	16	600
4.	8	1,024	720	8
5.	6,588	32,256	9,765,625	729

Page 173

1. a. 7,812   b. 100   c. 4,096   d. ${}^-$531,360
2. a. 7   b. 625   c. 4,160   d. 6,561
3. a. 4   b. 392   c. 7,776   d. 279,936
4. a. 1,000,0000   b. 4,096   c. 3,250   d. 49,152
5. a. 343   b. 387,420,489   c. 1,000,000,000   d. 320
6. a. 7,560   b. 10   c. 512   d. 48

Mixed Practice

	a	b	c	d
1.	45	$x = 3$	$5\frac{11}{15}$	1.38
2.	$\frac{4}{21}$	2.5	$21.60	${}^-21$

Page 175

1. Charles – Red   Terry – Blue   Tony – Green
2. Martin – 119   Anna – 101   Julie – 123
3. Raul–215   Samantha–275   Pablo–260   Mateo–130
4. Vanessa – Volleyball   Yolanda – Tennis
   Kimberly – Softball   Nicole – Cheerleading

Page 176

1. 018   2. 512 miles   3. 300 feet
4. 128   5. $173   6. 135
7. 243 free throws   8. 557 people

Page 177

	a	b	c	d
1.	30	0	6	85
2.	${}^-5$	10	3	8
3.	15	28	4	2
4.	9^2	z^3	17^2	
5.	30	${}^-3$	${}^-1\frac{4}{5}$	
6.	31	119	${}^-32$	
7.	9,400,000	1,230	570,000	89,000
8.	3	$y = 8$	$t = 2$	
9.	$z = {}^-10$	$m = 6$	12	
10.	$q = 6$	$x = 144$	$s = 2$	

11. The number is 14.   12. $10.75

Page 178

	a	b
1.	yes	no
2.	yes	yes
3.	domain: $\{{}^-10, {}^-2, 1, 9\}$	domain: $\{{}^-2, 1, 7\}$
	range: $\{{}^-1, 3, 4, 5\}$	range: $\{{}^-3, 6, 8\}$
4.	domain: $\{{}^-1, 0, 4\}$	domain: $\{1, 2, 5\}$
	range: $\{{}^-6, {}^-5, 0, 9\}$	range: $\{{}^-2, 1, 9\}$

Page 179

1. a. C $(0, {}^-4)$ b. D $({}^-1, {}^-3)$ c. E $(1, {}^-3)$
   d. F $({}^-2, 0)$ e. G $(2, 0)$
2. a. H $(3, 5)$ b. J $(5, 7)$ c. K $({}^-5, 7)$
   d. L $({}^-2, 1)$ e. M $(3, {}^-1)$
3. a. [graph]   b. [graph]

Page 180

1. $(3, {}^-12)$ 2. $({}^-2, 3)$
3. $\{(6, {}^-1), (14, 1)\}$ 4. $\{({}^-5, 0), (1, {}^-3), ({}^-9, 2)\}$

Page 181

	a	b	c
1.	$({}^-1, 4)$	$({}^-3, 5)$	$(5, 1)$
2.	$(3, 5)$	$(0, 11)$	$({}^-1, 13)$
3.	$({}^-4, {}^-2)$	$({}^-5, {}^-1)$	$({}^-9, 3)$

Page 182

1.

x	y
0	5
1	3
3	${}^-1$

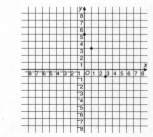

2.

x	y
⁻2	⁻2
0	⁻4
3	⁻7

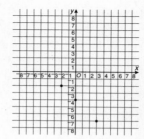

3.

x	y
⁻1	⁻1
0	2
1	5

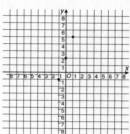

Page 183

Solution points will vary, but line graphs will be the same.

1.

x	y
0	⁻2
1	1
2	4

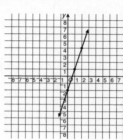

2.

x	y
⁻6	0
0	6
⁻4	2

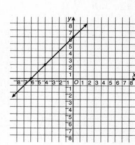

3.

x	y
0	⁻2
4	0
8	2

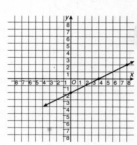

Page 184

1. $\frac{1}{3}$, positive   2. $\frac{7}{2}$, negative   3. $\frac{1}{3}$, negative

Page 185

	a	b	c
1.	$-\frac{1}{3}$	2	⁻1
2.	2	$-\frac{3}{4}$	$\frac{1}{2}$
3.	$\frac{-6}{5}$	$\frac{5}{9}$	3

Page 186

	a	b	c
1.	>	<	>
2.	>	>	<
3.	<	>	=
4.	=	<	>
5.	true	false	true
6.	false	true	false
7.	false	true	true

Page 187

	a	b	c
1.	$x > 16$	$x \le 15$	$x < 25$
2.	$x \le 7$	$x > 3$	$x \ge 6$
3.	$x > 15$	$x \le 24$	$x > 23$
4.	$x > 24$	$x \ge 25$	$x \ge 35$
5.	$x < ⁻2$	$x \ge ⁻4$	$x < 9$
6.	$x \ge ⁻2$	$x > ⁻8$	$x \le ⁻5$

Page 188

	a	b	c
1.	$x < 20$	$x \ge ⁻16$	$x \le ⁻18$
2.	$x > 5$	$x \ge ⁻5$	$x < 4$
3.	$x < 3$	$x < 7$	$x \le ⁻4$
4.	$x < 6$	$x \ge 7$	$x > 5$
5.	$x \le ⁻5$	$x > ⁻9$	$x > 9$

Page 189

1. 8.5 feet   2. 5 days   3. $2,300   4. $240

Page 191

1. June, December
2. February, April, July, and November
3. November–December
4. June–July
5. January and September
6. 15   **7.** 55   **8.** 55

Page 192

1. $-\frac{1}{2}$ 2. $x < 35$ 3. Tonya is 4.   4. $t \ge 14$
5. 4 days   6. April has a higher rate of growth.
7. (10, 5)   8. No more than $290

Page 193

1. yes, Domain: {⁻1, 1, 2, 3}   Range: {2, 4, 6}
2. no, Domain: {⁻4, 1, 5}   Range: {⁻3, 1, 6, 7}
3. Solutions for the ordered pairs will vary, but the line graphs will be the same.

a.

x	y
0	⁻6
3	0
4	2

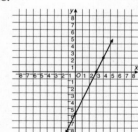

Page 193 (cont.)

b.

x	y
7	0
5	1
3	2

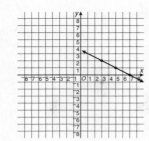

	a	b	c
4.	⁻3	2	⁻1
5.	$x > 32$	$x \leq 66$	$x \geq {}^-5$
6.	$x < 2$	$x > 4$	$x \geq 2$

Page 194

	a	b	c	d
1.	ray	line	point	line segment

2. a. parallel lines b. intersecting lines
c. perpendicular lines d. intersecting lines

Page 195

	a	b	c	d
1.	∠GHI	∠T	∠XYZ	∠ABC
2.	obtuse	straight	acute	right

Page 196

1. a. isosceles b. equilateral
c. isosceles d. scalene
2. a. acute b. right
c. obtuse d. obtuse

Page 197

1. a. regular b. irregular
c. regular d. irregular
2. a. irregular b. irregular
c. regular d. irregular
3. a. triangle b. quadrilateral
c. pentagon d. octagon
4. a. hexagon b. hexagon
c. pentagon d. quadrilateral

Page 198

1. 28.8 centimeters **2.** 50 inches
3. 164 meters **4.** 0.204 kilometers
5. 22 yards **6.** 310 feet

Page 199

1. 44 feet **2.** 2 kilometers
3. 232 centimeters **4.** 558 centimeters
5. 5.2 kilometers **6.** 216 inches

Page 201

1. $270 **2.** 576 inches
3. 34 meters **4.** 980 inches

Page 202

1. 160 square meters **2.** 4,567.5 square feet
3. 4,800 square meters **4.** 375 square kilometers
5. 17.5 square meters **6.** 137.5 square inches

Page 203

1. 55.2 square meters **2.** 384 square inches
3. 2,480 square centimeters
4. 300 square meters **5.** 150 square meters
6. 2,268 square feet **7.** 80 square inches
8. 13.2 square meters

Page 204

1. 550 square inches **2.** 72 square yards
3. 85.5 square meters

Page 205

1. 288 square feet **2.** 3,050 square centimeters
3. 1,332 square inches **4.** $57\frac{1}{4}$ square yards
5. 46 square feet **6.** 470 square centimeters
7. 9,400 square inches **8.** 18 square feet

Page 206

1. a. 70 square centimeters b. 6.75 square meters
c. 58 square yards
2. a. 2,887.5 square millimeters
b. 71.76 square feet c. 25 square inches

Page 207

	a	b	c
1.	168 sq. m	22.05 sq. yd	459 sq. in.
2.	625 sq. cm	1,950 sq. mm	304 sq. ft

3. 100 square inches **4.** $21\frac{1}{8}$ square feet
5. 252 square centimeters **6.** 128 square yards

Page 208

1. 5.4 cubic meters **2.** 343 cubic meters
3. 17,280 cubic feet **4.** 189 cubic yards
5. 59,675 cubic centimeters **6.** 960 cubic feet
7. 4,104 cubic inches **8.** 35 cubic meters

Page 209

1. 21.98 inches **2.** 219.8 centimeters
3. 1,099 millimeters **4.** 10.99 yards
5. 19.78 meters **6.** 143.53 centimeters

Page 210

1. 38.465 square feet **2.** 615.44 square inches
3. 38.47 square meters **4.** 13.8474 square meters
5. 7 gallons **6.** 55.39 square centimeters

Page 211

1. 40.00 cubic yards **2.** 2.3079 cubic meters
3. 10.99 cubic inches **4.** 1,038.56 cubic meters
5. 67.31 cubic meters **6.** 953.78 cubic centimeters

Page 213

1. 5 centimeters **2.** 1 foot
3. 4 inches **4.** 6 inches
5. 300 square meters **6.** 864 square inches
7. 4,800 cubic inches **8.** 1,800 cubic inches

Page 214

1. 125 feet **2.** 6 meters
3. 10 yards **4.** 22 feet
5. 12 inches **6.** 12.5 centimeters
7. 120 yards **8.** 16 inches

Page 215

	a	b	c	d
1.	right	acute	straight	obtuse
2.	regular	irregular	irregular	regular

3. *a.* equilateral **b.** scalene
c. obtuse **d.** right
4. 48,230.4 cubic centimeters
5. 94 square yards
6. 75 square feet **7.** 40 inches

Page 216

	a	b	c
1.	3 ft 3 in.	4 ft 4 in.	1 T 500 lb
2.	2 lb 3 oz	3 lb 12 oz	3 mi 270 yd
3.	8 qt 1 pt	3 pt 1 c	5 gal 1 qt
4.	216 in.	48 in.	10,560 ft
5.	128 oz	192 oz	6,000 lb
6.	29 c	32 c	40 pt

Page 217

	a	b	c
1.	15 m	4 mm	3 km
2.	5 m	20 cm	200 cm
3.	700 cm	150 mm	1,200,000 m
4.	22,500 cm; 225,000 mm	136,000 m	8,400 cm
5.	1.2 m	4.346 km	89 cm
6.	93 cm; 0.93 m	0.750 km	0.11 m

Page 218

	a	b	c
1.	1 g	4 kg	100 kg
2.	500 g	5 kg	20 g
3.	10,000 g	4,800 g	760 g
4.	4 g	1,092 g	305,000 g
5.	0.0028 kg	0.007 kg	3.094 kg
6.	0.925 kg	0.05243 kg	0.061 kg

Page 219

	a	b	c
1.	60 L	750 mL	350 L
2.	300 mL	50 mL	3 L
3.	700 mL	8,000 mL	1,600 mL
4.	421,000 mL	3,090 mL	424 mL
5.	8.883 L	0.3907 L	0.014 L
6.	0.0125 L	0.208 L	0.079 L

Page 220

	a	b		a	b
1.	$\frac{1}{3}$	$\frac{1}{7}$	**2.**	$\frac{1}{2}$	$\frac{1}{2}$
3.	$\frac{1}{4}$	$\frac{4}{5}$	**4.**	5	$\frac{5}{4}$
5.	$\frac{17}{20}$	$\frac{5}{3}$	**6.**	1	$\frac{1}{2}$
7.	2	1			

Page 221

1. $\frac{1}{9}$ **2.** $\frac{1}{16}$ **3.** $\frac{1}{125}$
4. $\frac{27}{64}$ **5.** $\frac{8}{27}$ **6.** $\frac{100}{1}$

Page 222

	a	b	c
1.	true	false	true
2.	false	true	true
3.	true	true	false

Page 223

	a	b	c
1.	$x = 20$	$x = 6$	$x = 12$
2.	$x = 27$	$x = 30$	$x = 10$
3.	$x = 3$	$x = 16$	$x = 100$
4.	$x = 21$	$x = 2$	$x = 2$

Page 224

1. $36.10 **2.** $1.30 **3.** $4.00
4. $290.40 **5.** 50 miles **6.** $26.25

Page 225

1. 50; 100; 150; 200; 250
2. 20; 40; 60; 80; 100; 120; 140
3. 6; 12; 18; 24; 30; 36; 42

Page 226

	a	b	c	d
1.	YZ; 3	XZ; 4	YZ; 3	XZ; 4

2. a. $\frac{AC}{XZ} = \frac{AB}{XY}$; $\frac{2}{4} = \frac{1}{2}$
   b. $\frac{BC}{AB} = \frac{YZ}{XY}$; $\frac{1.5}{1} = \frac{3}{2}$
   c. $\frac{YZ}{BC} = \frac{XZ}{AC}$; $\frac{3}{1.5} = \frac{4}{2}$
   d. $\frac{XY}{AB} = \frac{XZ}{AC}$; $\frac{2}{1} = \frac{4}{2}$

3. a. $\frac{XY}{XZ} = \frac{AB}{AC}$; $\frac{2}{4} = \frac{1}{2}$
   b. $\frac{YZ}{XZ} = \frac{BC}{AC}$; $\frac{3}{4} = \frac{1.5}{2}$
   c. $\frac{AC}{BC} = \frac{XZ}{YZ}$; $\frac{2}{1.5} = \frac{4}{3}$
   d. $\frac{AC}{AB} = \frac{XZ}{XY}$; $\frac{2}{1} = \frac{4}{2}$

Page 227

1. $XY = 21$ in. **2.** $XY = 3\frac{2}{3}$ ft **3.** $BC = 8$ m
4. $BC = 8$ cm **5.** $XY = \frac{1}{2}$ yd **6.** $YZ = 2$ ft

Page 228

1. 50 feet tall **2.** 555 feet tall
3. 40 feet tall **4.** 100 feet tall

Page 229

	a	b	c
1.	$c = 13$	$b = 24$	$c = 5$
2.	$a = 9$	$c = 2$	$b = 8$

Page 231

1. $281.25
2. 72 centimeters long
3. 2,258 people
4. Diane is 15; her brother is 3.
5. Raheem, Richmond; Harold, Brookdale; Katarina, Montague
6. $64.80

Page 232

	a	b	c
1.	0.06	48	0.016
2.	2	10,000	5 ft 6 in.
3.	3000	42,410	5,200
4.	$\frac{1}{2}$	$\frac{7}{13}$	
5.	true	false	true
6.	$x = 20$	$x = 10$	$x = 35$

7. 45 minutes   8. 2 inches
9. $\frac{1}{27}$ 10. 30 feet

Page 233

1. **a.** 8 thousands   **b.** 0 tens
   c. 2 tenths   **d.** 6 thousandths

	a	b	c	d
2.	9,554	31,759	466	2,091
3.	864	142,725	26 R1	92
4.	253	1,713	10,575	
5.	8,532	56	41 R1	

	a	b	c	d	e
6.	$\frac{2}{5}$	$\frac{3}{2}$	$\frac{1}{3}$	$\frac{14}{3}$	$\frac{3}{25}$

	a	b	c	d
7.	1	$14\frac{1}{10}$	$3\frac{7}{24}$	$\frac{7}{30}$

8. $43\frac{3}{4}$ yards   9. $0.69

Page 234

	a	b	c	d
10.	10	16	$3\frac{3}{4}$	
11.	$1\frac{1}{2}$	$8\frac{1}{4}$	$\frac{3}{2}$	
12.	$\frac{3}{10}$	$1\frac{17}{100}$	$\frac{9}{1,000}$	$\frac{1}{100}$
13.	0.8	0.23	0.05	0.008
14.	7.57	69.106	7.27	8.01
15.	117.78	0.9997	0.2475	6.7
16.	$0.35 = \frac{7}{20}$	$0.08 = \frac{2}{25}$		
17.	20	20%		
18.	90	36		
19.	$15.75	$85.20		

Page 235

	a	b	c	d
20.	$^-2$	11	$^-75$	4
21.	1	$-\frac{9}{11}$	$^-6$	

	a	b	c	d
22.	acute	straight	right	obtuse
23.	regular	irregular	regular	irregular
24.	isosceles	scalene	equilateral	isosceles

25. 54 square meters   26. 120 yards

Page 236

	a	b	c
27.	$(^-3, 9)$	$(1, 1)$	$(4, 5)$
28.	2 gal 2 qt	16 c	650,000 cm
29.	1ft 4 in.	3,000 lb	0.006 L
30.	4,000 g	23 cm	9,000 mL

	a	b	c	d
31.	$x = 22$	$x = 5$	$x = ^-6$	$x = 10$
32.	$x = 9$	$x = 6$	$x = 14$	$x = 36$
33.	$x = 8$	$x = 6$	$x = 5$	$x = 13$
34.	$\frac{7}{12}$	$\frac{1}{8}$		

	a	b	c	d
35.	$x \geq 3$	$x > 15$	$x > 3$	$x \geq ^-40$

36. 8 cm   37. $\frac{1}{3}$